THE UNIVERSITY OF CHICAGO
SOCIOLOGICAL SERIES

FIRST PUBLISHED IN 1928
REISSUED, 1965, BY RUSSELL & RUSSELL
A DIVISION OF ATHENEUM PUBLISHERS, INC.
BY ARRANGEMENT WITH RUTH SHONLE CAVAN
L. C. CATALOG CARD NO: 64-66390
ISBN: 0-8462-0555-6
PRINTED IN THE UNITED STATES OF AMERICA
BY SENTRY PRESS, NEW YORK

SUICIDE

By

RUTH SHONLE CAVAN, Ph.D.

New York

RUSSELL & RUSSELL

PREFACE

The subject for this study was chosen because of an interest in human nature in the midst of perplexities and because of a curiosity as to why people, even when perplexed, commit suicide. A preliminary exploratory jaunt into published material on suicide revealed a few general treatises by European writers, many monographs by French and German psychiatrists and physicians, and almost nothing by English, and particularly by American, writers. It showed further a tendency to treat suicide statistically, a neglect of life-histories, which are perhaps not so exact as statistics, but which give vastly more insight into, and understanding of, human nature, and an emphasis on cases showing some mental abnormality. The normal person who committed suicide was overlooked, as though the popular prejudice were indeed true that suicide is *ipso facto* proof of abnormality.

A further survey of material revealed numerous sources of data, many of which had scarcely been touched by previous writers. Collecting these data meant searching through hundreds of books on dusty library shelves in the hope of garnering a sentence here, a paragraph there, not of itself valuable but exceedingly revealing when compared with other statements. Much of the historical and ethnological material was thus gathered piecemeal, although the studies by Westermarck and Lecky aided materially and are referred to freely and frequently in chapters ii and iv. This historical and ethnological approach gave a perspective to the whole problem difficult to obtain in any other way. Suicide appeared in its relation to other customs, to attitudes toward life and religion, to political and social changes. There was made possible, not a mere chronicling of facts, but an analysis of suicide as a social phenomenon.

Statistics furnished the best method of comparing suicide rates of different groups, of tracing trends, and of discovering what factors are associated with suicide. Many of the tables used had been compiled by other writers. They have been brought as nearly down to date as possible; and in the case of the United States and certain cities in the United States, new combinations of tables and new compilations have been made. The statistical study of suicide is still, however, in a preliminary state. Few students have attempted to go beyond simple rates and a few sets of correlations. There is here a vast untapped fund of material for further analysis.

The bulk of the study consists of an analysis of individual cases of suicide, their classification into types, and the establishment of certain generalizations regarding them. Just as the historical and ethnological study showed suicide as a concomitant of other social phenomena, so the life-histories revealed suicide as a concomitant of such personal experiences as severe crises, certain emotional states, and certain tolerant attitudes toward suicide.

The book is, therefore, what its title states, a study of suicide in its relation to social and personal disorganization. It is intended to appeal both to those working with disorganized persons and to students of the theory of human nature.

The book was made possible only by the assistance rendered by certain officials in charge of public and semipublic records and of students and friends who assisted in gathering material and in preparing the manuscript. Foremost in the

PREFACE

list of those to whom the writer feels indebted is Ellsworth Faris, Professor of Sociology at the University of Chicago, to whom is due in part the inception of the study and whose counsel has guided the writer throughout, both in the organization and analysis of material and in the formulation of a sound theoretical background. Official records furnishing the case histories and the raw material for the statistics of Chicago were made available by Oscar Wolff, coroner of Cook County, Illinois, Dr. Herman N. Bundesen, commissioner of health of the City of Chicago, M. J. Karpf, formerly head of the Jewish Social Service Bureau of Chicago, Joel L. Hunter, head of the United Charities of Chicago. Dr. Berthold Laufer, of the Field Museum, very kindly placed at the writer's disposal several books on suicide in China, not otherwise obtainable. Many students at the University of Chicago assisted in collecting material: of these, particular mention should be made of Bertha Zahren, Fumi Jo, and P. P. Diefenderfer. Louis Wirth supplemented certain case records from the Jewish Social Service Bureau and Evelyn Buchan aided by having students at Ohio State University fill out questionnaires on wishes for death. Ruth McKinney read the manuscript and offered many valuable suggestions, and Jordan Cavan has assisted in the revision of the manuscript and in the arduous task of reading proof and compiling the index. Finally, mention should be made of Louis I. Dublin, of the Metropolitan Life Insurance Company, and of Albert and Charles Boni, Inc., both of whom have permitted the inclusion in this study of material from their publications.

RUTH SHONLE CAVAN

CHICAGO
August 1, 1927

INTRODUCTION

The readers of this book will learn many interesting things about suicide, but the book will not answer all the questions that might be asked. It should be the first of a series of studies, and sociologists and the public would be the gainer if Dr. Cavan could devote several years more to the study of some of the problems which she has raised in this work.

But the reader will learn much more than interesting facts and generalizations about suicide. The discussion includes valuable material on personal disorganization and the facts here presented form a chapter in social psychology which to the discerning will yield much and suggest more. Suicide is committed by individual persons, but this study reveals that suicide is not wholly an individual phenomenon. It occurs in two noticeably different situations. In one of these it is demanded by the group in accordance with custom, as in Japan, some parts of Africa, and formerly in India, according to which the man who failed, or a widow, was expected to commit suicide. The other kind of society where suicide is most prevalent is not in favor of the practice, but condones it, and in these Dr. Cavan has found evidences of disorganization. The extent and form of disorganization and the circumstances which accompany it constitute one of the central problems around which this book has been written.

We have here, then, a concrete investigation which contributes something toward the solution of the very ancient and very difficult problem, namely, the relation of the individual to the group, the relative importance of custom and public opinion as compared with individual motives and temperament.

The long road of social and philosophical theorizing is strewn with the wrecks of abandoned enterprises which have reduced the principles governing human life to one single motive or force. There are some of us who have never quite understood the enormous prestige of the number "one." Perhaps it arises from our desire to simplify the complex and from the satisfaction which we feel when differences are found to be disguised resemblances. To bring order out of a chaotic world means to find likenesses where they are not at first apparent; and if we continue this process and reduce all the differences to ultimate likenesses, we finally arrive at a monistic explanation. But if this monistic explanation fails to explain, we call it false, and it becomes a monistic fallacy. The unity which we have found has been purchased at the cost of refusing to see significant differences, and the simplification and unification, proceeding too far, defeats its own purpose. Attempting to simplify life the better to deal with it, it has been oversimplified, and the discovery is made that we cannot deal with it so well. But how long it has taken to learn this lesson!

It would be tedious to run through the list of these, but some are still current and are advocated by prolific and influential writers. Consider the instinct philosophers. Their best-known exponent did not originate the conception of instincts, but he has the doubtful honor of proposing that the instincts, which are of course hypothetical constructs, be regarded as the causes of individual human behavior and the ultimate explanation of our institutional and collective life. This view has forced its advocates to adopt strange and devious expedients. The instincts, being the universal hered-

INTRODUCTION

itary tendencies, are in the lower animals essentially universal and invariable, but the institutions and the customs which they were held to create being so protean and contradictory, the instinct philosophers were ultimately led to the ludicrous assumption that Frenchmen and Englishmen, for example, do not have the same instincts; or, more accurately, have such significant variations in the strength of the basic instincts that the variant culture patterns are thus adequately accounted for. And one of the "proofs" of this scheme that has been played up prominently has been the differential suicide rate which is present in differing racial groups. Dr. Cavan's work has not been extensive enough to answer all the questions about racial differences which we would like to see answered, but enough has been done to form a conclusive refutation of the monistic fallacy called instinctivism.

The disciples of Buckle—and a revival of Bucklism is now being promoted—favored another type of the monistic or particularistic fallacy. The soil, the climate, the amount of sunshine or shadow, the presence of hills, and the size of them were assumed to influence in some direct way the lives of men. Quite recently the explanation of the high suicide rate in San Diego, California, was seriously presented as the effect of too much sunshine! The details of this view are familiar to scholars, and in Dr. Cavan's work there can be found many facts which such a theory cannot possibly explain.

But the effect of the research done in the preparation of this work is not all negative. There is implied here a view, indeed explicity formulated, which goes further than mere refutation. It concerns the central problem of the one and the many, the individual and society, the person and the group.

INTRODUCTION

Suicide is in some situations "in the mores." In those groups where it is not expected or required it is a symptom of disorganization; but such groups differ widely in the prevalence or rate of self-destruction. This in turn depends upon the state of public opinion and various collective attitudes which are shown to be sometimes religious, sometimes moral, which are not accessible to interpretation by means of research in individual psychology. The mores grow up like folk-tales or proverbs, and individuals who are affected by them can only be understood if they be regarded as living their lives over against the background of a certain cultural situation.

Moreover, there are suggestions in the abandoned formulations which are not without value. The mores are after all attached to the soil; but apparently many kinds of soil are hospitable to essentially the same species of culture patterns. The mores, when they are sufficiently old, and if they are sufficiently isolated, do operate as forces of nature with which they are so often confused. The instinct fallacy is easily explained by the tendency of naïve minds to regard as natural any tendency which is so old that its origin is forgotten. The African widows who die in the husband's grave are not a conspicuously reflective lot. Yet if they be questioned regarding their action, the answer one often gets is that it is perfectly natural so to do. The instinctivists have not listed an instinct of suicide, but their reasoning is hard to account for the omission.

Now in attempting to answer the conundrum of the priority of the hen or the egg it seems easier to defend the statement that what we do "instinctively" is decided by the customs of our people. The institutions and the mores in which we have lived our lives mold our habits and fashion our sentiments. It is difficult for us to imagine ourselves capable of any other sort of behavior than that which has always satisfied our fellows and our fathers. But the social psychologist is at once challenged by the problem of how the institutions arise and what originated the mores and folk-ways. If they did not arise in the tendencies and instincts of human nature it seems absurd to look for them anywhere else. Perhaps the simplest answer would be that the mores and institutions are never the result of the activities of in-fants. They arise on rare occasions reflectively but nearly always unwittingly, when the adult and responsible mem-bers of the group meet a new crisis or solve an unprec-edented difficulty, and here appears the impossibility of the ancient and too facile solutions. For an institution arises in a given area and at a given time in the lives of men already grown to maturity and therefore organized into habitual responses and with defined sentiments and interests. An institution thus arising is the result of a unique constella-tion of forces and tendencies which has never been exactly equaled or matched anywhere at any time.

The present work, by the comparison which it has made of differential rates of the same group in different sections of the United States and in different sections of the city, has thrown much-needed light and ought to attract inter-ested investigators to a fruitful field of research.

The work of Dr. Cavan differs from her predecessors in this field of study also in her emphasis on, and use of, the case method. The individual records of the experience of suicides who have left documents, of unsuccessful attempts at suicide, and facts collected about cases where suicide was contemplated but never overtly attempted, furnish data for valuable formulations of the theory of personal disorganization. The organized personality has a certain equilibrium between his desires and the possibilities of their fulfilment. At least in his dreams and reveries the future holds a promise that what he aspires to may in some fashion be achieved. In cases of disorganization this conviction is lost, and the world he lives in, which we may call his life-organization, collapses, ceases to exist. His cosmos is wrecked and only chaos remains. Sometimes this is a very temporary condition which soon improves if the opportunity for self-murder is absent or is frustrated; but in other cases the brooding is long continued and the solution is definitely abandoned. The various types of disorganization are highly illuminating as set forth in this work, but further study would doubtless result in the refinement of the concepts and the sharpening of the distinctions.

One significant correlation is that between disorganization and "mobility," as it has come to be called, by which is meant, not the ability to move, but the actual frequency and extent of movements in space by the members of a group and the incoming members of other groups. Nothing seems more clear than the tendency toward stability and fixity of customs if the members of a society remain relatively fixed in their abode and are undisturbed by immigrants into their area. The further analysis of the factors in mobility which produce personal disorganization ought to reveal significant relations; but enough has been done to disprove some of the older formulations and to suggest more defensible theories.

The opening statements of this study will come to many readers as a revealing surprise. The fact that in America, where the homicide rate is very high, the suicide rate is 50 per cent greater makes the problem not only of theoretical

INTRODUCTION

interest but gives it a practical humanitarian appeal; and it
is the assumption of those who make scientific studies in
sociology that if we could sufficiently understand and completely interpret such a phenomenon as suicide we should be
practically ready for a program of control. Thus the most
objective research, if sufficiently successful, will pay its debt
to the society which made it possible and will definitely contribute to the amelioration of our social life.

ELLSWORTH FARIS

UNIVERSITY OF CHICAGO

TABLE OF CONTENTS

TABLE OF CONTENTS

PART II. SUICIDE AND PERSONAL DISORGANIZATION

TABLE OF CONTENTS

TABLE OF CONTENTS

LIST OF TABLES

LIST OF TABLES

LIST OF FIGURES

LIST OF MAPS

PART I
SUICIDE AND SOCIAL DISORGANIZATION

CHAPTER I

SUICIDE TRENDS

What is suicide? Superficially considered, suicide is the intentional taking of one's own life or the failure when possible to save one's self when death threatens. Within this broad definition there are types. At one extreme is the highly institutionalized form of suicide which is just passing out of the customs of oriental peoples; at the other, the equally highly individualized suicides of contemporary Europe and America.

Japan, China, and India until recently each had forms of suicide which were socially approved, committed in public with ceremony, and whose omission was not only "bad form," but cause for disgrace. The Hindu widow who burned herself on the funeral pyre of her husband or the Chinese widow who hanged herself in public may not have felt sufficiently grieved to kill herself; yet many widows in both India and China have killed themselves and been publicly honored for so doing. The Japanese warrior who killed himself when he and his lord faced defeat may have had many reasons for wishing to continue to live; yet he followed the code of his class and died at his own hand, sometimes with hundreds of his comrades. The relation of these highly formalized suicides to personal wishes on the one hand and to the social organization on the other is discussed in detail in a later chapter. It will suffice here to note that these suicides are performed at the command of the social group and are usually related to crises in the life of the group; they have only an indirect relation to personal interests and wishes.

Contrasted to this institutionalized form of suicide is the secretly committed, socially condemned suicide which characterizes Europe and America. The typical situation which causes a European or an American to commit suicide is intensely personal. It is not something which has happened to the group of which he is a member; it is something which has happened to him personally, and the interpretation he has placed upon it is not wholly that of society. The man who has been jilted may be sympathized with, advised to move to another city, to become interested in other girls, to turn his attention to his profession; but rarely is he advised to kill himself. Yet often he does commit suicide under such circumstances. The entire psychological process involved in the development of a suicidal wish as a solution to personal difficulties is discussed in Part II. It is evident that the personal suicide of Europe and America is very different from the social suicide of the Orient, with regard to the occasions when it occurs, the motives which underlie it, and the relation of social customs and moral values to it.

Between these two extremes—suicide in conformity to the mores and suicide against the mores—lie many intermediate types.[1] One such type which was more prevalent a few hundred years ago than at present is the religious martyr. All persons who die for a cause, whether religious or otherwise, cannot be classed as suicides. But the religious martyrs of a few centuries ago often actively sought death, sometimes returning again and again to a community where they knew they would be persecuted by an unfriendly but

[1] Mores are customs which have received the approval of the group where they are practiced; they have moral value and are the right ways of behaving, in the experience of the group. The term was first used by W. G. Sumner in *Folkways*, 1906.

dominant group. Suicide was forbidden to the early Christian sects; but martyrdom offered an honorable release from life, an effective escape into a hereafter thought to be filled with glory, and an undeniable testimony to the truth of sectarian beliefs. Martyrdom tended toward the institutional type of suicide. It offered relief from a critical social situation and it was approved by the religious group to which the martyr belonged.[1]

In occidental civilization has developed, too, the tradition that the captain shall remain on his ship when, through the accidents of war or weather, it is sinking. The captain under such circumstances acts in conformity to a social code which he has adopted as his own, and hence is very close to the oriental warrior who committed hara-kiri.

During the early part of the Christian era, also, girls who committed suicide to avoid physical violation were highly honored, even canonized, and an attitude developed which tended to call forth suicide on such occasions.[2]

While these and similar customs regarding the desirability of suicide upon given occasions have tended to die out, the suicide rates in Europe and America have increased.

The increasing rate.—The tables and graphs which follow are somewhat misleading in that the lowered rate during the war years gives the appearance of a great decrease in suicides during the past decade. But in those instances in which statistics are available for recent years, the trend is upward. The United States trend is again tending upward, as is that

[1] See James Truslow Adams, *The Founding of New England*, p. 271, for the case of a Quaker martyr in Massachusetts. Also, see W. E. H. Lecky, *History of European Morals from Augustus to Charlemagne*, II, 45-46.

[2] Lecky, *History of European Morals from Augustus to Charlemagne*, II, 46.

of Belgium, Switzerland, France, and Italy; while the rate
in Germany, after a downward dip during the war years, is
again equal to what it was before the war. It is to be expected, then, that during the next decade the rate of suicide will

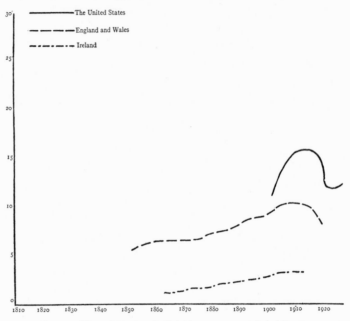

FIG. 1.—The suicide trend. Suicides per 100,000 inhabitants

again be upward and that from a long perspective the war
may be regarded as a temporary disturbance. It may be
assumed then, that the trend of suicide is in reality the trend
existing prior to the war. In 1914 suicide rates were rapidly
increasing in the following countries for which data are available: the United States, Sweden, Finland, Netherlands,
Austria, Hungary, Belgium, France, Spain, Italy.

In addition to these, Germany and Switzerland were

maintaining extremely high suicide rates—among the highest in the world—but with no appreciable trend either up or down.

Of all the countries of Europe for which rates were avail-

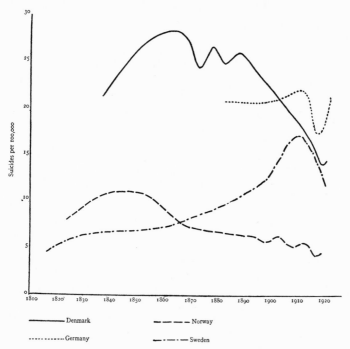

Fig. 2.—The suicide trend. Suicides per 100,000 inhabitants

able, only two, Norway and Denmark, had a downward trend prior to the war.

For the Orient rates are not easily obtained. Japan for the past fifty years has maintained a high rate, above the rate in the United States and approaching some of the highest European rates.

Although rates are in general increasing, they show a wide divergence from country to country. In recent times Germany, Austria, France, Switzerland, and Japan have led the world in frequency of suicide (approximately 23 suicides per

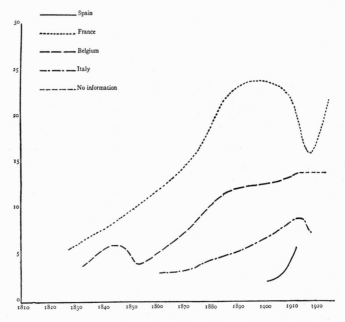

FIG. 3.—The suicide trend. Suicides per 100,000 inhabitants

100,000 population). The United States, Sweden, Belgium, Denmark, and Australia have held a middle position with about 16 suicides per 100,000. Norway, Finland, Netherlands, Spain, Portugal, Italy, England, Scotland, and Ireland are at the foot of the list, with from 4 to 9 suicides per 100,000. Below these countries stand the primitive peoples, among whom suicide is almost nonexistent.

TABLE I

SUICIDES PER 100,000 INHABITANTS FOR VARIOUS COUNTRIES*

Year	United States	Massachusetts	Connecticut	Rhode Island	Vermont	New Hampshire	Sweden	Norway	Finland	Netherlands	Denmark	German Empire	Prussia	Saxony	Austria	Hungary Kingdom	Hungary Proper	Belgium	France	Spain	Italy	Switzerland	England and Wales	Ireland	Australia	Japan
1816-20							4.8						7.4										(6.2)	(1.4)		
1821-25							5.8						8.3										6.7	1.5		
1826-30								8.0			21.3		8.9	15.8					8.5		(2.8)		6.5	1.8		
1831-35																		4.6					(5.7)	1.8		
1836-40		6.3					6.0						10.3					6.4					6.4	2.1		
1841-45		(7.8)	(12.1)	(5.6)	(8.8)	(8.2)	6.0	8.5										5.5					6.6	2.4		
1846-50																										
1851-55	6.3		4.6	5.7	5.7		5.7	10.9	5.8	5.6	24.5		11.0	33.3	19.7			7.0	12.4		5.0	22.1	7.0	2.2	14.6	
1856-60	8.0	6.1					5.7	11.0		6.2	24.8		13.0	38.3	17.3	8.4		7.0	10.0		4.9	22.7	7.5	1.8	16.0	
1861-65	6.9						6.7	10.7	4.0	6.7	27.6		12.4	35.6	16.2		(7.6)	6.3	13.5		4.1	23.3	7.4	3.3		
1866-70		6.1	5.5	8.4	7.6		7.6	6.5	4.0	5.6	26.1		12.3	32.3	16.0	10.1	(10.2)	6.6	14.6		3.0	22.1	6.6	1.5	9.7	
1871-75		7.4	6.6	6.3	9.0		7.5	5.5	3.3	6.4	24.3	21.0	13.4	30.5	15.8	10.6	17.7	7.0	15.0		3.5	22.2	6.3	1.8	12.4	
1876-80		7.5	8.7	8.2	8.0		7.2	5.5	3.9	5.5	27.2	20.2	13.0	32.5	17.3	16.3	19.1	6.3	16.8		4.1	24.3	7.4	2.3	12.5	
1881-85		8.7	10.3	10.1	9.0		8.1	6.4	3.3	5.5	25.8	20.3	12.3	32.5	17.3	16.3	17.6	6.0	20.4		4.9	23.0	7.9	3.3	13.5	
1886-90			(9.5)				8.5	7.2	4.4	5.6	27.6	21.1	13.0	35.5	17.3	19.0	17.0	6.3	21.7		5.3	24.3	7.5	3.1	11.6	
1891-95			0.0	8.3	0.0		9.2	7.5	4.8	5.5	23.8	21.1	13.5	34.1	18.2	16.3	17.6	7.0	22.8		5.5	24.7	8.0	3.5	12.4	
1896-1900			13.0	13.0	10.0		9.4	7.1	4.7	6.0	24.1	20.7	14.2	30.5	15.8	17.7	17.7	6.6	23.2		6.3	18.2	8.9	3.8	12.4	
1901-05	11.5	13.0	13.6	12.0	10.7	10.1	11.0	6.6	6.6	6.0	25.0	21.1	20.7	31.1	15.9	16.1	(13.2)	6.9	24.1	4.6	5.7	20.1	9.9	2.9	10.2	
1906-10	15.1	13.1	13.0	11.8	10.2	13.0	10.4	6.7	8.7	6.2	26.1	20.5	12.3	32.3	16.1	19.0	(10.2)	8.8	21.6	4.5	7.9	22.1	8.9	2.4	11.6	15.9
1911-	15.0	13.1	18.0	11.8	13.0	13.0	17.6	4.6	6.0	5.8	18.9	21.7	20.0	31.5	16.0	10.1		6.1	21.6	4.5	8.1	22.1	7.0	2.4	11.6	15.9
1913	15.5	13.4	17.4	14.6	16.3	18.3	18.3	6.6	9.3	6.0	18.2	22.5	20.5	32.3	20.2	10.5		9.3	21.3	4.6	8.5	23.3	9.0	3.8	13.6	18.2
1914	16.1	13.5	17.4	15.3	17.3	17.3	17.0	6.4	10.8	6.4	22.8	23.2	19.5	30.5	15.8	16.3	(19.2)	8.0	23.0	5.5	6.3	22.2	9.6	3.5	13.5	18.5
1915	16.2	13.3	15.1	15.1	16.5	15.9	15.9	5.0	11.8	6.0	18.3	21.8	20.3	32.5	17.3	17.6	19.1	5.0	21.1	2.2	8.1	24.3	10.3	3.4	12.6	20.1
1916	13.8	12.3	15.0	14.4	13.5	13.1	18.0	4.6	6.9	5.8	15.8	21.7	20.8	33.3	19.7	16.1	(10.2)	6.1	17.1	2.8	6.9	21.5	7.8	2.7	11.8	17.4
1917	13.1	13.3	16.7	11.7	17.8	18.0	16.4	4.6	7.8	6.2	13.8	16.4	20.5						16.7	4.6	5.5	21.1	8.9	3.8	10.2	16.4
1918	12.3	13.0	14.5	13.6	15.4	15.4	14.5	3.8	12.5	6.0	12.8	15.7	19.5						13.5	5.5	5.3	24.7	9.6	3.5	10.0	16.1
1919	11.4	13.3	14.5	13.3	13.0	11.1	14.3	5.1	7.8	6.0	12.0	15.7	19.3					13.2	12.8	5.3	5.3	19.8	7.4	3.3	10.3	17.8
1920	10.2	11.1	14.1	12.5	12.5	9.7	11.3	5.0	9.9	6.0	14.3	17.3	21.1					13.2	20.4	5.3	5.0	18.6	7.8	3.3	10.3	20.3
1921	12.5	10.2	14.3	10.4	13.6	13.5	10.4	5.6	11.3	5.8	14.3	17.1	21.6						20.7	5.9	6.9	21.5	7.3	2.7	11.8	17.4
1922	11.8	11.4	12.8	12.2	15.0	12.1	14.5		7.8		14.5		21.4		20.2									8.0	11.8	
1923	11.6	11.2	13.2	15.0	15.0	9.8	21.0	10.5			14.5	21.0			21.1			21.9						9.0	10.7	10.0
1924	12.1	11.9	10.4	10.9	13.9	14.5	11.4		11.3		20.7	21.4													11.6	10.7

* Rates for the United States (registration states only) from *Special Reports of the Census Office, Mortality* (1900-1904), pp. ckiv-v; *Mortality Statistics* (1922), p. 68; *Mortality Rates* (1910-20), pp. 62 ff.; and *Mortality Statistics* for states from R. Fisher, *Statistical Association*, n.s. III (1892-93), 163, and from *Mortality Statistics* (1909), p. 93 ff.
Rates for European countries, Australia, and Japan from J. R. Miner, "Suicide and its Relation to Climatic and Other Factors," *American Journal of Hygiene*, Monographic Series, No. 2, pp. 3–5, and for recent years from the official yearbooks of the various countries. Re-garding the sources of his data, Miner states, "the rates prior to 1871 are from Morselli's Table II (p. 22), except for the English rates, which are calculated from material in the reports of the Registrar General. From 1871 the rates are quoted from Knibbs ('Suicide in Australia: A Statistical Analysis of the Facts,' *J. Royal Soc. New South Wales*, XLV, 1912), with additions from the official publications of the various countries."

† "This sudden decrease is due to the fact that cases of poisons self-administered for purposes of abortion have been excluded" (Miner, *ibid.*, p. 3).

Why study suicide?—Except for a few articles in periodicals and some fragmentary statistical studies, suicide in the United States has received very little attention.[1] This is perhaps due to the fact that the rate is not only low as compared with suicide rates in Europe, but is also low when compared with other causes of death in the United States. Some four or five physical diseases each cause the deaths yearly of eight to sixteen times as many people as die by suicide.

Suicide cannot, however, be compared fairly with deaths due to physiological disorders. Suicide belongs in another series: deaths due to sociological and psychological causes. Homicides and many types of accident belong in the same series, and, with suicide, are largely due to defects in social control. In its own series, suicide ranks above homicides, of which there were 7,878 in the registration area in 1923 (more than 3,000 less than the number of suicides). It ranks above railroad accidents, which contributed 7,100 deaths to the 1923 total, and not far below automobile accidents, which caused 14,411 deaths in 1923.

Although suicide may be classed with homicides and accidents as a product of the social organization, it is not explicable by the same processes which produce homicides and accidents. The trend of these types of death for the last twenty-five years is illustrative. For many years prior to about 1915 the trend for suicide rates had been steadily upward in the United States. The war caused a decided decrease in suicides and the trend has scarcely yet reasserted an upward direction. Homicides and automobile accidents, however, have steadily increased, and if anything have become aggravated during the post-war period.

[1] For the most recent statistical study of suicide in the United States, see Adolph Dominic Frenay, *The Suicide Problem in the United States.*

Homicide, with fewer deaths, has been included in general studies of crime, and accidents are receiving increased attention. Suicide, because of the number of deaths and the probable upward trend, should also be recognized as a serious problem for study.

TABLE II

RATES OF DEATHS DUE TO SPECIFIED CAUSES IN THE
REGISTRATION AREA
(PER 100,000 POPULATION)*

Year	Suicide	Homicide	Automobile Accidents
1901–5.........	13.9	2.9	
1906–10.......	16.0	5.9	1.0†
1911..........	16.3	6.6	2.2
1912..........	16.0	6.5	2.9
1913..........	15.8	7.2	3.9
1914..........	16.6	7.4	4.3
1915..........	16.7	7.0	5.9
1916..........	14.2	7.1	9.6
1917..........	13.4	7.7	9.0
1918..........	12.2	6.8	9.3
1919..........	11.4	7.5	9.4
1920..........	10.2	7.1	10.4
1921..........	12.6	8.5	11.5
1922..........	11.9	8.4	12.5
1923..........	11.6	8.1	14.9
1924..........	12.2	8.5	15.7

* From United States mortality statistics for the various years. As the registration area changes from year to year, the same area is not represented throughout.
† Not given separately from other accidents.

Moreover, if the United States is taken not as a unit, but as a collection of states, the rates for the individual states run the entire gamut of European rates, from 3 suicides per 100,000 in certain southern states to 24 suicides per 100,000 on the Pacific Coast. These high rates deserve serious attention.

The attempts which have been made to study suicide in

both the United States and in Europe are limited in scope. On the one hand are statistical studies, which are of value chiefly in locating problems for further study as to causation. On the other hand are the studies of physicians and psychiatrists, whose chief interest is in pathological cases and whose profession leads them to seek for causes in physical or mental disorders.

There is opportunity, then, for a survey of suicide in its relation to social as well as physical conditions, and also for a study of the special conditions which prevail in the United States.

The desire to explore many possible factors led to a threefold approach: through historical and descriptive material, through statistical data, and through life-histories. These various types of material supplement and corroborate each other and act as a check against too hastily formed conclusions.

The chapters that follow in Part I give the attitudes and traditions which lie in the background of present-day suicide, the influence of various social factors in Europe and America on the suicide rates, the effect of simple primitive culture on suicide, and, by way of contrast, the factors favoring high suicide rates in a modern city. Or, to put the whole matter in the form of a question, Part I answers the query: What phases of social organization develop the tendency to commit suicide, and what phases control and inhibit it or build up alternative types of conduct?

CHAPTER II

EUROPE: WHY SUICIDE IS NO LONGER SINFUL

While there is evidence of very early practice of suttee (widow suicide) in several parts of Europe—a custom which died out before the period of historical records—sufficient background to recent suicide trends in Europe may be gained by beginning with Grecian attitudes and customs and tracing the subsequent changes.

The history of suicide in Europe is a study in social attitudes. While there are no exact figures of suicide frequency prior to 150 years ago, descriptive comments indicate a direct relation between suicide frequency and the attitudes commonly held toward the values of life, toward individual freedom, toward high authorities, whether the state or God.

A relation is also apparent between frequent suicides and times of great social change, when not only are attitudes in flux, but when the control of institutions and customs over the conduct of individuals has been slackened.

The Grecian decline and the rise of suicide cults.—There are indications that the early Grecian attitude toward suicide was that of disfavor, except, perhaps, under a few specific circumstances.

From the religious point of view suicide was regarded always as a crime, a violation of the social order. . . . . The Greek language hardly distinguishes between self-murder and murder of kin (the worst offense). The suicide belongs to the class of the victims of violent and untimely death . . . . the murdered, the dead on birth or in nonage, the unborn victim of abortion, regarding the fate of whom the popular mind was peculiarly sensitive. It seems probable that these religious grounds, and not any speculative theories, were the really active motives at all periods of ancient Greece in condemning the practice of suicide.[1]

In Athens, Sparta, and Thebes, while there were none of the special laws such as were later found in the Middle Ages in Western Europe, honors were denied the suicide at the time of burial, and in Athens a special burial place was provided.[2]

The early philosophers of Greece—Pythagoras, Plato, and Aristotle—all condemned suicide. Pythagoras regarded it as an encroachment on the right of God; Plato had a similar conception; while Aristotle condemned it on civic grounds.[3]

But even during the period when suicide met with disfavor, certain occasions calling for suicide were recognized. In harmony with the practice of disposing of weak infants was the voluntary death of old people by drinking poison hemlock.[4]

As early as the fifth century B.C. compulsory suicide was used as a means of execution. Poison hemlock was the favorite method for this type of suicide. Theramenes, in 403 B.C., and Socrates, in 399 B.C., are classic examples.[5]

It is evident, then, that hidden in the early Greek philosophy and customs were elements which tended toward the

[1] A. W. Mair, "Suicide," *Encyclopedia of Religion and Ethics* (hereafter referred to as *E.R.E.*), XII, 30–31. Note the similarity of this early Grecian attitude to the attitudes of preliterates of more recent times. See pp. 67 f.

[2] *Ibid.*, 29.

[3] Lecky, *History of European Morals from Augustus to Charlemagne*, I, 212.

[4] Mair, *op. cit.*, p. 29.

[5] *Ibid.*, pp. 28–29.

approval of suicide on such occasions as illness, old age, or the occurrence of crime.

The fourth century B.C. is significant. The power of Greece was declining, values of life were lowered, and a philosophy developed which went from the extreme of disregard of material values among the Stoics to an overemphasis on physical pleasures among the Epicureans.

Suicide became almost a dogma with many philosophical sects. The rigid control by the state (the social group) over the individual members of the state was weakened, and for allegiance to the state was substituted great concern with individual pleasures and pains. A part of this growing individualism was the right of each person to decree for himself whether or not he should continue to live. Suicide tended to become an accepted and approved method of ending difficulties, even trivial ones. And there is reason to believe that in the period of social disorganization attending Greece's `changed status difficulties of personal adjustment were increased in number and intensity.[1]

One philosophical sect, the Cyrenaics, founded 365 B.C., in general opposed suicide; but one of its members was perhaps the strongest advocate of suicide.

One of the most striking figures that a passing notice of Cicero brings before us is that of Hegesias, who was surnamed by the ancients "the orator of death." A conspicuous member of the Cyrenaic school which esteemed the pursuit of pleasure the sole end of a rational being, he taught that life was so full of cares, and its pleasure so fleeting and so

[1] Suicide as a life-philosophy and panacea for all ills will be noted in individual cases among contemporary Americans. See chapter x. The Grecians carried the process to a logical extreme and incorporated it into a definite code of behavior. These Grecian suicides did not reach a point of complete institutionalization, such as existed in the Orient, but tended in that direction.

alloyed, that the happiest lot for man was death; and such was the power of his eloquence, so intense was the fascination he cast around the tomb, that his disciples embraced with rapture the consequence of his doctrine, multitudes freed themselves by suicide from the troubles of the world, and the contagion was so great that Ptolemy, it is said, was compelled to banish the philosopher from Alexandria.[1]

The Cynics, whose philosophy was formulated about 360 B.C. by Anthistenes, and who included Diogenes among their members, "professed to be absolutely indifferent to life and death as to everything else and are accused of killing themselves by extraordinary methods for little or no reason. . . . ."[2]

Although the Epicureans were not indifferent to the pleasures of life they saw no reason to continue living after those pleasures were abated. Thus Epicurus exhorted men "to weigh carefully, whether they would prefer death to come to them, or would themselves go to death."[3]

The Stoics (who will be considered in more detail in Roman life) developed a philosophy of indifference to emotions and of allegiance to duty which at times taught that death was more worthy than living.

Stoicism taught men to hope little, but to fear nothing. It did not array death in brilliant colors as the path to positive felicity, but it endeavored to divest it, as the end of suffering, of every terror. Life lost much of its bitterness when men found a refuge from the storms of fate, a speedy deliverance from dotage and pain. Death ceased to be terrible when it was regarded rather as a remedy than as a sentence. Life and death in the Stoical system were attuned to the same key. The deification of human virtue, the total absence of all sense of sin,

[1] Lecky, *History of European Morals from Augustus to Charlemagne,* I, 215-16.

[2] H. J. Rose, "Suicide," *E.R.E.,* XII, 24.

[3] Lecky, *op. cit.,* I, 214-15.

the proud stubborn will that deemed humiliation the worst of stains, appeared alike in each.[1]

The history of suicide in Greece is the first of a series repeated in the case of Rome and in the Renaissance. A period of marked social change destroyed old customs and ancient ideals of conduct. Life could no longer follow routine paths, and difficulties of a personal nature increased. There had never been in Greece strong inhibitions to suicide. In this period of change suicide gradually came to be accepted as an expedient means of adjustment of the individual to his problems. Not only did the social disorganization contribute to suicide by destroying customary ways of living and creating difficulties, but the very attitude toward suicide as possible and commendable human conduct changed, and with its change suicide greatly increased.

Rome, a repetition of the Grecian situation.—Rome, as the cultural heir of Greece, inherited her philosophical sects with their favorable attitudes toward suicide as a means of adjustment to personal problems. Prior to the fall of the Roman Republic, however, suicide held a place similar to that in Greece prior to its decline. Suicide was permissible as an escape from intolerable shame or in the name of a great cause. Its promiscuous use was frowned upon; yet the tradition of certain occasions for suicide left the needed loophole for the entrance of the suicide cults from Greece.[2]

In the tumultuous period during which the Republic fell and the Empire was established, Stoicism taught suicide as a natural means of ending life that had become intolerable. To endure when honor, political causes, or zest of living was gone was no honor. Rather honor lay in choosing death un-

[1] *Ibid.*, I, 222–23.
[2] See Mair, "Suicide," *E.R.E.*, XII, 31.

der such circumstances, and by a brave, even a spectacular, death proving one's bravery and disregard for a worn-out life.[1]

The public attitude found its expression and formulation into a doctrine of conduct in the writings of various leaders. Musonius, Epictetus, and Seneca are typical in expressing the sentiment which Seneca worded as follows:

> If I can choose between a death of torture and one that is simple and easy, why should I not select the latter? As I choose the ship in which I will sail, and the house I will inhabit, so I will choose the death by which I will leave life. . . . . In no matter more than in death should we act according to our desire. . . . . Why should I endure the agonies of disease, and the cruelties of human tyranny, when I can emancipate myself from all my torments, and shake off every bond? For this reason, but for this alone, life is not an evil—that no one is obliged to live. The lot of man is happy, because no one continues wretched but by his fault. If life pleases you, live. If not, you have a right to return whence you came.[2]

The law likewise was in harmony with public sentiment.

As a general proposition, the law recognized it as a right, but two slight restrictions were after a time imposed. It had become customary with many men who were accused of political offenses to commit suicide before trial, in order to prevent the ignominious exposure of their bodies and the confiscation of their goods; but Domitian closed this resource by ordaining that the suicide of an accused person should entail the same consequences as his condemnation. Hadrian afterwards assimilated the suicide of a Roman soldier to desertion.[3]

As had been the case earlier in Greece, so now in Rome, certain leaders—Virgil, Cicero, Apuleius, Caesar, and Ovid

[1] See Lecky, *op. cit.*, I, 168–69.

[2] *Ibid.*, I, 217–18.

[3] *Ibid.*, I, 218–19.

—were opposed to suicide and sought to stem the tide of opinion favoring it.[1] The suicides of certain noted men, however, were extolled as heroic and set a precedent for others to follow. Cato and Marcus Brutus both committed suicide. Otho, who killed himself (69 A.D.) to avoid being the cause of a second civil war, was imitated by some of his soldiers who committed suicide before his corpse. Petronius, "one of the most famous voluptuaries of the reign of Nero (54–68 A.D.)" permitted himself slowly to bleed to death in the midst of friends assembled at a great banquet.[2]

In Rome, as in Greece, an early semi-indifferent attitude toward suicide, stabilized by a well-balanced social organization, flared into approval of suicide and its marked increase when the controls of custom and institutions failed.

Christianity as a prophylaxis to suicide.—Christianity came as an antidote to the lax moral ideals and disintegrating social control of Rome, although many years were required for its influence thoroughly to permeate the Roman culture. The attitudes of Christianity toward death were directly opposed to the pagan attitudes. To the pagan, death was the end of suffering and fear. To the Christian, for the majority of people, death was the entrance upon a period of torturing punishment.[3] The early Christian church took a stand against various formerly approved forms of violent death, such as infanticide, the performances in the arena, and abortions, as well as against suicide.[4] In time, suicide came to be regarded as a sin of the first magnitude.

This change from the moral lassitude and heightened

[1] *Ibid.*, IV, 213.

[2] *Ibid.*, I, 219–20; note, p. 215.

[3] *Ibid.*, I, 208–9.

[4] *Ibid.*, II, 20.

individualism of Rome to the stern repression and control of the individual exerted by the church was not accomplished without disagreement among the early leaders of the church.

At first the church approved certain forms of suicide: to procure martyrdom, to avoid apostasy, or to retain virginity.[1] Famous for suicide to retain virginity are Domnina and her daughters, and Pelagia, who was later made a saint.[2]

Gradually, however, all suicides were condemned. St. Ambrose (340–97) and St. Jerome (340–420) both condemned suicide to preserve chastity. St. Augustine (354–430) made an especial attack on the custom and "his opinion of the absolute sinfulness of suicide has since been generally adopted by the Catholic theologians, who pretend that Pelagia and Domnina acted under the impulse of a special revelation."[3]

This doctrine [of St. Augustine] which assimilated suicide with murder was adopted by the Church. Nay, self-murder was declared to be the worst form of murder . . . . already St. Chrysostom had declared that "if it is base to destroy others, much more is it to destroy one's self." The self-murderer was deprived of rights which were granted to all other criminals. In the sixth century a Council at Orleans enjoined that "the oblations of those who were killed in the commission of any crime may be received, except such as laid violent hands on themselves"; and a subsequent Council denied self-murderers the usual rites of Christian burial. It was even said that Judas committed a greater sin in killing himself than in betraying his master Christ to a certain death.[4]

[1] Edward Westermarck, *The Origin and Evolution of the Moral Ideas*, II, 251.

[2] Lecky, *op. cit.*, II, 46.

[3] *Ibid.*, II, 47; Rose, "Suicide," *E.R.E.*, XII, 23.

[4] Westermarck, *op. cit.*, II, 251.

These attitudes toward suicide came in time to be incorporated into law. Suicide became not only a sin, but a crime.

The old Pagan legislation on this subject remained unaltered in the Theodosian and Justinian codes; but a Council of Arles, in the fifth century, having pronounced suicide to be the effect of diabolical inspiration, a Council of Bragues, in the following century, ordained that no religious rites should be celebrated at the tomb of the culprit, and that no masses should be said for his soul; and these provisions which were repeated by later Councils, were gradually introduced into the laws of the barbarians and of Charlemagne. St. Lewis originated the custom of confiscating the property of the dead man, and the corpse was soon subjected to gross and various outrages. In some countries it could only be removed from the house through a perforation specially made for the occasion in the wall; it was dragged upon a hurdle through the streets, hung up with the head downwards, and at last thrown into the public sewer, or burnt, or buried in the sand below high-water mark, or transfixed by a stake on the public highway.[1]

Medieval philosophy unfavorable to suicide.—During the Middle Ages, which may be considered a continuation of the early Christian period, the opposition to suicide was strengthened both by the teachings of the church leaders and by secular legislation. Thus St. Thomas Aquinas denounced suicide as (1) unnatural, being contrary to the charity which every man bears toward himself, (2) an offense against the community, (3) a usurpation of God's power to kill and make alive,[2] arguments rooted for the most part in the Christian conception of the sacredness of human life, the subordinate relation of the human being to God, and the importance of death as the entrance upon a new kind of life.

[1] Lecky, *op. cit.*, II, 50.

[2] H. J. Rose, "Euthanasia," *E.R.E.*, V, 600; Westermarck, *The Origin and Development of the Moral Ideas*, II, 253.

Laws providing for special treatment of the bodies of suicides continued in force and were found in England and Scotland as well as in countries on the Continent.[1]

While there are no statistics of suicide rates for these early periods of European history, there is general agreement that suicide came to be extremely rare, a fact undoubtedly traceable in part to the rigid condemnation by the church. But it may be recalled also that the Middle Ages were extremely static as to social movements. Stable customs and institutions were paramount, and the disturbances caused by numerous contacts between people of diverse customs or by great political changes were absent. Under these circumstances the two types of suicide which tended to appear spasmodically during the Middle Ages are important.

One situation calling for suicide was a critical period which exceeded the ability for adjustment of those involved. Suicide was prevalent during the last, dissolute period of the Spanish Gothic kingdom; many instances occurred during a widespread pestilence which swept through England in the seventh century and at the time of the Black Death in the fourteenth century. Suicide ended the lives of many of the wives of priests when they were separated from their husbands by order of Hildebrand, and the witches of Europe, faced with torture on earth and the prospect of eternal damnation, frequently killed themselves. At the time of the Reformation in Germany, when the old order of living was breaking up and a new set of customs and morals had not fully evolved, suicide became noticeable among the Protestants.[2]

[1] Westermarck, *op. cit.*, II, p. 254.

[2] J. Janssen, *History of the German People at the Close of the Middle Ages,* VI, 304; XVI, 168–74; Lecky, *History of European Morals from Augustus to Charlemagne,* II, 51–52, 54.

Here again, as in Greece and Rome, suicide was a function of marked disturbances in the social organization, when habit and custom were inadequate to effect personal adjustment. The attitude, compelling as it was, that suicide was sinful proved insufficiently strong to withstand the disruptive effects of marked social disturbances.

The second type of suicide found during the Middle Ages resembles an unmotivated epidemic or mania for suicide. Such epidemics occurred among certain of the monastic orders, and there were at times manias for martyrdom which approached suicide. The dancing manias which swept over Europe at intervals during the Middle Ages also led at times to wholesale suicide at the height of the feverish excitement which attended the phenomenon.[1]

The Renaissance and the revival of suicide.—The attitude that suicide was sinful, which became "set" in the first three centuries of the Christian era, continued through the centuries until the time of the Renaissance, when there occurred a general upheaval of the static social organization of the Middle Ages. Contacts between different cultural groups were enormously increased, resulting in confusion of customs and morals and the disorganization of social institutions and of personal norms of conduct which accompany such a condition. Moreover, the writings of the Roman philosophers, coming into the hands of Renaissance philosophers, gave a ready justification for the individualism and right to commit suicide which was advocated.

A long list of philosophers defended suicide. More, in his *Utopia*, advocates it under certain circumstances. Other

---

[1] Sumner, *Folkways*, p. 219; Lecky, *History of European Morals from Augustus to Charlemagne*, II, 49–55; J. F. C. Hecker, *Epidemics of the Middle Ages*, pp. 95, 111–12.

writers who favored it were Donne and Hume (1711–76) in England; Montesquieu (1689–1755), Voltaire (1694–1788), and D'Holbach (1723–89) in France; and Schopenhauer in Germany. Their attitudes are so similar that any one may be taken as typical.[1]

Thus Schopenhauer cites the attitude of Pliny, the Stoics, and the Hindus to prove that suicide is not a crime. Any moral objection to suicide is that it "is opposed to the attainment of the highest moral goal, since it substitutes for the real emancipation from this world of sorrow, a merely apparent one." The ascetic ideal of the church that suffering is the true purpose of life had never been embraced by European philosophers. "We shall find on the whole that as soon as the terrors of life counterbalance the terrors of death man makes an end of his life." Thus an excess of pain or anxiety makes death a relief. He sums up his position as follows:

We have to hear, accordingly, that suicide is the greatest cowardice, that it is only possible in madness, and similar twaddle, or even the entirely senseless phrase that suicide is "wrong," whereas obviously no one has a greater right over anything in the world than over his own person and life.[2]

An uneasy fear of suicide shows itself in the writings of a few philosophers, notably Paley, Hegel, and Kant.[3]

Again the changed attitude toward suicide found expression in law, this time either in the repealing of former laws

[1] Lecky, *History of European Morals from Augustus to Charlemagne*, II, 57; Westermarck, *The Origin and Development of the Moral Ideas*, II, 258–60; David Hume, *Philosophical Works*, IV, 558–68; B. d'Holbach, *System of Nature*, II, 137 ff.

[2] A. Schopenhauer, *Selected Essays*, p. 357.

[3] Westermarck, *op. cit.*, II, 260–61.

punishing suicide or in their disregard.[1] Suicide, which had ceased to be a sin, was no longer a crime.

In this brief survey of the history of suicide in Europe two points are important. In the first place, the dependence of suicide upon attitudes regarding it is clear. When death was regarded as a natural event leading on to a desirable phase of life, as it was regarded in pagan Greece and Rome, suicide was easily justified. The Christian attitude that life belongs to a superhuman power and that death may lead to suffering made suicide repulsive and almost nonexistent. The individualism of the Renaissance again placed the right to die in the hands of the individual.

The second point is the coincidence of outbreaks of suicide with periods of social disorganization. The decline of Grecian power, the fall of the Roman Republic, the freedom of the Renaissance—all mark periods of change and of confusion when accustomed ways of doing and thinking were no longer adequate to meet the problems of the social situation in which people found themselves. The same relation of suicide to social crises is shown on a smaller scale in the occurrence of suicide at times of crisis during the static Middle Ages.

[1] Westermarck, *op. cit.*, II, 261.

CHAPTER III

EUROPE AND THE UNITED STATES: SOME CONTEMPORARY FACTORS

The twentieth-century heritage.—Modern Europe and America are joint heirs to two lines of tradition which affect the attitude toward suicide. There is on the one hand the attitude fostered by the church throughout the Middle Ages, and now carried forward principally by the Catholic church, that life is sacred and that suicide is a sin. On the other hand, there is the tradition of individualism which gives one the right to dispose of his own life when and how he pleases.

This sharing by America of the European thought currents, the fact that the United States are peopled by those of European blood, and the parallel industrial development in the two countries makes it possible to draw data from both in attempting to ferret out some of the influences which contribute to variations in the suicide rate.

Is climate a factor?—Morselli, who wrote some fifty years ago, on the basis of the suicide rates then existing in Europe, concluded that the warm climate of Southern Europe deterred people from committing suicide, while the rigors of Northern Europe increased suicides.[1] More recent tendencies in European suicide rates prove the fallacy of this general assumption. The highest rates are not in Northern, but in Central, Europe; Norway has a rate as low as some of the countries which share the mellow Mediterranean air; and

[1] Henry Morselli, *Suicide: An Essay on Comparative Moral Statistics,* pp. 36–51.

France, well to the south, has a suicide rate as high as any in Europe. Australia, with a low rate, also contradicts the generalization.

In the United States even the most brief thought forces one to question how climate affects suicide, when one considers among the southern states alone the difference in rates between Mississippi (3.1. suicides per 100,000) and Florida (7.77). (See Table III and Map I.) Or the field of comparison may be widened, and the Pacific Coast, second in mellowness of climate, considered. But this is the region of highest rates, with the warmest state, California, highest of all. Among the northern states as little correlation between climate and suicide rates can be maintained. Of the states represented, Maine, New Hampshire, and Vermont have perhaps the most rigorous climate. Yet their rates are no higher than the rates for New Jersey, Missouri, Illinois, and Indiana, with less trying climates, and very little higher than for any of the eastern or plains states. Moreover, one could scarcely contend that Utah and Idaho have climates which differ radically from the climates of adjacent states, although their suicide rates are but half those of neighboring states. If, then, climate is at all a factor, it is secondary to other factors which, when present, nullify it.

The fallacy of the racial-temperament theory.—A favorite theory to explain the differences in suicide rates in Europe and one in harmony with the biologically tinged thinking of the past generation has been racial temperament.

The concept of temperament is that it is an inherited "bent" or an innate, characteristic way of reacting. Theoretically, such a concept, being biological and inheritable, is entirely compatible with the concept of race. Race presupposes descent from a common ancestral group, itself of

TABLE III

SUICIDES PER 100,000 INHABITANTS FOR THE UNITED STATES

	1918–22*	1910†
Mississippi‡	3.10	
South Carolina	3.86	
North Carolina	4.00	
Louisiana	5.74	
Georgia§	5.80	
Tennessee	6.15	
Virginia	7.20	
Kentucky	7.74	
Florida‡	7.77	
North Dakota¶	7.9	
Idaho§	8.10	
Utah	8.64	10.7
Delaware‡	8.80	
Rhode Island	10.38	14.7
Pennsylvania	10.60	12.7
Michigan	10.94	13.6
Kansas	11.44	
Nebraska‖	11.58	
Maryland	11.58	10.3
Massachusetts	11.62	12.6
Wisconsin	11.84	14.1
Ohio	12.08	14.2
Minnesota	12.58	11.6
New Hampshire	12.68	12.5
New Jersey	12.68	17.1
Maine	12.80	11.4
New York	12.86	16.8
Missouri	12.86	
Vermont	12.98	13.2
Indiana	13.14	14.1
Connecticut	13.24	17.8
Illinois	13.46	
Iowa**	13.6	
Colorado	15.46	20.8
Oregon	15.50	
Montana	16.20	
Wyoming§	16.90	
Washington	17.34	20.1
California	24.42	29.0

* Average of suicide rates for 1918–22, as given in *Mortality Statistics* (1922), pp. 68–69; rates for North Dakota and Iowa from *Mortality Statistics* (1924), p. 69.
† *Mortality Rates* (1910–20), pp. 238 ff.
‡ Based on four years, 1919–22. § Rate for 1922 only.
‖ Based on three years, 1920–22. ¶ Rate for 1924 only.
** Based on two years, 1923–24, inclusive.

MAP I

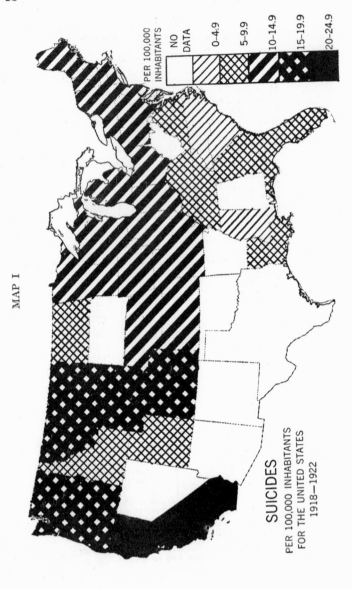

SUICIDES

PER 100,000 INHABITANTS
FOR THE UNITED STATES
1918—1922

PER 100,000 INHABITANTS

NO DATA
0–4.9
5–9.9
10–14.9
15–19.9
20–24.9

a definite biological type. Races are distinguished on the basis of physical characteristics, of which certain ones have been found to be inherited without great variability, e.g., skin color, hair texture, hairiness of the body, the cephalic index, the nasal index, the degree of prognathism, the color of the hair and of the eyes. When a group of physical characteristics is found throughout a large group of people with a certain degree of consistency that group is assumed to be of one race, and a second group with the same characteristics is assumed to belong to that race also.[1] Thus, the American Indians and the Mongoloid people of Asia, although widely separated in space and differing in customs, are generally considered to have come from the same parent stock. Racial temperament is thought of as another biological trait, inherited more or less consistently throughout the group.

It is necessary to realize, of course, that races are not sharply delimited, that the meeting places of even unfriendly races are also the meeting places of lovers, that political conquest of one race by another means also the conquest of the women of the defeated race, and that all racial frontiers are marked by racial hybrids. In some cases whole nations and new biological groups which may almost be called new races have been created. And it is assumed that no race is entirely pure. Nevertheless, certain divisions can be made on the basis of the physical traits listed previously, and the following races and subdivisions have been distinguished by anthropologists:[2] (1) Caucasian or white race, including Nordic, Alpine, Mediterranean, Hindu. (2) Mongoloid, or yellow race, including Mongolian, Malaysian,

[1] A. L. Kroeber, *Three Essays on the Antiquity and Races of Man*, University of California, Syllabus Series No. 119.

[2] *Ibid.*, p. 68.

American Indian. (3) Negroid or black race, including Negro, Melanesian, Dwarf black. (4) Of doubtful classification: Australian, Vedda, Polynesian, Ainu.

Denmark
Norway
Sweden } ......Nordic race
Northern Germany
Austria

England................Predominantly Nordic, but with ancient Alpine and perhaps Mediterranean strain

France...................Nordic, Alpine, and Mediterranean races

South Germany
Russia
Czechoslovakia
Jugoslavia
Roumania } ....Alpine race
Poland
Bulgaria
North Italy

Southern Italy
Greece
Ireland (predominantly) } ....Mediterranean race
Northern Africa

Japan
China } ....Mongoloid race
American Indians

Political units (with their language groupings) do not correspond to racial lines with any degree of consistency. Yet for practical purposes it is necessary to speak in terms of political units; hence for certain of the civilized countries the overlapping boundaries of race and nation have been merged as well as possible (see Table on p. 30).[1]

The Jews, except for such mixture as has taken place, are Alpine.

The United States represents a mixture of all the primary races and most of the subdivisions, although it is not as yet a very homogeneous mixture.

Race is a biological attribute which can be changed only through interbreeding with another race. Temperament is also a biological attribute, and inheritable. The hypothesis of racial temperament assumes that while all types of temperament are present in every race, some races tend to have a predominance of a certain type of temperament. With reference to suicide, the hypothesis further assumes that certain types of temperament are conducive to suicide (or to personal disorganization), and that therefore a high rate of suicide in a race is due to the predominance of a suicidal temperament in that race. The argument is extremely weak, since the phenomenon to be explained (suicide) is used as proof of the hypothesis of explanation (a certain type of racial temperament).

The foundation upon which this hypothesis has rested is statistical; and the means of shaking it are also statistical.

If the concept of racial temperament has any value at all in explaining human behavior, it must be assumed to act with some consistency and constancy. As evidenced by races it should be operative throughout a historical period and in varying social situations. If temperament is changed by changing social conditions, its value as a constant and

---

[1] Kroeber, *Three Essays on the Antiquity and Races of Man*, p. 70, and Humphrey J. Johnson, "Race, Language, and Nationality in Europe," in A. L. Kroeber and T. T. Waterman, *Source Book in Anthropology*, pp. 180 ff.

innate factor is at once invalidated and social customs and experiences take precedence as more powerful determining factors than temperament—hence as crucial factors.

In Table I and Figure 2 the rates for Sweden, Norway, and Denmark cover almost a hundred years, a period of time sufficiently long, it would seem, to obtain a trend. The suicide rate for Norway has been cut in half during that period; the rate for Sweden has doubled; while the rate for Denmark has followed the trend in Norway, but on a higher level, the rates for Denmark being consistently twice those for Norway. These three countries are of the Nordic race, and Norway and Sweden in particular have similar climates, topography, occupations, and general social customs. The explanation of these changes in trend and variations in frequency of suicide in nations of the same racial stock is not indicated by the statistics, nor is it available to an American investigator; but it is obvious that racial temperament is not a good explanation for such wide variations within the limits of one racial group. The people of Prussia are also Nordic. A hundred years ago they had a rate of 7 or 8 suicides per 100,000 population; in 1914, by a fairly steady increase, they had achieved a rate of more than 20 suicides per 100,000 population, a rate much above that of the Norwegians for the same year.

Other illustrations of opposed trends in nations peopled by the same race are obvious in the table, but less striking. Australia is for the most part peopled by the English. Yet the suicide rate in Australia is consistently about a third higher than that of England and Wales. For people with a strong Nordic strain, the English have a low suicide rate: 7–10 per 100,000, as compared with 20 in Germany for the same period of time.

In general, Southern Europe has had lower suicide rates than Northern Europe, a fact which led to the conclusion that the Mediterranean races were temperamentally indisposed to suicide. But the peculiar ranking of suicide frequency in Europe which made this conclusion possible when Morselli and his contemporaries wrote no longer exists. Italy, which is Alpine and Mediterranean in race, while it had in 1866–70 a suicide rate of 3, from 1912 to 1915 had a rate of more than 8, which compares favorably with the highly Nordic Norway. France, presumably a mixture of all three races, between 1826 and 1913 increased from a rate of 5.4 to a rate of 23 suicides per 100,000, and hence stands in the same rank as the pure Nordic countries.

Hence a comparison of European nations of the same race either at the same period or with regard to the trends of their suicide frequency, as well as the varying trend in any given nation, dispels the hypothesis that the variations in suicide frequency are due to racial temperament. It is probable that variations and trends cannot be traced to any one factor, and the complexity of the situation and need for intimate knowledge prevents any analysis here of the European situation.

The ease with which rates vary for people of the same race and cultural group when social conditions are changed is shown by a comparison of the rates for Europe and the rates for European immigrants in America[1] (see Table IV and compare with Table I). In all cases the rates for immigrants in this country are two or three times as high as the rates for their brethren in Europe, whether the comparison is made for the same dates or whether the suicide rates in the United States are compared with rates at an earlier

[1] See Frenay, *The Suicide Problem in the United States*, pp. 132–41.

period in Europe when conditions were more nearly the same as when the immigrant lived there and came under the influence of current European customs and beliefs. The suicide rates for the different European immigrants vary greatly,

TABLE IV

SUICIDE RATES IN CERTAIN CITIES, ACCORDING TO COUNTRY OF BIRTH (RATES PER 100,000 OF THE POPULATION)

Place of Birth	New York City* 1911–20	Chicago† 1919–21	Philadelphia§ 1916–24	Boston‖ 1911–15 and 1918–19
Total rate................	15.4	15.2	No data	17.0
United States............	8.1	9.4	9.3	12.7
All foreign countries.......	No data	28.8	20.1	21.3
Canada..................	No data	27.9	23.8	21.5
England.................	30.6	17.7	23.5	31.5
Ireland..................	15.3	8.1	10.3	15.3
France..................	33.8	No data	18.4	No data
Italy....................	10.5	15.8	10.5	10.9
Russia..................	17.8	19.3‡	16.1	16.0¶
Austria.................	No data	56.9	No data	No data
Hungary................	No data	47.3	No data	No data
Germany................	64.2	43.4	53.2	68.9
Scandinavia.............	No data	37.4	25.6	57.5**
Poland..................	No data	11.3	11.2	No data

* Frenay, *The Suicide Problem in the United States*, p. 134.
† Based on records in the office of the coroner of Cook County, Illinois, and the *Fourteenth Census of the United States*, II, 291, 739. For a more detailed table, see Table XV, p. 80.
‡ Includes Lithuania.
§ Frenay, *op. cit.*, p. 136.
‖ *Ibid.*, p. 137.　　　　　¶ Includes Poles.　　　　** Swedes only.

but without any great correspondence to race. German immigrants in the United States have high rates; Scandinavian, Austrian, and English come next; the Irish and Russian groups follow, while the Italian immigrants have almost as low a rate as native-born Americans. Native-born Americans, it should be recalled, are a mixture of several races, but principally of the Nordic groups. Their suicide rate is not, however, of the type considered typical of the Nordic race.

It is possible to carry the inquiry of shifting rates and racial groups a step farther. What of the offspring of immigrant parents, racially pure? Such information is not available for the entire United States. For Chicago in 1919–21 the suicide rate of the offspring of foreign-born parents was slightly lower than the rate for offspring of native parents; that is, in one generation the suicide rate in the same racial groups had dropped not only from the high rates of the immigrant groups, but far below the rates of the racial groups in Europe from which many of the immigrants came. The Chicago rate for foreign born in 1919–21 was 28.8 suicides per 100,000; for native white of native parentage, 11.1; for native white of foreign parentage, 9.1; and for native white of mixed parentage, 6.7 per 100,000 in each group.

While there may be noted a general tendency for the countries of Northern Europe to have a high suicide rate, those of Southern Europe a low rate, and those classed as Alpine an intermediate rate, the variations within each race and the contradictory trends of nations of the same race suggest that the explanation is to be sought in changing social conditions rather than in fixed temperamental qualities. Such a conclusion is supported by the unusually high rates of European immigrants in America and the low rates of their American children, as well as the generally low rate of Americans, who are the offspring of European races several generations removed, and in particular are the descendants of Nordic peoples.

The Orientals in America, in the Hawaiian Islands, and in China and Japan afford another but less clear-cut instance of the variation of suicides in the same racial groups under different social conditions.

Mortality statistics are not available for China as a whole. For Pekin the rate was 15.5 per 100,000 in 1917.[1] If the relation of urban to rural rates which exists in Europe and America holds also for China, the rural rate and the rate for China as a whole would probably be lower than the Pekin rate. In the Hawaiian Islands, where the Chinese numbered 23,507 in 1920, the rate for 1918–22 was 34.00 per 100,000,[2] double the Pekin rate for 1927.

In Japan the rate in 1917 was 16.4; in 1918, 17.8; and in 1923, 19.7 suicides per 100,000 (see Table I). In the Hawaiian Islands the rate for 1918–22 for the Japanese, who numbered 109,274 in 1920, was 28.4 suicides per 100,000.[3]

In California, while only an approximation can be reached and the Japanese and Chinese rates cannot be separated, it is evident that the rate for Oriental suicides is much higher than either the white rates in California or the Oriental rates in the Hawaiian Islands. The California rate for 1919–21 for whites was 23.9 per 100,000. For the entire colored group (Negroes, Indians, Chinese, Japanese, and miscellaneous), the rate was 34.57. The Negroes and Indians would both normally have a lower rate than the white group;[4] hence the excess in the rate of colored over white must be due to the Chinese and Japanese. As with the Europeans, the Chinese and Japanese in a foreign environment have suicide rates higher than those found in the home countries.

[1] S. A. Gamble and J. S. Burgess, *Pekin: A Social Survey*, pp. 116–17.

[2] Compiled from *Mortality Statistics* for 1918, 1919, 1920, 1921 and the *Fourteenth Census of the United States*, III, 1172.

[3] *Ibid.*

[4] For Negroes, see Table IX; for Indians, see Commission of Indian Affairs, *Annual Reports of the Department of the Interior*, from 1898 through 1906.

The data presented seem to frustrate conclusively the assertion that suicide is the result of innate temperamental traits which characterize races. The variations in Europe and America at any one time seem to be related to national groups rather than to racial groups. National groups are social rather than biological, and hence the producers and carriers of social attitudes generated by the peculiar history and social conditions of the group.

TABLE V*

SUICIDES PER 100,000 INHABITANTS IN CALIFORNIA, BY RACES
(1919–21)

	Population	Annual Average Number of Suicides	Rate per 100,000
White population.............	3,264,711	779	23.9
Negroes........38,763 Indians........17,360 Chinese........28,812 Japanese.......71,952 Other colored... 5,263	162,150	56	34.6

* Compiled from *Mortality Statistics* for 1919, 1920, 1921, and *Abstract of the Fourteenth Census of the United States* (1920), pp. 102, 104.

Again, social disorganization looms large in the case of immigrant groups, and suicide again appears as a concomitant of weak social control.

As a partial alternative to the racial-temperament hypothesis may be offered certain data on religious and urban communities.

Does religion prevent suicide?—When Morselli's book on suicide was translated into English in 1881, the statistics of suicide in the three major religious groups of Europe were such as to enable him to state confidently that with regard to frequency of suicide the religions stood in the order of Protestant first, Catholic second, with the Jews contributing the fewest suicides.[1] This relationship was in general continued until about 1890. Since that time, however, the rates

TABLE VI

SUICIDES PER 100,000 OF EACH RELIGIOUS GROUP*

Year	Catholic		Protestant		Jewish	
Prussia						
1849–55	5.0		16.0		4.6	
1869–72	6.9		18.7		9.6	
1891–1900	9.3		24.7		24.1	
1901–7	10.1		25.2		29.4	
Percentage of increase.		102%		57.5%		539.1%
Bavaria						
1844–56	4.9		13.5		10.6	
1870–79	7.4		19.5		11.5	
1880–89	9.5		22.2		18.6	
1890–99	9.3		21.0		21.2	
1900–8	10.2		22.2		25.3	
Percentage of increase.		108.2%		64.4%		138.7%
Württemberg						
1844–60	8.0		11.4		6.6	
1873–80	13.5		17.7		9.8	
1881–90	11.8		16.9		13.8	
1891–1900	11.2		15.5		26.3	
1901–7	11.7		19.3		21.5	
Percentage of increase.		46.3%		69.3%		225.8%
Baden						
1864–70	12.1		15.9		9.5	
1871–80	15.5		21.3		15.1	
1881–90	16.0		23.7		22.2	
1891–1900	15.9		25.0		22.9	
1901–5	16.9		26.8		26.9	
Percentage of increase.		39.7%		62.9%		183.2%

* R. Weichbrodt, *Der Selbstmord. Abhandlungen aus der Neurologie, Psychiatrie, Psychologie, und Ihren Grenzgebieten*, Heft 22 (1923), p. 19.

of suicide in the three religions have increased in an extremely uneven manner, at least in some parts of Europe (see Table VI).

In the four German states for which rates are given over

[1] Morselli, *Suicide: An Essay on Comparative Moral Statistics*, pp. 122 ff.

a period of fifty-eight years, the Protestants show the most regular increase, amounting to about 60 per cent. The Catholic increase in two states exceeds the Protestant increase in the same states. The Jewish increase has been most marked and most erratic, varying in the four states from 138.7 per cent to 539.1 per cent. A similar comparison for Hungary reveals an increase of about 400 per cent for both Catholics and Protestants and an increase of about 700 per cent for the Jews from the middle of the nineteenth century to the first decade of the twentieth century. At both periods the Protestants rank highest; but the Jews have shifted from a rate only half that of the Catholics to a rate double the Catholic rate.[1]

From these figures and from the undifferentiated figures for the suicide trend by nations (Table I) it is apparent that until very recently Catholicism and Judaism acted as restraints to suicide in most parts of Europe, and that even yet in many sections this relationship prevails. The variation in the rates of increase in the four sections of Germany, however, prevent any dogmatic statement as to the effect of religion, as does also a comparison of the rates of nations predominantly Protestant or Catholic.

Spain, Bosnia, Ireland, Portugal, Italy, Serbia, and Roumania, all Catholic countries, while their rates differed considerably and were in all cases on the increase, had rates which so far as available data show did not exceed ten suicides per 100,000 of the population per year for the years prior to the war. With regard to religion, exceptions are of extreme importance. Hence France deserves attention; for

[1] See Morselli, *Suicide: An Essay on Comparative Moral Statistics*, p. 122; J. Kollarits, "Ein Erklärungsversuch für die Selbstmordhäufigkeit der Protestanten," *Ztschr. f. d. ges. Neurol. und Psychiat.*, XLIX (1919), 357.

in spite of the fact that it is in part a Catholic country, its suicide rate had reached 23.2 per 100,000 in 1912. Belgium, another Catholic country, by an increasing rate had reached a rate of 13.5 in 1912.

As for the Protestant countries, their suicide rates tend to be high. Germany and Sweden, both with increasing rates, had between 18 and 24 suicides per 100,000 in 1913. Protestant Denmark, in spite of a decreasing rate, had 18.3 suicides per 100,000 in 1914. One mixed Protestant-Catholic country had an increasing rate, on a high level: Switzerland, with a rate of 24.7 per 100,000 in 1913. The kingdom of Hungary, with mixed Catholic and Protestant population, had an increasing rate which had reached 19.9 per 100,000 in 1913. Two exceptions among the Protestant countries should be noted: Norway with a decreasing rate, never high, which had sunk to 6.4 suicides per 100,000 in 1913, and England and Wales, with a fluctuating rate showing a slight tendency to increase, with a rate of 9.6 in 1913.

Fragmentary as this information is, it is evident that while Catholicism and Judaism have tended in the past to maintain a lower suicide rate among their members than Protestantism, there is no magic in any of the three religions which prevents suicide. It is also obvious that religion operates within a larger social organization and that comparisons of religious groups to be valid ought to be in the same larger social group and hence subject to the same influences.

A part of the low rate among Catholics is undoubtedly due to the positive attitude against suicide which the church teaches.

Positive and direct suicide perpetrated without God's consent always constitutes a grave injustice towards Him. To destroy a thing is to dispose of it as an absolute master and to act as one having full and independent dominion over it; . . . . God has reserved to himself direct dominion over life; . . . . Consequently, suicide is an attempt against the dominion and right of ownership of the Creator. . . . . That suicide is unlawful is the teaching of Holy Scripture and of the Church which condemns the act as a most atrocious crime, and, in hatred of the sin and to arouse the horror of its children, denies the suicide Christian burial.[1]

To the orthodox Jew of Europe, also, suicide is sinful. Suicides are not buried in the same cemetery as other Jews, but are given graves near the fence, and certain prayers are omitted from the burial services.[2]

While Protestant churches and nations formerly had similar penalties, they have tended to repeal or to disregard them.[3]

But these positive teachings against suicide which create an attitude of repulsion toward it are not the only effect of certain religions. The Catholic and Jewish religions are organized on a group rather than an individual basis. Before a Jewish synagogue can be established, ten heads of households must meet together and the frequent meetings of the orthodox Jewish community necessitate close proximity of residence to the synagogue. Thus the mere establishing of a synagogue calls for a neighborhood group of ten families as a minimum. The rabbi in the Jewish community is a learned man who is regarded with respect, to whom troublesome questions of conduct are brought. By assimilating into their personal codes of conduct the teachings of the rabbi,

[1] A. Vander Heeren, "Suicide," *Catholic Encyclopedia*, XIV, 326; see also chap. ii.

[2] Information given by Dr. Louis Wirth, Department of Sociology and Anthropology, University of Chicago.

[3] See chap. ii.

a homogeneous community of one moral standard and one system of customs is built up and the people find their lives organized through their religion. Under such conditions they have little opportunity for personal disorganization so long as the Jewish community remains culturally isolated from non-Jewish contacts. Moreover, the Jewish religion and the Jewish religious community recognize many of the major needs of life and provide for them. Rules of health, dress, food, recreation, occupation, philanthropy, the rituals of funerals, food preparation, of obtaining a wife, are all prescribed.

In the Catholic groups the situation is very similar. The Catholic church is organized on a parish system, with a priest and his assistants to look after not only the moral welfare but many other interests of the parishioners. The church prescribes for the people what their attitudes shall be, not only on strictly church matters, but on many types of human conduct: on marriage, on birth control, on type of schooling, on suicide. Catholics are forbidden to marry outside the church or to attend any other than churches of their own faith. Thus, even in a mixed community there is a tendency for the church to dominate the lives of the members, while in a homogeneous Catholic community the people have their interests and attitudes fixed by the church, their urgent needs provided for, and their troubles dissipated through confession and the advice and help of the priest.

Religions such as the Catholic and the Jewish are more than religions; they are systems of social organization which (1) mold the personalities and dictate the dominant interests of their members; (2) furnish the means of satisfying the needs thus created; and (3) provide means for reorganizing the few individuals who do become disorganized.

In America there are few communities of any size which are organized on the basis of such a religious organization. There are and have been, however, many small ones, such as the Quaker communities, Amish communities, Shaker villages, and many other less well-known communities. The Mormons have the largest, most concentrated, and best organized of these community-organized religions, and it is significant that the two most thoroughly Mormon states, Utah and Idaho, have suicide rates which are only one-half as high as the rates of the surrounding western states.[1]

The manner in which the religious groups just mentioned, as well as the large number of sects, have thrived in a Protestant country points to one peculiarity of Protestantism which undoubtedly contributes to the high Protestant suicide rate. Protestantism is an individualistic religion. Theoretically, anyone may interpret the Bible according to his own intellect and interests. Thus the individual does not have his attitudes firmly set by an institution which in the case of the Catholics and Jews not only saves the person from becoming confused and disorganized but also fosters homogeneity of beliefs throughout the group. Even the orthodox Protestant thinks and does much more as he pleases than does the orthodox Catholic or Jew. In like manner, he finds fewer customs and institutions to satisfy his needs.

In places where there is little conflict[2] between the religious groups and where contacts are numerous the control of orthodox religions tends to break down, and with the loss of the severe social control, not only are the attitudes

[1] See Table III and Map I.

[2] Conflict tends to unify the opposing groups and to strengthen the social organization of each.

against suicide lost, but personal disorganization becomes more frequent. France is an example of a Catholic country in which Catholicism has ceased to dominate all classes of people.

With reference to the increasing Jewish rate in Europe, Fishberg, who has made an intensive study of his own people, states that in Eastern Europe, where the old Jewish mores still function, suicide is less frequent among Jews than among Christians, and that in Western European cities the suicide rate for Jews has increased as they have grown away from the old customs and traditions during succeeding generations and have adopted the attitudes and ways of living of their Christian and urbanized neighbors.[1]

From the data here presented it is evident that the outstanding effect of religion on suicide is not solely through church doctrines which may hold that suicide is sinful, but also through the organizing effect of an orthodox religion on the adherents to that religion. In the United States data are not available for the religion of suicides, nor are there adequate data at hand for a recent estimate of the membership of the numerous religious sects.[2] In general, the South is Baptist; moreover, the southern Baptists are "fundamentalists," that is, they are orthodox and accept the dictates of the church and live their lives accordingly. It is suggested that the conservatism and organizing effect of the Baptist religion may be one factor in the low rate of suicides in the southern states. The northern and eastern states have more Catholics than any one Protestant sect. Their suicide

---

[1] Maurice Fishberg, *The Jews: A Study of Race and Environment*, p. 40.

[2] The last national religious census was made in 1916. It is based on church membership, not always an adequate indication of the religious character of a community.

rate is only moderately high. The Middle West tends toward Methodists and Presbyterians and has a suicide rate about equal to the eastern states. The West, with its abnormally high suicide rate, is dominated by no particular religious groups. So far as percentages of the population who adhered to any religion whatever is concerned, the Far West tended in 1916 to have a smaller proportion of church members than the other sections of the United States. The varying rates of Europe and the United States cannot be explained solely on the basis of religion; but undoubtedly religion is a factor, on the basis of its organizing and conservative tendencies and ability to create a homogeneous community as well as its attitudes toward suicide as a sin.

Suicide and the urban trend.—A statement made by Morselli a half-century ago is still a valid generalization regarding the relation of suicide to urban and rural communities in America as well as in Europe.[1]

The proportion of suicides in all Europe is greater amongst the condensed population of urban centres than amongst the more scattered inhabitants of the country. Nevertheless, this influence of cities is not uniform and exclusive, nor, as might be supposed, is it ever according to ratio with the mass of inhabitants. Town life is a powerful modifier of the human will, but it does not neutralize all the other social and individual factors.

Recent statistics show the same relation between rural and urban areas which was evident fifty years ago. The rate of suicide in cities of 10,000 and over in the United States, when considered *en masse* for the registration states, is consistently year after year approximately 50 per cent higher than the rate for cities and towns of less than 10,000 and

[1] Morselli, *Suicide: An Essay on Comparative Moral Statistics*, p. 169. For rate of suicide in cities at the time Morselli wrote, see *ibid.*, pp. 172–73.

rural population taken *en masse*. From 1910 to 1922 the rate for small towns and rural sections, taken together, has been between 8.5 and 13.3 suicides per 100,000 population, while the rate for cities of 10,000 and over has been from 12.0 to 19.5 per 100,000.

In order to examine the material with more precision than a simple urban-rural division permits, a three-part divi-

TABLE VII

SUICIDES PER 100,000 INHABITANTS IN URBAN
AND RURAL COMMUNITIES

Country	Years	Urban Rate	Rural Rate
Sweden*.......	1901–10	24.04	12.45
	1911–15	24.32	14.39
Norway†.......	1917	6.8	3.8
	1918	4.8	3.4
	1919	6.6	4.7
Finland‡.......	1919–23	18.38	8.6
United States	1920	12.0	8.5
(reg. states)§..	1921	15.0	10.1
	1922	14.3	9.5

* *Annuaire Statistique de la Suède* (1921), p. 55.
† *Annuaire Statistique de la Norvège* (1922), pp. 7, 32.
‡ *Annuaire Statistique de Finlande* (1925), p. 65.
§ *Mortality Rates* (1910–20), pp. 234 ff.; *Mortality Statistics* (1922), p. 68.

sion was made for each state in the registration area into (1) rural and towns under 10,000, referred to here as rural; (2) cities from 10,000 to 100,000 population, referred to here as secondary cities; (3) cities with population over 100,000, referred to here as principal cities. Further, the rates for all cities of 100,000 and over in the registration states for 1921 were computed separately.

From these data it becomes apparent that while in general the rate increases from rural through secondary cities to the principal cities, there is on the one hand no definite and consistent ratio between the three rates, and on the other there are numerous exceptions, cases in which the secondary

TABLE VIII

SUICIDES PER 100,000 INHABITANTS IN CITIES
AND RURAL DISTRICTS IN REGISTRA-
TION STATES*

Year	Total	Cities of 10,000 and Over†	Cities under 10,000 and Rural
1900..........	10.2	11.8	8.3
1901..........	10.4	11.7	8.7
1902..........	10.3	11.7	8.5
1903..........	11.3	12.8	9.4
1904..........	12.2	13.9	10.1
1905..........	13.5	15.0	11.6
1906..........	12.8	14.9	10.4
1907..........	14.5	16.7	11.9
1908..........	16.8	19.6	13.7
1909..........	15.9	19.0	12.6
1910..........	15.3	17.9	12.4
1911..........	15.9	19.2	12.6
1912..........	15.5	18.2	12.7
1913..........	15.4	18.6	12.1
1914..........	16.1	19.5	12.8
1915..........	16.2	19.2	13.3
1916..........	13.8	17.0	10.9
1917..........	13.1	16.2	10.4
1918..........	12.2	14.2	10.3
1919..........	11.4	13.6	9.5
1920..........	10.2	12.0	8.5
1921..........	12.5	15.0	10.1
1922..........	11.8	14.3	9.5

* From *Special Reports of the Census Office, Mortality, 1900–1904*; *Mortality Statistics, 1909*; *Mortality Rates, 1910–20*; *Mortality Statistics, 1922*.

† Figures for 1910–20 are based on cities of 10,000 or more in 1920.

cities and even the rural sections rank higher than the principal cities. In the third place, the rural rate in some states is much higher than the rate of the secondary and even of the principal cities in other states. Mere ruralness or urbanness does not fix the rate, although in adjacent states (that is, under similar social conditions) a certain relationship may be detected. Thus, in the West, Middle West, and South the tendency is for the principal cities to exceed the secondary cities, which in turn exceed the rural districts (see Table IX).

In the northeastern states another pattern tends to predominate. In New Jersey, for instance, the rate for principal cities is 12.8 suicides per 100,000; for secondary cities, 11.9; and for rural sections, 13.7. The same relationship and almost the identical rates hold for New York. Rhode Island, Massachusetts, New Hampshire, and Vermont all have rural rates which equal or exceed the rates not only of secondary cities but of primary cities as well, while in Maine rural sections and cities have almost identical rates.

The highness or lowness of rates and the relation of rural to urban rates, in so far as any classification can be made, conform to sections of the country more nearly than to any consistent pattern based on population groupings. It must be concluded then that while urban rates tend to be higher than rural rates, there are conditions which affect both urban and rural rates. The influences of these wider conditions is seen also in the trends of rural and urban rates, which, although on different levels, have been in the same direction over a long period of time.

If it be assumed that mere size of the local group creates conditions conducive to suicide, it might be expected that the suicide rate for cities would increase along with the size of cities. A study of the suicide rates for all cities of 100,000 population and over in the registration states in 1920 confirms the statement of the previous section—that the variations are regional—much more than it confirms the statement that the larger the city the higher the rate. Thus the

TABLE IX

SUICIDES PER 100,000 OF THE POPULATION BY CLASSES OF CITIES
(1919–21)*

	Cities of 100,000 and Over	Cities of 10,000–100,000	Cities under 10,000 and Rural
Far West			
California................	27.6	24.3	21.5
Oregon..................	18.2	21.4	11.5
Washington.............	22.6	18.5	14.7
Montana................		21.4	14.8
Utah...................	13.0	18.6	5.8
Colorado...............	20.5	19.1	11.8
West			
Kansas.................	14.2	15.2	10.4
Missouri................	19.1	16.0	8.9
Nebraska†..............	20.3	16.5	10.1
Middle West			
Minnesota..............	15.7	16.8	10.8
Wisconsin..............	15.0	10.6	11.2
Michigan...............	10.8	11.2	10.5
Illinois.................	15.3	14.1	11.7
Indiana................	15.5	13.4	12.0
Ohio...................	13.7	10.6	11.1
East			
Pennsylvania...........	12.3	10.4	8.6
Delaware...............	11.9		6.5
New Jersey.............	12.8	11.9	13.7
New York..............	12.8	9.9	13.7
Rhode Island...........	11.2	7.7	11.6
Massachusetts..........	11.7	10.7	11.7
New Hampshire........		11.0	12.7
Vermont...............		12.5	13.1
Maine.................		12.9	12.5

		Cities of 100,000 and Over	Cities of 10,000–100,000	Cities under 10,000 and Rural
South‡				
	⎰Total...	13.4	10.4	8.0
Maryland......⎨White...		14.5	12.0	9.7
	⎱Colored.		5.2	0	1.7
	⎰Total...	15.9	10.0	6.0
Kentucky......⎨White...		18.1	11.6	6.3
	⎱Colored.		5.0	2.1	2.6

TABLE IX—*Continued*

		Cities of 100,000 and Over	Cities of 10,000–100,000	Cities under 10,000 and Rural
South—Continued				
Tennessee	Total	11.3	11.0	5.1
	White	15.6	13.7	5.6
	Colored	3.1	4.1	2.4
Louisiana	Total	12.5	10.1	3.2
	White	14.8	10.1	5.3
	Colored	5.9	10.0	0.5
Mississippi	Total	....	10.1	2.7
	White	....	15.0	4.5
	Colored	....	3.0	1.1
North Carolina	Total	....	6.4	3.5
	White	....	8.3	4.2
	Colored	....	2.3	1.9
South Carolina	Total	....	7.7	3.5
	White	....	10.9	6.4
	Colored	....	2.9	1.1
Florida	Total	....	12.7	5.7
	White	....	17.1	7.9
	Colored	....	4.1	1.3

* Based on *Mortality Statistics* for 1919, 1920, and 1921 and *Abstract of the Fourteenth Census*.

† Based on two years, 1920 and 1921.

‡ The percentage of whites used in obtaining the population base for cities under 10,000 and rural is that given in the *Fourteenth Census* for towns under 2,500 and rural; the percentage of whites used here for cities of 10,000–100,000 is that given in the *Fourteenth Census* for all towns and cities over 2,500; the white and colored population for cities over 100,000 is based on actual figures given in the *Fourteenth Census*. The population of Negroes and whites upon which rates were figured in the first two groups is an estimate, but probably an accurate one.

five highest rates are those of San Francisco, Spokane, Oakland, Los Angeles, and Seattle, none of which can be considered cities of prodigious size. Reading, Pennsylvania, for some unexplained reason ranks next, after which come other western cities, Omaha, Kansas City, Missouri, St. Louis, and Denver. Toledo follows, and then Portland. It is significant to note that five of the six distinctly southern cities are above the median rate, and that the sixth is not far below. Apparently the extremely low southern rates are due to the extensive rural population. The numerous cities of the East and Middle West follow in heterogeneous order, yet with certain minor regional groupings. Thus all seven of the Massachusetts cities are in the lower 50 per cent of the cities, and all except two (Boston and Springfield) are in the lower third, while three are the lowest of all, except for Yonkers, New York. The difference between the lowest rate for a Massachusetts city and the highest is 7.1 suicides per 100,000, not a great variation as the rates run. Connecticut has three cities whose rates are almost identical but considerably higher than those of the Massachusetts cities. Other instances might be pointed out. On the other hand, adjacent cities may vary considerably in rate: Minneapolis, for instance, has a rate of 21 suicides per 100,000, while St. Paul has a rate of but 16. Kansas City, Kansas, has a rate of 17.7 and Kansas City, Missouri, a (white) rate of 25.3.

A very slight tendency for the smaller cities to have low rates may perhaps be detected. Seven of the fourteen smallest cities are in the lower third of the series, while the four lowest rates fall to four of these seven small cities. It happens, however, that three of these small, non-suicidal cities at the bottom of the series are in Massachusetts, which has been noted to have a low rate throughout.

As for the three mammoth cities, New York City, Chicago, and Philadelphia, all fall well toward the middle of the series, and New York and Philadelphia in particular are equaled or surpassed in rate by many smaller cities in the same regions of the country.

A general and somewhat obscure tendency was noted for suicide rates to vary according to rates of growth of cities

TABLE X

SUICIDES PER 100,000 OF THE POPULATION TEN YEARS OF AGE AND
OVER FOR CITIES OF 100,000 AND OVER IN THE REGISTRATION
STATES (1919–21), AND ADDITIONAL INFORMATION*

| | SUICIDES PER 100,000 | | | PERCENTAGE OF GROWTH WHERE ESPECIALLY HIGH OR LOW† |
	Total	White	Colored	
San Francisco............	38.0	....	....	69
Spokane.................	29.5	....	....	424
Oakland.................	28.2	....	....	344
Los Angeles.............	28.1	....	....	1044
Seattle..................	25.9	....	....	636
Reading.................	25.0	....	....	....
Omaha..................	24.5	....	....	36
Kansas City, Mo.........	23.9	25.3	11.8	....
St. Louis.............\...	22.1	23.9	4.9	71
Denver..................	23.8	....	....	....
Toledo..................	21.6	....	....	199
Portland................	21.5	....	....	457
Louisville...............	18.8	21.7	5.7	46
Memphis................	14.3	21.1	3.8	....
Minneapolis.............	21.0	....	....	....
Norfolk.................	14.4	20.8	4.1	....
Trenton.................	20.5	....	....	....
Hartford................	20.3	....	....	....
Chicago.................	19.0	....	....	....
Cincinnati..............	18.8	....	....	35
Milwaukee..............	18.7	....	....	....
Bridgeport..............	18.5	....	....	194
Indianapolis............	18.4	....	....	198
New Haven.............	18.2	....	....	....
Baltimore...............	16.5	18.2	6.2	69
New Orleans............	15.1	18.0	7.1	59
Newark.................	17.9	....	....	....
Kansas City, Kan........	17.7	....	....	....
Cleveland...............	17.4	....	....	205
Albany.................	17.4	....	....	19
Boston.................	16.7	....	....	67
Paterson................	16.4	....	....	....
Salt Lake City..........	16.4	....	....	....
New York City..........	16.4	....	....	....
Grand Rapids...........	16.3	....	....	....
Philadelphia............	15.4	16.3	5.8	74
Nashville...............	12.2	16.2	3.3	....

TABLE X—*Continued*

	SUICIDES PER 100,000			PERCENTAGE OF GROWTH WHERE ESPECIALLY HIGH OR LOW†
	Total	White	Colored	
St. Paul.................	16.0	....	....	....
Springfield..............	15.1	....	....	193
Rochester...............	14.9	....	....	....
Dayton..................	14.8	....	....	....
Syracuse................	14.7	....	....	....
Wilmington.............	14.6	....	....	....
Richmond...............	10.7	14.6	2.2	....
Camden.................	14.4	....	....	....
Akron...................	14.4	....	....	653
Pittsburgh..............	14.0	....	....	....
Worcester...............	13.9	....	....	....
Providence..............	13.9	....	....	....
New Bedford............	13.5	....	....	198
Youngstown............	13.4	....	....	299
Detroit.................	13.2	....	....	383
Buffalo.................	12.9	....	....	....
Jersey City.............	12.5	....	....	....
Columbus...............	11.8	....	....	....
Scranton................	10.9	....	....	....
Cambridge..............	10.4	....	....	57
Lowell..................	10.2	....	....	45
Fall River..............	9.6	....	....	62
Yonkers.................	8.0	....	....	213

* Suicide rates based on data in *Mortality Statistics* for 1919, 1920, and 1921 and in Vol. III of the *Fourteenth Census of the United States*. Cities are ranked according to the rates of the white population. For practical purposes this is the total rate in all except southern cities.

† Percentage of increase in population from 1890 to 1920.

during the past few decades. Of the fifteen cities which have made the greatest gain in population between 1890 and 1920, six are among the twelve most suicidal cities. On the other hand, the second most rapidly growing city, Akron, with an increase of 653 per cent in thirty years, has a low rate: 14.4 suicides per 100,000 in a series that runs from 8.0 suicides as the lowest rate to 38 as the highest. New Bedford, Youngstown, Detroit, and Yonkers are also rapidly growing cities and each has a lower rate than has Akron.

Moreover, of the fifteen cities which have showed the least increase in the last thirty years, four have distinctly high rates, three distinctly low rates, and the others are scattered in rather indiscriminate fashion throughout the series. San Francisco is a particularly outstanding exception to the tendency for rapid increase in population growth to create suicide conditions. It has increased only 69 per cent in the last thirty years, yet has a suicide rate of 38 per 100,-000, almost ten suicides per 100,000 above the second city, Spokane, with a rate of 29.5 per 100,000 and a rate of increase of 424 per cent in thirty years.

Without detailed case studies of cities it is almost impossible to know why the suicide rate varies from city to city, and why in some sections—the East, for instance—the rural rate equals or exceeds the city rate. Certain general statements are possible as to the higher rates in cities in general than in surrounding rural areas. Rural areas approximate the religious communities of Europe; they have settled ways of living, established moral codes, a narrow range of interests, but fairly adequate ways of caring for the interests they have. There are few newcomers, few transients, only a small degree of mobility, and consequently little disturbance to the rigid social control of the family, neighborhood, and institutions. People do not commit suicide without a cause, and in the rural areas there is less of the disturbance to accustomed ways of living which constitutes a major cause of personal disorganization in urban centers.

The dominance of social factors.—Climate and racial temperament are minor factors if they are direct factors at all in determining the suicide rate. Influential in determining the rate are the attitudes and customs of national groups, the breakdown of such customs among immigrants, the organizing effect and the creeds of religious groups, and the conditions of urban or rural life.

Following this chapter comes a discussion of suicide in very primitive and very rigid social organizations and then a chapter devoted to a detailed analysis of suicide in an urban community. And finally, in the concluding chapter of Part I, the contrasting influences of stable, simple cultures and of mobile, unsettled cultures are assembled and placed in order.

CHAPTER IV

SUICIDE IN PRELITERATE[1] AND ORIENTAL GROUPS

The surveys, historical and contemporary, of Europe and America show that when attitudes exist which make suicide extremely distasteful, suicides occur infrequently; and also that in communities where disorganization prevails and at periods of great social change suicides increase. Europe and America have been considered somewhat as one great cultural unit. Two other types of cultural life may be distinguished: preliterate and oriental. The first is simple and very static; the second, highly organized but also very static. What form does suicide take under these social conditions?

Preliterate people non-suicidal.[2]—There is positive proof of the relative absence of suicide in certain preliterate groups. In the Caroline Islands (Micronesia) the natives are

---

[1] Preliterate is a word suggested by Professor Ellsworth Faris, of the University of Chicago, as a substitute for primitive. Primitive is something of a misnomer for the people usually so designated, for these simply organized tribes have an old culture and are not primitive in the sense of being more primeval than more highly organized groups. Preliterate (before writing) refers to a very significant lack in their culture. The acquisition of writing is one of the important steps in the transition from a simple tribal to a civilized type of social organization.

[2] Surveys of suicide among primitive people which have, however, been limited largely to reciting instances of suicide have been made by Westermarck, *The Origin and Development of the Moral Ideas*, and by S. R. Steinmetz, "Suicide among Primitive People," *American Anthropologist*, VII (1894), 53. References in this chapter to Westermarck and Steinmetz are to these sources.

reported as laughing at the mere idea of a man killing himself,[1] while in the Pelew Islands (Micronesia) suicide is regarded as the "expression of the will of a free man."[2] No other references were found for Micronesia.

In Australia suicide is unknown, according to Ratzel;[3] queries regarding suicide brought laughter as the only reply to another investigation;[4] while a third writer reports that suicide is rare and "if a native wishes to die, and cannot get anyone to kill him, he will sometimes put himself in the way of a venomous snake, that he may be bitten by it."[5]

For the Andaman Islanders only one reference to suicide was found, and that to the effect that it was unknown among them until after they had come into contact with "the alien population," that is, Hindus or Europeans.[6]

In Malaysia suicides are reported among the Bontoc Igorots[7] and the Bukidnon[8] of the Philippines, the Karo Bataks,[9] the Tonapo and Tobado of Central Celebes,[10] the

[1] Westermarck, op. cit., II, 230, quoting Von Kotzebue, Voyage of Discovery into the South Sea, III, 195.

[2] Steinmetz, "Suicide among Primitive Peoples," American Anthropologist, VII (1894), 58, from Kubary, Die Verbrechen und das Strafverfahren auf den Pelau Inseln.

[3] F. Ratzel, History of Mankind, I, 346.

[4] Westermarck, op. cit., II, 248, from Grey, Expeditions of Discovery in Northwest and Western Australia.

[5] Ibid., p. 230, from Dawson, Australian Aborigines, p. 62.

[6] E. H. Man, "On the Aboriginal Inhabitants of the Andaman Islands," Journal of the Anthropological Institute, XII, 111.

[7] A. E. Jenks, The Bontoc Igorot, p. 74.

[8] Professor Fay-Cooper Cole, Department of Anthropology and Sociology, University of Chicago, interview, April, 1925.

[9] Steinmetz, op. cit., p. 58.

[10] Steinmetz, op. cit., 58.

Dyaks[1] and Kayans[2] of Borneo; but it is reported to be rare or unknown among certain of the tribes of Central Borneo.[3] Among the Malays is also found the interesting custom of running amok, which has certain suicidal aspects,[4] and on the islands of Bali and Lombok suttee is still occasionally practiced.[5]

For the mainland of southern Asia suicide is noted in Cambodia,[6] Siam,[7] among the Karens of Burma,[8] among the Hos of Bengal,[9] both the Sema and the Angami Nagas,[10] the Todas,[11] and the Kafirs in Hindu-Kush.[12] It is interesting to note that while suicide occurs among these tribes, none of them has the highly institutionalized form of suttee, or widow-suicide, found among the Hindus.

For Melanesia there are two types of reports: one con-

[1] H. L. Roth, *Natives of Sarawak and British North Borneo*, I, 117–18, 140, quoting Brooke Low and Sir Spencer St. John.

[2] Charles Hose, "A Journey up the Baram River to Mount Dulit and the Highlands of Borneo," *Geographical Journal*, I (1893), 199.

[3] Carl Lumholtz, *Through Central Borneo*, pp. 180, 198, 275, 302.

[4] Gilmore Ellis, "The Amok of the Malay," *Journal of Mental Science*, XXXIX, 331. Also, Professor Fay-Cooper Cole, interview, April, 1925.

[5] *Cyclopedia of India and of East and South Asia*, II, 784–85.

[6] R. Lasch, "Die Behandlung der Leiche des Selbstmörders," *Globus*, LXXVI (1899), 63.

[7] *Ibid.*, p. 63.

[8] Westermarck, *The Origin and Development of the Moral Ideas*, II, 231; H. I. Marshall, *The Karen People of Burma*, p. 150.

[9] E. T. Dalton, *Descriptive Ethnology of Bengal*, p. 206; Westermarck, *op. cit.*, II, 231; R. W. Russell, *The Tribes and Castes of the Central Provinces of India*, II, 264.

[10] J. H. Hutton, *The Sema Nagas;* J. H. Hutton, *The Angami Nagas*, pp. 229–30 and note, p. 229.

[11] W. H. R. Rivers, *The Todas*, p. 555.

[12] Westermarck, *op. cit.*, II, 230, quoting Scott Robertson, *Kafirs of the Hindu-Kush*, p. 381.

cerning suicide for personal motives which is reported for several places;[1] the other concerning a form of suttee by which the widow strangles herself or permits herself to be strangled at the funeral of her husband.[2] The latter is reported specifically for New Hebrides,[3] the Eddystone Island of the Solomons,[4] and Fiji,[5] while Codrington refers to essentially the same custom, except that burying alive is used instead of strangling.[6] This same writer also attributes to the Melanesians the practice of sometimes burying alive the sick and aged, with their own consent, a practice which must be regarded as a form of suicide.[7]

The situation in Melanesia is repeated in Polynesia; suicide for personal reasons is noted for several parts of Polynesia,[8] while strangling of the widow is specifically mentioned for Tonga[9] and the Maoris.[10] In the Hawaiian Islands it is reported that sometimes retainers killed themselves

[1] Westermarck, *The Origin and Development of the Moral Ideas*, II, 230, note, quoting Haddon; Rivers, *The History of Melanesian Society*, p.237; Charles Gabriel Seligmann, *Melanesians of British New Guinea*, p. 571; R. H. Codrington, *The Melanesians*, p. 243.

[2] Thomas Williams, *Fiji and the Fijians*, I, 123.

[3] George Turner, *Samoa a Hundred Years Ago*, pp. 324, 326.

[4] A. M. Hocart, "The Cult of the Dead . . . . , Part I, *Journal of the Royal Anthropological Institute*, LII, 74 ff.

[5] Westermarck, *op. cit.*, II, 235; Edward B. Tylor, *Primitive Culture*, I, 415.

[6] Codrington, *op. cit.*, pp. 288–89.

[7] *Ibid.*, p. 347.

[8] R. L. Stevenson, *The South Seas*, pp. 31–33 (for Marquesas Islands); Turner, *Samoa a Hundred Years Ago*, p. 305 (Island of Niue); Ralph Linton, Field Museum, Chicago, interview, tradition of suicide in Hawaii.

[9] R. H. Lowie, *Primitive Religion*, pp. 236–37, quoting Martin, *An Account of the Natives of the Tonga Islands*, p. 295.

[10] Edward Tregear, *The Maori Race*, p. 390.

when their chief died, and one man customarily met death as part of the ritual of maintaining secrecy for the chief's burial place.[1]

In preliterate Africa references to suicide from personal motives were found for all parts of the continent except for the Bushmen and Hottentots, for whom no references of any kind were found.[2]

In addition, three types of suicide enforced by custom but agreed to by the suicides were found. In four tribes near the Niger River, the Ibo, Egba, Yoruba, and Tshi,[3] suicide upon certain occasions is required as a punishment. Among the Tshi suicide may also be used as a means of revenge, the person who has caused one to commit suicide through some mistreatment being held responsible for the death, much as though a murder had been committed.[4] Among the Bankundo suicide is sometimes used as a threat which has in it an element of revenge: if one man owes another man a debt which he does not pay, the creditor may threaten and then proceed actually to hang himself, his death being laid at the door of his debtor.[5] In seven tribes the custom exists, or did exist until recently, of the widow permitting herself to be killed at the funeral of her husband, usually by being

[1] Laura C. Green and Martha W. Beckwith, "Customs and Beliefs Relating to Sickness and Death," *American Anthropologist*, XXVIII, 181–82; Davida Malo, *Hawaiian Antiquities*, pp. 141–43.

[2] Drawn from about twenty sources.

[3] J. G. Frazer, *Dying God*, p. 41; N. W. Thomas, *Anthropological Report on the Ibo-speaking People of Nigeria*, pp. 86, 88; Frazer, *op. cit.*, p. 41 (the Yoruba); A. B. Ellis, *Tshi-speaking People of the Gold Coast of West Africa*, p. 302.

[4] *Ibid.*, pp. 301–3.

[5] Professor Ellsworth Faris, Department of Anthropology and Sociology, University of Chicago, interview.

buried alive,[1] while in five others the widow was killed,[2] whether willingly or unwillingly is not stated. In most cases either of willing or unwilling suicide of the widow, other human sacrifices were made of slaves or attendants, and both widow and slave sacrifice attended usually only the deaths of principal men of the tribe. For the Ashanti it is also recorded that a man of low rank who marries into the royal family is required to kill himself at the death of his wife or upon the death of a male child.[3]

In South America only three records of suicide were uncovered. One is to the effect that the Yahgans of Tierra del Fuego do not commit suicide,[4] and others that suicide of the personal type is found among the Araucanian[5] and Guiana

[1] Unyoro tribe: R. G. Pasha, *Seven Years in the Soudan*, p. 115.

Mundu, Abukaya, and Abaka tribes: W. Junker, *Travels in Africa during 1875-78*, p. 296.

Bairo tribe: Sir Harry Johnston, *Uganda Protectorate*, II, 610.

Yoruba tribe: Samuel Johnson, *History of the Yorubas*, pp. 55-56.

Zulus: G. M. Theal, *History and Ethnography of Africa South of the Zambesi*, p. 88.

[2] Awemba tribe: J. H. W. Sheane, "Some Aspects of Awemba Religion and Superstitious Observances," *Journal of the Anthropological Institute*, Vol. XXXVI.

Ibo tribe: A. G. Leonard, *The Lower Niger and Its Tribes*, p. 162.

Aragga tribe, Nigeria: A. J. N. Tremearne, "Notes on the Kagora and Other Nigerian Headhunters," *Journal of the Royal Anthropological Institute*, XLII, 168.

Boloki: J. H. Weeks, *Among Congo Cannibals*, pp. 103, 319-20.

Warua tribe: V. L. Cameron, *Across Africa*, p. 333.

[3] Ellis, *Tshi-speaking People of the Gold Coast of West Africa*, p. 287.

[4] Westermarck, *The Origin and Development of the Moral Ideas*, II, 229, from Bridge, *South American Missionary Magazine*, XIII, 211.

[5] Steinmetz, "Suicide among Primitive Peoples," *American Anthropologist*, VII (1894), 56, from Ochsenius, *Chile, Land und Leute*, p. 119.

Indians.[1] Bancroft records suicide of the same type for the Indians of the east coast of Central America.[2]

Among North American Indians suicide seems quite generally found and is recorded for many tribes of the plains and the northwest coast[3] by writers who knew the Indians in their early culture. Only a few tribes in either North or South America practiced anything which approached the socially accepted and prescribed suicides, such as the suttee of the Pacific Islands and Africa or suicide for punishment. Among the Natchez it was customary at the death of one of the members of certain families of the three highest social castes for the widow or widower and other chosen ones to commit suicide by permitting themselves to be strangled, all with a definite public ritual.[4] Among the Northern Kwakiutl, Sikanni, Carrier, and Tsimshian Indians a debatable form of incipient suttee existed, whereby the widow was required to lie upon or permit herself to be pushed into the funeral pyre of her dead husband. The same custom applied to the widower among the Carrier Indians.[5] Among some of the northwest-coast Indians slaves deemed it an

[1] W. E. Roth, "An Introductory Study of the Arts, Crafts, and Customs of the Guiana Indians," *38th Annual Report of the Bureau of American Ethnology*, p. 560; W. E. Roth, "An Inquiry into the Animism and Folklore of the Guiana Indians," *ibid., 30th Annual Report*, p. 227.

[2] H. H. Bancroft, *The Native Races*, I, 744.

[3] From several dozen different sources.

[4] H. C. Yarrow, "Study of the Mortuary Customs of the North American Indians," *First Annual Report, Bureau of American Ethnology*, pp. 187–89; John R. Swanton, "Indian Tribes of the Lower Mississippi Valley . . . . ," *Bureau of American Ethnology, Bulletin 43*, pp. 139 ff.

[5] W. C. MacLeod, "Certain Mortuary Aspects of Northwest Coast Culture," *American Anthropologist*, XXVII, pp. 122 ff.

honor to be killed at the burial of their masters, since their bodies were buried with those of their masters.[1]

The Aztecs used human sacrifices to the gods which sometimes attained the character of voluntary sacrifices. The young man killed each spring as an offering to the god Tezcatlipoca was chosen to this office a year in advance of his death, and during the year impersonated the god and received homage from the people. He chose his own hour of death and proudly stepped up to the death stone when his time came.[2] The Aztecs also sacrificed attendants and, in the case of chiefs, wives at the time of burial, but it is not clearly stated whether these were voluntary or genuine sacrifices.[3] For the Mayas suicide of the personal type has been recorded for recent times, but human sacrifices were rare and there appears no record of sacrifices at the time of burial.[4] For other Central American tribes voluntary death of wives, attendants, slaves, and friends is reported.[5] Among the Incas when a chief died attendants and wives willingly met death to accompany the dead chief into the next world.

[1] A. P. Niblack, "The Coast Indians of Southern Alaska and Northern British Columbia," *Report of the U.S. National Museum* (1888), p. 356. This report covers several tribes, including the Kwakiutl, Tlingit, Tsimshian, and Haida, and it is not stated to which tribe the before-mentioned practice belonged.

[2] Bernardino de Sahagun, *Historia General de los cosas de Nueva España*, I, 56.

[3] T. A. Joyce, *Mexican Archeology*, pp. 104–5; Yarrow, *op. cit.*, p. 190.

[4] Thomas W. F. Gann, "The Maya Indians of Southern Yucatan and Northern British Honduras," *Bureau of American Ethnology, Bulletin 64*, p. 35; Joyce, *op. cit.*

[5] Yarrow, "Study of the Mortuary Customs of the North American Indians," *First Annual Report, Bureau of American Ethnology*, p. 190, quoting Bancroft, *Native Races of the Pacific States*, III, 513.

After the death of the last great Inca at the hands of the Spanish invaders his wives rushed into the Catholic funeral which was under way and cried out that such was not a fit burial for an Inca and demanded their right to die with him. Turned out of the Catholic church, some of them committed suicide.[1]

The Eskimos, in addition to a certain amount of suicide from personal motives, had well-recognized suicide of the sick and aged.[2] Their attitude toward this latter type of suicide is well illustrated in the story of a girl who explained to the missionary that she had given proof of her love for her neighbors. "Once an old woman who was ill but could not die offered to pay me if I would lead her to the top of the steep cliff from which our people have always thrown themselves when they are tired of living; but I, having ever loved my neighbors, led her thither without payment and cast her over the cliff."[3]

A statement regarding the tribes of northern Siberia completes the survey of suicide among preliterate people. Suicide of the aged is recognized as legitimate among the people of the Aleutian Islands, the Yakuts, and the Chukchi, while the Votyaks sometimes kill themselves for revenge,[4]

[1] W. H. Prescott, *History of the Conquest of Peru*, II, 489; also *ibid.*, I, 32–33.

[2] Steinmetz, "Suicide among Primitive Peoples," *American Anthropologist*, VII (1894), 55, from Hall, *Life with the Esquimaux*, II, 101, 317; Franz Boas, "Central Eskimo," *Seventh Annual Report, Bureau of American Ethnology*, p. 615; F. Nansen, *Eskimo Life*, p. 267.

[3] F. Nansen, *Eskimo Life*, p. 170.

[4] Sumner, "Yakuts," *Journal of Anthropological Institute*, XXXI, 65; Steinmetz, *op. cit.*, p. 54; Westermarck, *The Origin and Development of the Moral Ideas*, II, 231; W. Bogoras, "Chukchi of North Eastern Asia," *American Anthropologist*, III, 106.

believing that their ghosts will persecute the offender. In these various places suicide from personal motives is also known.

The suicides found among preliterate people fall into two distinct groups. Suicides for personal motives are reported from so many sources that it must be assumed that they occur in all except the most isolated groups with extremely simple cultures, such as the Andamans, the native Australians, and some of the Micronesians. The ·second type of suicide is socially accepted and often socially enforced, such as the widow suicides. As found among preliterate people this type includes the voluntary death of the widow, the voluntary death of attendants and followers upon the death of their leader, the voluntary death of the widower upon the death of his wife, suicide as punishment decreed by the group, suicide as a means of revenge upon an offending party, suicide of the aged or sick, and "running amok." Some of these forms seem to be almost local in their development: running amok is confined to certain parts of Malaysia; suicide of the sick and aged, to the Arctic peoples; suicide for punishment and for revenge, to a certain section of east Africa. In some cases these local developments are clearly related to some other feature of the social organization and conditions of life. The relation of suicide of the sick and aged to the sparse food supply and highly developed communistic spirit of the Eskimos and the tribes of Northern Asia is clear. Running amok is related to the Mohammedan faith, which prohibits self-murder but not the murder of others, especially if those others be of another faith. The suicide is indeed indirect, since it comes from the hands of another in response to the series of murders committed, but it appears to be suicide none the less.[1] The suicide of widows is the most widespread form, being found in at least eight places in the Pacific Islands, seven parts of Africa, and several parts of America. Obviously suicide for personal motives and suicide as a social custom are very different acts and represent different phases of culture.

Suicide from personal motives.—Suicide from personal motives is very similar among preliterate people and civilized people. In many cases the same situations call forth suicide among both preliterate and civilized people. Quarrels, ridicule, scolding or punishment, marriage of a girl to a man she disliked, commission of a crime, injuries and illness are all given as occasions for suicide in preliterate tribes. Suicide cases in Chicago for 1923 yielded the following external situations: economic failure, extreme poverty, arrest, change of location, as removal from the country to the city, pain and illness, intoxication, insanity, domestic difficulties, lovers' quarrels, death of a loved one.[2] It is, of course, difficult to know whether the motives are the same. In addition to these similar situations there are many dissimilar ones which are capable of causing suicide because of

[1] Running amok as a form of insanity is denied by both Dr. Gilmore Ellis, *Journal of Mental Science*, XXXIX, 331, and Professor Fay-Cooper Cole, of the University of Chicago. Professor Cole states that in the Malay states and Dutch Indies if a man feels aggrieved he starts out to kill people and continues until he is himself killed. This conduct has been standardized. The British and Dutch at first gave orders to kill anyone who ran amok, but the malady increased; there was glory in such a death. When these men were taken alive, put in chains, and made to work on the road, the malady decreased among the others. Professor Cole also states that a native Mohammedan of the South Philippines sometimes takes a vow before the native local priest to kill so many Christians before he is himself killed. He shaves his eyebrows and is called *juramentado* (having taken an oath).

[2] See chap. xiii.

their particular meaning in the tribe where they occur. Thus, among the Bukidnon in north-central Mindanao in the Philippines it is immoral for a man other than a woman's husband to touch her little fingers, elbows, or heels. In one instance a man in trying to make love to a woman during her husband's absence touched her little fingers. So great was her shame that she committed suicide by driving a bamboo spike through her neck.[1] This occurrence, which would have had no significance to a civilized European or American, was of immense importance in the group where it occurred.

So far as suicides from personal motives are concerned, the great difference between preliterate and civilized groups lies in the number of suicides. While there is no objective proof of the number of suicides occurring among preliterates, the general assumption of anthropologists is that relatively few occur there, and no evidence to the contrary can be found.

One, perhaps the minor, deterrent to suicide among preliterates lies in certain adverse attitudes toward suicide held by many of these groups. Suicide is not, apparently, regarded as sinful or evil, but as non-understandable. Witchcraft is believed to cause suicide in certain parts of Africa. In numerous places in both Africa and the Pacific Islands and among some tribes of India a person who commits suicide is not buried in the same place nor in the same manner as other people, while among certain North American Indian tribes the life after death of the suicide is thought to differ from that of the person who dies a normal death. These discriminations are not in the nature of a punishment, however, for often the suicide simply shares the fate of anyone

[1] Professor Fay-Cooper Cole, interview, from his personal knowledge.

killed by violence, and sometimes of mothers who die in childbirth. Suicide is not understood; it is mysterious and perhaps unclean. Nevertheless this attitude must act as a deterrent to the extent at least of prohibiting indiscriminate suicide from becoming approved by the group.[1]

The second reason that suicide tends not to occur among preliterate people is that few occasions for it arise. In the relation of the individual to social organization, the undisturbed preliterate village is almost the antithesis of the modern city. The opportunities for personal disorganization among preliterates are few. There is, for one thing, in each group a relative homogeneity of culture. Children grow up with one set of standards which they accept completely and implicitly; they follow evenly along the routinized ways of life that are traditional. The chief interests of life are usually cared for quite adequately. Marriage is provided for, food is obtained by the group and divided among all, children are either accepted as a part of nature or infanticide is approved. In short, there tends to be a prescribed way for doing everything and there is little occasion for the individual to find himself either confused by a multiplicity of choices or lonely, hungry, or unappreciated.

Obviously, the situations previously listed as occasions for suicide among preliterates are those in which the social organization fails in some way to provide for the individual. The best efforts of the shamans and medicine men cannot always cure illness; the offended and disgruntled person is often left to recover as best he can from his injured feelings. The linking of suicide to social disorganization is further shown in times when semi-epidemics of disease occurred

[1] Data from sources already quoted in this chapter. Also see Bibliography for additional sources for information on preliterates.

among the American Indians. A traveler among the Mandans and neighboring tribes almost a hundred years ago wrote of the conditions following a smallpox plague.

Very few of those who were attacked recovered their health; but when they saw all their relations buried, and the pestilence still raging with unabated fury among the remainder of their countrymen, life became a burden to them, and they put an end to their wretched existence, either with their knives and muskets, or by precipitating themselves from the summit of the rock near their settlement. The prairie all around is a vast field of death, covered with unburied corpses, and spreading, for miles, pestilence and infection.[1]

A similar occurrence is related in the calendar history of the Kiowa Indians.

The next notable event in Kiowa history is the cholera epidemic of 1849. It was brought from the east by California emigrants and ravaged all the tribes of the plains. The Kiowa remember it as the most terrible experience in their history, far exceeding in fatality the smallpox of nine years before. Hundreds died and many committed suicide in their despair.[2]

In the before-mentioned times the social organization broke down because of the intrusion of an outside factor which could not be controlled. Such occurrences differ from the single instances of suicide only in magnitude and because a number of people feel their inability to adjust to the situation and seek release in suicide.[3]

Institutionalized suicide.—The socially enforced suicides of the preliterates, such as the voluntary death of the wife

[1] R. G. Thwaites, editor, *Early Western Travels*, XXII, Part I of Maximilian, *Prince of Wied's Travels in the Interior of North America, 1832–34*, pp. 34–35.

[2] James Mooney, "Calendar History of the Kiowa Indians," *17th Annual Report, Bureau of American Ethnology*, p. 173

[3] See chap. ii, p. 21, for similar occurrences in Europe during the Middle Ages.

at the funeral of her husband, are best discussed in relation
to similar customs found in the Orient and in the historical
records of Europe.

To these suicides the term "institutional" has been applied. While not all suicides which occur at the command of
the group, especially among preliterates, have reached the
stage of complete institutionalization, they have certain
characteristics of institutions, and if developed along logical
lines would become completely institutionalized. Completely institutionalized suicides have group approval and usually
participation of the group in the commission of the suicide;
the suicide is performed in a certain manner and usually
with a definite ritual; and it is related to some concept or
attitude of a traditional group character.

India, China, and Japan have had the most highly developed forms of institutional suicide. Suttee, the sacrifice of
the widow on the funeral pyre of her husband, was a religious
rite in India which was forcibly stopped by the British in
1828. In China institutionalized suicides included suicide
for revenge, an event so well recognized that legal provision
was made for the punishment of anyone who by nagging
or mistreatment caused another to commit suicide;[1] suicide
as punishment; suicide of attendants at the death of their
lord, or of statesmen at the death of the emperor; suicide
following military or political defeat (approaches institutionalization), suicide of widows. In Japan institutionalized
suicides included junshi, or suicide of attendants and followers when their lord died; hara-kiri or seppuku, to avoid
capture after military defeat; seppuku for punishment; while
other types, especially suicide as a protest against some

[1] Ernest Alabaster, *Notes and Commentaries on Chinese Criminal Law*,
pp. 304–7, 315–18.

wrong, and the double suicide of lovers, approached institutionalization.[1]

The institutionalized suicides no longer exist in the east except perhaps for sporadic occurrences. They belong to the days when eastern culture was isolated, homogeneous, unimpaired by contacts with the dissimilar traditions and customs of the West. The ceremonial suicides of the East have become a part of history, fortunately of a history preserved in tangible form and hence capable of reconstruction.

Europe has only a small part in the history of institutionalized suicides. The only form which seemed at all widespread was suttee, or widow sacrifice, found in ancient times among the Danish northmen, the Scandinavians, the Slavonians, and the Greeks. Scythia and Thrace before the Christian era also practiced widow sacrifice, whether always of the voluntary kind is not certain.[2]

[1] For material on suicide in India, see: *Cyclopedia of India and of Eastern and Southern Asia*, Vol. II; A. Coomaraswamy, *The Dance of Siva: Essay on Status of Indian Women;* J. G. Frazer, "Sati," *Encyclopedia of Religion and Ethics*, XI, 207; E. W. Hopkins, *Religions of India;* A. A. MacDonell, "Vedic Religion," *Encyclopedia of Religion and Ethics*, XII, 601–18; J. T. Wheeler, *The History of India.*

For material on suicide in China, see: J. D. Ball, *Things Chinese or Notes Connected with China;* J. H. Gray, *China;* Wm. Gowland, "The Burial Mounds and Dolmens of the Early Emperors of Japan," *Journal of the Royal Anthropological Institute*, XXXVII, 10; J. J. Matignon, *Superstition, Crime et Misère en Chine.*

For material on suicide in Japan, see: Tasuku Harada, "Suicide," *Encyclopedia of Religion and Ethics*, XII, pp. 35–37; W. E. Griffis, *The Mikado's Empire;* James Murdoch, *A History of Japan, from the Origins to the Arrival of the Portuguese in 1542 A.D.,* I; I. O. Nitobe, *Bushido, the Soul of Japan;* Hisho Saito, *A History of Japan.*

[2] See Otto Schrader, *Prehistoric Antiquities of the Aryan Peoples*, p. 390; Westermarck, *The Origin and Development of the Moral Ideas*, I, 473 ff.; *Cyclopedia of India and of Eastern and Southern Asia*, II, 781; H. Schetelig, *Traces of the Custom of Suttee in Norway during the Viking Age*, reviewed in *L'Anthropologie*, XXI (1910), 559; Wheeler, *History of India*, pp. 69–70.

When institutionalized suicides are considered over a long period of time and a world-wide spread of people it becomes apparent that only one type is or has been at all common: the suicide or voluntary sacrifice of widows at the funeral of their husbands. Such suicides were probably rather common at one time in Europe; they reached a high development in India and China, and probably spread from there into the islands of the Pacific. Widow sacrifice is found also throughout the central portion of Negro Africa and was practiced in the most aristocratically developed tribes of American Indians. While it is not possible to assert that this wide range of a custom similar in meaning and often in execution spread from a single point of origin, it is possible to trace historically diffusion in certain places and also to point out certain relations between the custom of suttee, human sacrifices, and social organization which seem general for all groups where widow suttee is practiced as a group custom.

1. The areas where widow suicide is found are also the areas of human sacrifice. In the Orient the sacrifices are a matter of history and are often recorded as accompanying the widow suicide. Among the preliterates, the sacrifices were noted in conjunction with the suicides by early white observers. Moreover, in few parts of the world was human sacrifice found except in the groups which also had suttee. Human sacrifice and suttee went hand in hand.

2. Widow suicide is found in groups with some social caste system and usually attended the death of only certain high castes. This fact was true both of preliterates and in the Orient. In America the only Indian groups having highly developed social castes were the Natchez, the Aztecs, and the Incas, and suttee was confined to two of these

groups. In all cases only certain men of high rank were honored by having their wives commit suicide at their deaths.

3. The suicide of widows is often accompanied by the suicide of attendants and followers of the dead man. This procedure was true of all groups, either historically or in recent times.

As for the meaning of suttee in the groups where it is practiced, a fairly general statement can be made. In Europe, and apparently in the first period of its use in India, it was associated with the provision of other possessions for the use of the dead man in his future life. Schrader says in this connection:

The closest connection, in my opinion, subsists between the house-master's unrestricted right of property in his wife and the awful doom which in Indo-European antiquity awaited the surviving wife, the widow. . . . . It is no longer possible to doubt that ancient Indo-Germanic custom ordained that the wife should die with her husband. This custom has its origin in part in the wish to provide the deceased in his grave with everything which was dear to him in life; and partly was designed to make the life of the house-father safe on all sides . . . . and to render him an object of perpetual care and anxiety to his family."[1]

In Scythia the sacrifice of the wife or concubine was accompanied by that of the master's cupbearer, cook, groom, waiting-man, messenger, and favorite horses.

In India there was survival of an earlier custom of burying the man's weapons with him, as well as his wife.

In Africa the sacrifice of the widow is frequently accompanied by that of slaves, and personal property is often placed in the grave.

Thus in the early European and Indian custom as well

[1] *Prehistoric Antiquities of the Aryan People*, p. 390.

as with the recent African custom, suttee was part of a larger custom which involved the sacrifice of personal servants as well as of the wife, and the provision of personal property. This custom is usually interpreted to mean that provision was being made for the master in future life.

In general the different types of ceremonial suicide tend to cluster, perhaps because one form has developed from another or from the same situation which nourished the first. Thus the suicide of widows and of attendants seems to originate in the same impulse or tradition.

Social factors making institutionalized suicide possible.— Institutionalized suicides imply first a scale of values which places the life of the individual lower than certain other values. In the case of widow suicide the life of the widow has value only in relation to the life of her husband, and for the comfort she can bring him. In the case of suicide to avoid military defeat in Japan, honor lay in dying a free man rather than in living a captured one. Among the Arctic peoples the welfare of the tribe takes precedence over the lives of aged and helpless members of the tribe. Such scales of values are held by the entire group and are a part of the group tradition, but they are accepted implicitly by each member to such a degree that individuals willingly give up their lives to support and maintain these values.

For this complete acceptance of group values a well-integrated and functioning social organization is necessary. It seems almost a paradox to assert, as was done in a previous section, that suicides from personal motives do not exist among preliterates because of the complete control of the group over the individual, and that institutional suicides do exist because of this same complete social control. But both statements imply that the group is paramount and that while the group remains isolated from adverse and disruptive influences the individual fits his life to the group dictates. If group custom provides that he shall live an uneventful life until he dies from old age or disease, he so lives. But if the group customs provide that upon a certain occasion he shall kill himself, he complies and kills himself more or less as a matter of course. From the point of view of the group, institutional suicide is a means of caring for a social crisis, just as marriage, war, hunting, and the like are group methods of providing for group needs. When, among the Arctic circle peoples, the individual becomes a burden to the group, it is his social duty to eliminate himself. When, in China, Japan, and certain parts of Africa, a man had by some misdeed threatened the order of society, it was his social duty to eliminate himself. When a man, particularly a man of importance, died, it was the duty of his wife and his followers to die also and provide for him in the hereafter as they had provided for him on earth.

Institutionalized suicide is disrupted when groups of dissimilar traditions meet and contradictory ideals of life become disseminated. China, Japan, and India no longer have institutional suicides. Their days of isolation and complete submission of the individual to one set of group customs and ideals are gone. Social control has been weakened and individual interests have arisen and take precedence over social values. Individualism has developed. In Europe when individualism developed during the Renaissance the old group attitude that suicide was a sin gradually was lost. In the Orient individualism has meant the disintegration of the group-demanded institutional suicide. In both cases the group control was lost and the individual was left free. He might commit suicide if he chose; but whether he did it or restrained himself, he was not acting wholly in response to group or community dictates.

The preliterate situation shows the effect of a simple, homogeneous social organization on personality. There is little disorganization and hence a small amount of personal suicide.

CHAPTER V

SUICIDE IN AMERICA'S SECOND CITY:
A STUDY OF URBAN CONDITIONS

Chicago, a "normal" city.—While descriptive and statistical studies covering wide areas and long reaches of time have value in giving perspective, trends, and some hint of far-reaching factors, there is need also for detailed case studies of suicide in specific localities. This chapter presents one such case study, of Chicago, a typical American metropolitan center.

With regard to suicide, Chicago is "normal," as cities go; in fact, in some respects it is almost "subnormal." When compared with the remainder of the state, Chicago has a higher rate than either the smaller cities or the small towns and open country.

TABLE XI*

SUICIDES PER 100,000 INHABITANTS FOR
CHICAGO AND ILLINOIS, 1919–21

Chicago................................... 15.3
Cities of 10,000–100,000..... .... 14.1
Towns of less than 10,000 and rural sections..... 11.7
*Taken from Table IX.

The Chicago rate does not, however, soar far above the rate for the rest of the state. Compared with all the cities of 100,000 or above in the registration area, Chicago has a medium rate. The lowest rate of cities in this group was held in 1922 by Cambridge, Massachusetts, which had 6.3 suicides per 100,000; the highest rates, by Los Angeles and San Francisco, which had 30.7 and 30.6 suicides, respectively, per 100,000 per year. Chicago in 1922 had a rate slightly higher than New York but below that of Philadelphia.

Chicagoans commit suicide with greater frequency in May and December, which is in accord with conditions elsewhere.[1]

Approximately three times as many men as women regularly commit suicide in Chicago, although there are approximately as many women as men living in the city. This relationship has been found to be common to America and Europe.[2]

With reference to age, the rate increases steadily with the advance of years. For some individual years there is a decrease in the age group of eighty years and over, but the average for ten years shows a continued increase in rate with increased age.[3]

In Chicago, as elsewhere, marriage and family life tend to lower the suicide rate, while the divorced rank higher than the widowed, who in turn rank higher than unmarried people.[4]

National and racial groups show approximately the same relation found for other cities in the United States.[5] Native-born whites in 1919–21 had a rate of 9.47 suicides per 100,-000, while the foreign born overtopped them with a rate of 28.8 suicides per 100,000, and the Negroes fell below with a rate of 7.7 suicides per 100,000.

With regard to specific immigrant groups the Central European countries rank high: Austria with a rate of 56 9 suicides per 100,000, Denmark with 48.1, Hungary with 47.3, Germany with 43.4, and Czechoslovakia with a rate

[1] See pp. 268 f.

[2] See pp. 306 ff.   [4] See pp. 317 ff, especially 320.

[3] See pp. 310 ff.   [5] See p. 34.

of 42.0. The Irish, Poles, Italians, Russians, Greeks, and English rank lowest of the immigrant groups in Chicago. This division corresponds in general with the ranking of

TABLE XII

SUICIDES BY SEX, CHICAGO, 1915–25*

Year	Total	Male	Female
1915...........	616	473	143
1916...........	533	398	135
1917...........	474	351	123
1918...........	444	328	116
1919...........	415	295	120
1920...........	365	253	112
1921...........	459	345	114
1922...........	398	275	123
1923...........	389	281	108
1924...........	443	328	115
1925...........	430	327	103

* From the Chicago Department of Health.

TABLE XIII

SUICIDES PER 100,000 POPULATION IN EACH AGE GROUP, CHICAGO, 1915–24*

Year	Under 20	20–29	30–39	40–49	50–59	60–69	70–79	Over 80	Total
1915....	1.9	23.3	32.0	46.5	54.3	63.5	78.0	54.1	25.0
1916....	1.8	20.0	27.5	34.6	47.7	56.0	76.4	66.2	21.2
1917....	1.0	20.3	23.6	36.1	35.5	44.9	35.9	51.9	18.4
1918....	0.9	13.0	20.4	26.1	50.5	50.8	64.5	50.8	16.9
1919....	1.3	13.2	22.4	27.4	33.2	40.2	40.3	49.8	15.5
1920....	1.0	11.8	16.2	24.5	29.8	28.2	67.7	85.5	13.4
1921....	1.8	10.7	23.9	29.0	37.3	41.5	74.7	36.0	16.5
1922....	0.9	12.6	17.2	26.2	34.4	29.9	51.6	70.6	14.0
1923....	0.7	11.1	16.5	24.0	27.3	53.3	32.0	103.9	13.5
1924....	1.7	11.3	19.3	29.4	28.9	48.8	52.3	34.0	15.1
Average	1.30	14.73	21.90	30.38	37.89	45.71	57.34	60.28	16.95

*From the Chicago Department of Health.

TABLE XIV

CHICAGO SUICIDES BY NATIVITY, 1919–21*

	AVERAGE ANNUAL NUMBER OF SUICIDES FOR 1919–21			POPULATION OF CHICAGO BY 100,000 FOR 1920			RATE PER 100,000		
	Male	Female	Total	Male	Female	Total	Male	Female	Total
Total	292.1	118.9	411.0	13.70	13.32	27.02	21.3	8.9	15.2
Native white Native parentage	44.0	27.5	71.5	3.23	3.20	6.43	13.6	8.6	11.1
Foreign parentage	52.6	27.9	80.5	4.34	4.54	8.88	12.1	6.1	9.1
Mixed parentage	8.2	8.7	16.9	1.22	1.30	2.52	6.7	6.7	6.7
Foreign-born white	179.0	53.2	232.1	4.32	3.74	8.05	41.4	14.2	28.8
Negroes	7.0	1.6	8.6	.56	.54	1.09	12.5	2.9	7.7
Chinese	1.3	.....	1.3	.....	.....	.02	.....	.....	65.0

* Based on material gathered from the coroner's records, Cook County, Illinois, and data in Vol. II, *Fourteenth Census of the United States*.

TABLE XV

SUICIDE IN CHICAGO AMONG FOREIGN BORN, 1919–21*

BIRTHPLACE	AVERAGE ANNUAL NUMBER OF SUICIDES, 1919–21			POPULATION FOR 1920			RATE PER 100,000		
	Male	Female	Total	Male	Female	Total	Male	Female	Total
England	3.0	1.6	4.6	13,972	12,466	26,438	21.4	13.3	17.7
Scotland	1.6	1.0	2.6	5 408	4 502	9 910	32.0	20.0	26.0
Ireland	3.0	1.6	4.6	26 566	30 220	56 786	11.1	5.3	8.1
Norway	6.3	1.0	7.3	9 913	10 568	20 481	63.3	10.0	36.5
Sweden	13.3	4.0	17.3	28 832	29 731	48 563	45.9	13.4	29.3
Denmark	4.3	1.0	5.3	6 359	4 909	11 268	71.7	20.0	48.1
Germany	34.3	14.3	48.6	56 456	55 832	112 288	61.2	25.5	43.4
Poland	21.6	4.0	25.6	75 311	62 300	137 611	28.8	6.5	11.3
Czechoslovakia	18.3	2.6	21.0	25 688	24 704	50 392	70.4	10.4	42.0
Austria	13.0	4.3	17.3	16 415	14 076	30 491	81.3	30.7	56.9
Hungary	8.0	4.3	12.3	13 634	12 472	26 106	57.1	35.8	47.3
Jugoslavia	1.6	.....	1.6	6 223	3 470	9 693	26.6	.....	.....
Russia and Lithuania	16.6	6.6	23.3	68 658	52 360	121 018	24.1	12.7	19.3
Greece	1.6	0.3	2.0	9 228	2 318	11 546	17.8	15.0	16.7
Italy	8.0	1.3	9.3	35 059	24 156	59 215	22.9	5.4	15.8
Canada	5.3	2.0	7.3	12 808	13 584	26 392	40.8	14.3	27.9

* Based on records in the office of the coroner of Cook County, Illinois, and the *Fourteenth Census of the United States*, II, 291, 739.

nationalities found in the United States, as well as with the ranking for the European nationalities.

So far as data are available on suicide among classes and groups of the population, Chicago has no peculiarities with reference to its suicide rate.

Communities in the suicide belt.[1]—Chicago has four suicidal areas: the "Loop" or central business district and its periphery of cheap hotels for men and sooty flats over stores (No. 1 on Map II); the Lower North Side, particularly the central part of this district, which includes a shifting population of unattached men and an equally shifting population of young men and women in the rooming-house area (No. 64 on the map); the Near South Side linking the Loop on the north with the Negro area to the south and having one-fourth of its population Negro (No. 2 on the map); and the West Madison area, with its womanless street of flophouses, missions, cheap restaurants, and hundreds of men who drift in aimless, bleary-eyed abandon (No. 40 on the map).

For purposes of statistical and community studies the city of Chicago has been divided into seventy-two areas.[2] While the statistical districts used in the census enumeration

---

[1] The basis of this discussion is Map II. Before making this map all residences of suicides occurring in the three years 1919–21 in Chicago as given in the coroner's records were plotted on a map. The communities as defined by the Sociology Department of the University of Chicago were marked on this map, the number of suicides in each community counted, and this number divided by three to obtain the yearly average. The rate of suicide for each community was then figured on the basis of population figures computed by the Sociology Department from data obtained from the census office. A second map (II) was then constructed showing by cross-hatching the suicide rate in each community. Transient suicides in hotels and hospitals were ommitted.

[2] For the purpose of this study finer divisions were made in a few cases than are used on the regulation community map of the Sociology Department.

have in part determined the boundaries of these areas, these small statistical districts have been combined in such a way that significant units are outlined. Usually the communities have natural boundaries, such as boulevards, railroads, street-car tracks, the river, or parks, which act as barriers to communication. In areas so bounded the people tend to be thrown together and to develop a feeling of loyalty for their particular community and, in well-integrated parts of the city, community consciousness and a definite social organization for their own control. Often these communities have as their nucleus some small town which Chicago has engulfed in its growth, and the names of these towns still cling. Ravenswood on the North Side, Hyde Park and Woodlawn on the South Side are examples. In some of the large communities there are distinct subsections with definite and describable characteristics. In some cases such communities have been subdivided for this study and the variation in rates shown. This was done for the community known as the Near West Side, which was divided into sub-communities Nos. 40, 41, and 49 on the map. In the text similar detailed analysis is given for Uptown (70), Lakeview (66), and the Lower North Side (64)—all communities in which it was known that the neighborhoods differed in nationality and interests, forming distinct little communities. No doubt other large communities might also be so subdivided.

Of these seventy-two communities as shown on the map, all but nine had in 1919–21 an average annual rate of suicide of less than 20 per 100,000, while all but thirteen had a rate less than the rate for the city as a whole. The sixty-three communities with a rate of less than 20 suicides per 100,000 per year comprise approximately eight-ninths of the area of

Chicago and include approximately 2,330,000 people, or eight-ninths of the population of the city. For only a minority of people, congregated in a small portion of the total area, does the suicide rate reach proportions sufficiently large to excite interest. Four of the nine high-rate communities have rates only slightly above the rates of the large number of low-rate areas, ranging from 20 to 24 suicides per 100,000 population per year. These communities are Uptown (70), North Albany (60), Oakland (13), and Lincoln (65). A glance at the statistical table will show that up to the rate of 24 suicides per 100,000 the variations in rates are very small. The rate next higher to 24 suicides per 100,000 is 35, a jump of 11 suicides per 100,000, held by the Lower North Side (64), which is followed by a rate of 40 suicides for the West Madison Street district (40), 59 suicides for the Near South Side (2), and the extremely high rate of 87 suicides per 100,000 people for the Loop (1).

When the community known as Uptown (70) is divided in order to isolate the white-light area of Wilson Avenue, the north half of the district has a rate of but 14 suicides per 100,000, while the gay Wilson Avenue section has a rate of 25 suicides per 100,000.

The Lower North Side (64), when divided in east and west halves, shows two distinct rates. Little Sicily, the western area, almost solidly Italian, has a rate of 27 suicides per 100,000 while the east section has a rate of 37 suicides per 100,000.

In addition to these distinctly suicidal areas, which have rates far in excess of the majority of the communities, interest attaches also to the non-suicidal communities. For the five years 1919 through 1923, Jefferson Park, Norwood Park, and Edison Park (61, 62, 63), with a combined population

TABLE XVI

SUICIDES PER 100,000 IN CHICAGO COMMUNITIES FOR 1919–21

COMMUNITY	TOTAL	M.	F.	NATIVE-BORN WHITE			FOREIGN BORN			NEGRO		
				Total	M.	F.	Total	M.	F.	Total	M.	F.
1. Loop...............	87	110	11	82	100	15	114	160	...	...	...	...
2. Near South Side......	59	75	36	73	84	50	86	130	...	15	14	17
3. Douglas.............	16	24	6	30	50	5	43	56	30	9	15	5
4. Armour Square, Bridgeport................	11	13	8	8	10	6	15	16	13	...	...	...
5. McKinley Park*......	8	...	...	...	...	...	...	...	...	...	...	...
6. Brighton Park*......	8	...	...	...	...	...	...	...	...	...	...	...
7. Archer Heights*.......	24	...	...	...	...	...	...	...	...	...	...	...
8. Mexico*.............	9	...	...	...	...	...	...	...	...	...	...	...
9. New City*...........	16	27	4	4	5	4	33	55	4	...	...	...
10. Canaryville*..........	7	...	...	...	...	...	...	...	...	...	...	...
11. Fuller Park*..........	14	...	...	...	...	...	...	...	...	...	...	...
12. Grand Boulevard......	15	19	11	16	20	12	36	47	24	4	3	5
13. Oakland.............	22	20	24	30	26	35	12	23	...	...	...	...
14. Kenwood............	16	23	11	18	24	14	18	30	9	...	...	...
15. Hyde Park..........	14	16	13	12	11	11	22	25	20	...	...	...
16. Washington Park......	11	17	6	7	10	5	22	34	9	14	19	9
17. Woodlawn............	14	19	10	13	15	9	23	40	6	...	...	...
18. South Shore*.........	1	...	...	...	...	...	...	...	...	...	...	...
19. Greater Grand Crossing	8	...	...	...	...	...	...	...	...	...	...	...
20. Englewood...........	8	9	6	6	7	5	18	20	10	...	...	...
21. West Englewood......	8	11	5	13	10	3	12	14	3	...	...	...
22. Chicago Lawn*.......	13	...	...	...	...	...	...	...	...	...	...	...
23. Clearing*.............	...	...	...	...	...	...	...	...	...	...	...	...
24. (Unnamed)*..........	...	...	...	...	...	...	...	...	...	...	...	...
25. Auburn-Gresham*.....	4	...	...	...	...	...	...	...	...	...	...	...
26. Chesterfield*.........	...	...	...	...	...	...	...	...	...	...	...	...
27. Avalon Park*.........	23	...	...	...	...	...	...	...	...	...	...	...
28. South Chicago........	9	16	2	4	7	...	20	29	4	...	...	...
29. East Side*...........	7	...	...	...	...	...	...	...	...	...	...	...
30. South Deering*.......	12	...	...	...	...	...	...	...	...	...	...	...
31. Pullman*............	...	...	...	...	...	...	...	...	...	...	...	...
32. Roseland*............	14	...	...	...	...	...	...	...	...	...	...	...
33. Washington Heights*..	20	...	...	...	...	...	...	...	...	...	...	...
34. South Beverly*.......	3	...	...	...	...	...	...	...	...	...	...	...
35. Morgan Park*.........	17	...	...	...	...	...	...	...	...	...	...	...
36. South Pullman........	15	18	11	15	15	16	16	27	...	...	...	...
37. West Pullman*.......	11	...	...	...	...	...	...	...	...	...	...	...
38. Riverdale*...........	10	...	...	...	...	...	...	...	...	...	...	...
39. Hegewisch*..........	...	...	...	...	...	...	...	...	...	...	...	...

TABLE XVI—*Continued*

COMMUNITY	TOTAL	M.	F.	NATIVE-BORN WHITE			FOREIGN BORN			NEGRO		
				Total	M.	F.	Total	M.	F.	Total	M.	F.
40. Madison St.**	40	...	...	...	...	...	...	...	...	...	...	...
41. Near West**	11	...	...	...	...	...	...	...	...	...	...	...
42. Lower West	18	27	8	7	5	12	32	52	8	...	...	...
43. South Lawndale	12	19	6	5	7	2	27	39	13	...	...	...
44. North Lawndale	11	16	5	5	8	2	18	25	10	...	...	...
45. East Garfield Park	10	12	7	10	12	5	10	11	8	...	...	...
46. West Garfield Park	12	12	11	10	12	7	22	15	29	...	...	...
47. Austin	6	6	6	4	4	4	17	14	19	...	...	...
48. West Humboldt Park	15	18	11	5	4	5	40	53	26	...	...	...
49. Negro area**	4	...	...	...	...	...	...	...	...	...	...	...
50. East Humboldt Park	14	23	4	4	9	...	26	40	10	...	...	...
51. Logan Square	8	11	6	5	6	3	15	20	11	...	...	...
52. South Avondale	11	14	7	5	10	...	29	27	29	...	...	...
53. Hermosa*	12	...	...	...	...	...	...	...	...	...	...	...
54. Belmont-Craigin*	5	...	...	...	...	...	...	...	...	...	...	...
55. Mount Clair*	5	...	...	...	...	...	...	...	...	...	...	...
56. West Dunning*	(	...	...	...	...	...	...	...	...	...	...	...
57. Portage Park*	7	...	...	...	...	...	...	...	...	...	...	...
58. South Irving, North Avondale	9	14	4	8	11	5	12	25	...	...	...	...
59. South Albany, North Irving Park	13	18	8	8	9	5	30	46	12	...	...	...
60. North Albany Park, North Park*	20	...	...	...	...	...	...	...	...	...	...	...
61. Jefferson Park*	...	...	...	...	...	...	...	...	...	...	...	...
62. Norwood Park*	...	...	...	...	...	...	...	...	...	...	...	...
63. Edison Park*	...	...	...	...	...	...	...	...	...	...	...	...
64. Lower North Side	35	47	19	28	35	21	48	71	16	...	...	...
65. Lincoln	24	36	13	14	19	9	45	63	25	...	...	...
66. Lakeview	15	19	12	12	11	12	24	38	9	...	...	...
67. Hamlin Park*	6	...	...	...	...	...	...	...	...	...	...	...
68. North Center*	6	...	...	...	...	...	...	...	...	...	...	...
69. Ravenswood	10	6	15	5	2	7	25	20	33	...	...	...
70. Uptown	20	29	13	16	21	12	39	61	19	...	...	...
71. West Rogers Park*	21	...	...	...	...	...	...	...	...	...	...	...
72. Rogers Park*	10	...	...	...	...	...	...	...	...	...	...	...

* Rates have been figured on the total population only for communities having a yearly average number of suicides of less than three.

** Communities numbered 40, 41, and 49 were considered one community by the Sociology Department. Hence it was not possible to make classified rates for each division. For the three communities combined the rates stand as shown in Table XVI A, page 86.

of 9,917, had no suicides. Had these communities had the suicide rate of the city as a whole (15.2 per 100,000) they would have had 7.5 suicides during these five years. Clearing–Garfield Ridge (23) also had no suicides for five years. With a population of 3,760 it should have had four suicides during these five years to equal the rate for the city as a whole. Chesterfield (26) with a population of 6,946, had no suicides in the same five years; five suicides during this period would have given it the rate for the city. South Shore (18), although it had only one suicide in 1919–21, had 3 in 1922 and 2 in 1923; these would, however, give a rate of only

TABLE XVI A

TOTAL	M.	F.	NATIVE WHITE			FOREIGN			NEGRO		
			Total	M.	F.	Total	M.	F.	Total	M.	F.
19	24	13	13	17	9	29	36	19	.....	.....	.....

3 suicides per 100,000 per year for the five-year period. Twenty-five suicides would have been necessary to bring the rate up to the general rate for the city.

Of peculiar interest are communities 49 and 3, both Negro areas. Fully 73 per cent of the population of Douglas (3), the larger of the two, is Negro. The Negroes of Chicago tend to become segregated into compact colored areas; hence the suicide rates for these communities show the tendency for Negro rates in general to be below the white rates. This tendency is further demonstrated by computing the rates for whites and Negroes separately for the community of Douglas. The annual rate for native-born whites in this community for 1919–21 was 30 per 100,000; for foreign born, 43; while for the Negroes it was only 9.

Except in a few instances the community rates for sui-

MAP II

MAP OF CHICAGO SHOWING RATES OF SUICIDE, 1919–21*

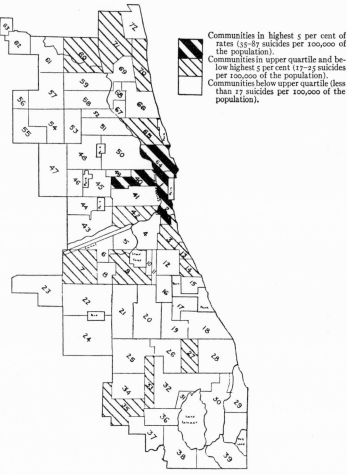

Communities in highest 5 per cent of rates (35–87 suicides per 100,000 of the population).

Communities in upper quartile and below highest 5 per cent (17–25 suicides per 100,000 of the population).

Communities below upper quartile (less than 17 suicides per 100,000 of the population).

* For Maps II, III, IV, and V the communities were ranked according to their rates for suicide, and in the cases of the last three maps, also for divorce, murder, and deaths from alcoholism, respectively. Communities falling in the highest 5 per cent of the rates are marked with heavy cross-bars. Those in the upper quartile and below the highest 5 per cent are marked with light cross-bars. Those below the upper quartile are unshaded.

cide do not show the national groupings with any clearness, although the statistical tables show that the foreign born as a group have in each community higher rates than the native born in the same community. The failure of the total rates, and hence of the map, to show nationality groupings is perhaps due in part to the fact that the national groups with high suicide rates (Germans, Swedes, and Danes especially) are scattered over the city and cannot be isolated into communities, while others, such as the Hungarians, are gathered here and there into neighborhoods too small to be treated as separate units. Some of the most concentrated groups of foreign born are those with low suicide rates. The Poles, who live in the east half of Logan Square (51) and East Humboldt (50), in the west half of the Lower West Side (42) and the east half of South Lawndale (43) and in the communities south of the river, have a rate of only 11.3 suicides per 100,000 for the city. This rate is lower than that for the city as a whole. The Russians and Italians, many of whom live in the Near West Side (41) have rates of 19.3 and 15.8 per 100,000 for the city. The Czechoslovakians, a group with high suicide rates, are interspersed among the low-rate Poles and Russians. And in all communities the children of these immigrants, who make up a large proportion of the population, have suicide rates far below those of their parents. It is because of this complex intermixture of the population that the community rates as figured on the total population do not clearly demonstrate what the classified rates show, namely, that the rate for the foreign-born is almost treble that for the native-born whites.

The foreign communities, instead of coinciding with the areas of high suicide rates, surround these areas, which are for the most part made up of native-born whites.

Since the foreign born, in spite of their high rate, do not account for the high suicide rates of communities 2, 40, and 64 and for the white rate in 3, other factors must be sought. In the first place these four areas are adult areas; their population is chiefly of the age groups which commit suicide most frequently.

Moreover, the males predominate in all four groups and to a degree not found elsewhere in the city. In the Loop (1), 78 per cent of the population is male; in the Near South Side (2), 58 per cent; in the West Madison district (40), 57 per cent; and on the Lower North Side, 55 per cent—a percentage which would be much higher for the American section considered alone. In no other community is the proportion of men so high as in these. The predominance of men in the suicidal communities contributes somewhat to the rate of the community as a whole. But it is by no means entirely responsible, for the statistical table (XVI) clearly indicates that in these communities the rates for women as well as for men tend to be higher than in other communities.

The result from considering the population classes in these communities of high suicide rates is mainly negative: immigrant groups, male predominance, adult groups, although known to contribute to high rates, do not seem to account for the high rates in these communities.

A second and more fruitful line of approach is through characteristic activities found in these areas in which suicide rates are high. To the five main areas already mentioned should be added Oakland (13) on the edge of the Negro area, and the Wilson Avenue district in the south half of Uptown (70). The attempt to find associated activities was for the most part by trial and error and consisted in examination of many maps on file in the research rooms of the Sociology

Department of the University of Chicago and comparison of these maps with the suicide map.

The lodging-house areas.—There were in 1923, 5,152 lodging-houses in Chicago listed with the Illinois Department of Public Health.[1] Of these houses, 1,817, adequate to the needs of 29,344 guests, were on the South Side, and all but a very few were in communities 2, 3, 10, and 13; 1,452 were on the West Side, chiefly in community 40; and 1,883 were on the North Side, especially in community 64, with a lessening number extending up into the east half of communities 65 and 66 and the southern part of 70. A map spotted with black dots, one dot for each rooming-house, is completely black in three tongues extending outward from the loop, but has only a bare scattering of dots for any other part of the city. The Loop (1), while it has comparatively few lodging-houses, has numerous hotels. (See Map VI.)

A detailed study of the Lower North Side[2] revealed the following pertinent facts about the rooming-house area in that community. It is concentrated between the thin line of wealthy residences along the lake front and the crowded family life of Little Sicily to the west. In this one area alone there are 1,139 rooming- and lodging-houses, with 23,007 people living in furnished rooms. A study of ninety blocks in the better rooming-house area disclosed that 71 per cent of all the houses in this district kept roomers; 52 per cent of these roomers were single men; 10 per cent were single women; and 38 per cent passed as married couples. There are few children and few old people in the community. In the

---

[1] From map in research rooms of Sociology Department, University of Chicago.

[2] See H. W. Zorbaugh, "The Dweller in Furnished Rooms: An Urban Type," *American Journal of Sociology, Papers and Proceedings of the 20th Annual Meeting*, XXXII, No. 1, Part II (1926), 83.

section east of Clark Street the young men and women are either clerical workers in the loop, or students in the North Side music schools, or more-or-less earnest followers of some profession in or bordering on the arts.

Lodging-house people are a restless, moving throng. The population on the Lower North Side has a complete turn-over every four months, and about half of the rooming-house keepers themselves move every six months.

Clark Street north of the river and south of Chicago Avenue is a part of the area of homeless men which has its other centers on South Clark and West Madison streets.

The West Madison Street area has many transient men looking for jobs in the many employment bureaus located in that neighborhood. They are here today, gone tomorrow; restless, yet aimless in their seeking.[1]

Another portion of the lodging-house area, in the southern part of the Loop (1), is also the home of unattached men, this time of men who work at petty jobs about the city and earn barely enough to live on. There are more women in this area than on West Madison, and no employment bureaus. The Pacific Garden Mission on South State typically has a third to a half of its audience women, and there are many men and women who are regular attendants.

South of Roosevelt Road [the southern boundary of the Loop (1)] the lodging-house area continues. Unfortunately no special study has been made of the lodging-house population in these further areas, but the more even division of the sexes in these communities suggests a more mixed lodging-house group.

Although there seem to be great differences in the personnel of these communities of lodging-house people, there

[1] See Nels Anderson, *The Hobo.*

are also certain general characteristics, both in the classes of people who live in these areas and in the type of life they live. For the most part they are either not married or at least are not living with husband or wife; and they are unencumbered with children. Men and women, even when married, often both work, which again prevents a home and family life in the old-fashioned sense of the words. There is in the rooming-house areas then a striking lack of the intimate type of group life which is considered by some sociologists the most fundamental both for the control of the individual and for the establishment of conventional norms of conduct, and for the satisfaction of interests and wishes.

Unincorporated into family groups, the lodging-house people are also without neighborhood life. People living in the same house scarcely come to know each other, due to the rapidity with which roomers move in and out, and also to the lack of opportunity for contacts. The old-time boarding-house with a common parlor and front porch and meals served in one large dining-room is gone. Chicago roomers in these areas usually see their fellow-roomers only in passing in the halls or on the stairway, if they see them at all. This condition means that the lodging-house has no standards and no traditions. The contrast to this comes in certain other institutions, such as social settlements or fraternity houses or college dormitories, where family life is also for the most part lacking, but where there are common meeting-places, wide interests which unite the individuals into effort for a common purpose, long-continued residence, and the gradual incorporation of newcomers into the group. Under such conditions traditions are established which control the newcomer, causing him to conform to the customs of the place. Moreover, he is made to feel a member of the group, his wishes and needs are considered, and provision is made for them. In lodging-houses the people are detached, uncontrolled by the opinions of their neighbors, and often very lonely.

Lodging-house life is quite naturally not conducive to neighborhood or community consciousness, and in this wider group there is in a lodging-house area little unanimity of opinion or effort.

Divorce areas (see Map III).—Divorces are an indication both of the breakdown of organized family life in the families in which they occur and also of the attitude that the family relationship is impermanent and subject to the wishes of the married couple themselves rather than to any ideal of social stability maintained through family life. Rates for Chicago communities show that in 1919 there were three small areas of high divorce rates, the Loop (1), the Wilson Avenue area in the Uptown community (70), and Oakland (13). An area of slightly less high rate includes the Lower North Side (64), the communities just west of the river, and a rather large area to the south. For the great number of other communities in Chicago the rate is relatively low.[1]

The high rate in these particular areas is all the more remarkable because of the dearth of family life in them. Where there has been no marriage there can be no divorce. Apparently the areas where family life thrives—the non-rooming-house areas—are also the areas in which there is stability, adjustment, and continuance of families. In the lodging-house areas the families which have been established tend to disintegrate, no doubt in part at least due to the individualism engendered by the non-group life and the in-

[1] E. R. Mowrer, *Family Disorganization*, chap. v.

MAP III

COMPARISON OF SUICIDE AND DIVORCE IN CHICAGO, BY COMMUNITIES

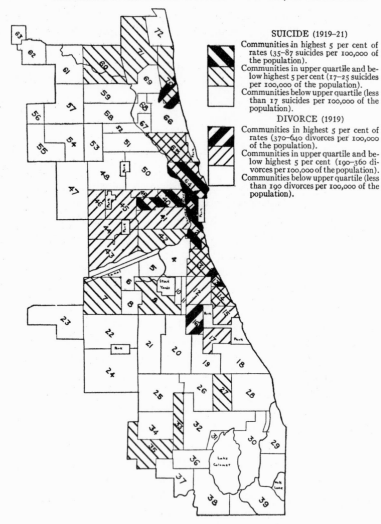

SUICIDE (1919–21)

Communities in highest 5 per cent of rates (35–87 suicides per 100,000 of the population).

Communities in upper quartile and below highest 5 per cent (17–25 suicides per 100,000 of the population).

Communities below upper quartile (less than 17 suicides per 100,000 of the population).

DIVORCE (1919)

Communities in highest 5 per cent of rates (370–640 divorces per 100,000 of the population).

Communities in upper quartile and below highest 5 per cent (190–360 divorces per 100,000 of the population).

Communities below upper quartile (less than 190 divorces per 100,000 of the population).

ability or unwillingness to sacrifice personal aspirations for the sake of family ideals.

Pawnshops (see Map VI).—It is not without significance that forty-four of the fifty-four pawnshops listed in the classified telephone directory for January, 1925, are within the areas of high suicide rates. Nine of these shops are on or near North Clark Street between the river and Chicago Avenue—within the limits of the Lower North Side (64) and in one part of the rooming-house area. Nine more are near the intersection of Halsted and Madison, in the heart of the West Madison Street area (40). Seven are on or near South Clark between 300 and 800 south, while nine more are a little farther north but on or near Clark Street. The fourth pawnshop center lies near State and Thirty-fourth streets, where ten pawnships are a part of the life of the community of Douglas (3). The other ten pawnshops listed in the telephone directory are scattered here and there and do not form centers, although there are many other business sections throughout the city.

The concentrating of one particular type of institution or industry into definite centers indicates that in those communities where the concentration occurs there is need for a definite kind of service.

For the most part these pawnshops are small, one-room establishments with three dingy balls above the door, often with old clothing hanging outside, and with the windows filled with such small articles as knives, watches, rings, banjos, and pins of various kinds. These petty articles, as well as the mere existence of the pawnshops, are an indication of the economic status of the people of the community. A hand-to-mouth existence and the possession of very little personal property are distinctive.

Murders (see map IV).—A map showing the rate of murder in the various communities of Chicago makes clear that certain sections of Chicago are almost free of murders, while in other parts the rate is very high.[1] Murders, as well as suicides, occur most frequently, in proportion to the population, in the Loop (1). The Lower North Side (64), the West Madison area (40), the Near South Side (2), Douglas (3), and Archer Heights (7), also have high rates. Here the correspondence between suicide and murders stops. For the other communities having high murder rates are certain of the immigrant communities south of the south branch of the river, in which the suicide rate is not high. The partial coincidence is, however, significant, for it indicates that in certain communities not only suicide, but other aberrant forms of behavior occur, and hence that these communities have those characteristics of mores and social organization which permit such behavior.

Other indications of personal disorganization (see Maps V and VI).—The phenomena just considered may be thought of as symptoms of lesions in the social organization and hence of weakness in the social control of the community. They are symptoms of social disorganization which often has its counterpart in the personal disorganization of the individuals in the community. Various overt types of activity are indexes of the degree of personal disorganization and even demoralization in a community. It has been possible, from studies made by other investigators, to localize certain of these types of conduct.

When deaths due to alcoholism in 1923–25 were spotted

---

[1] Based on map and computations made by P. P. Diefenderfer, University of Chicago. The basis is 533 cases of murder (not homicides) occurring in Chicago from July, 1918, to June, 1921.

MAP IV

COMPARISON OF SUICIDE AND MURDER IN CHICAGO, BY COMMUNITIES

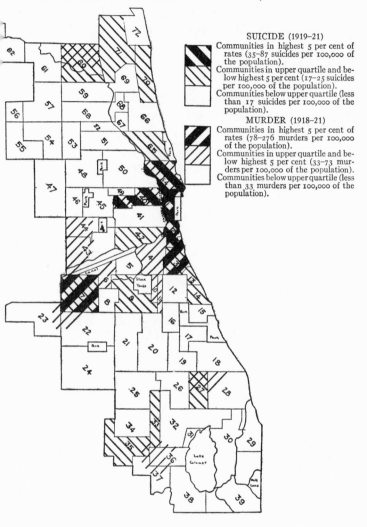

SUICIDE (1919–21)
Communities in highest 5 per cent of rates (35–87 suicides per 100,000 of the population).
Communities in upper quartile and below highest 5 per cent (17–25 suicides per 100,000 of the population).
Communities below upper quartile (less than 17 suicides per 100,000 of the population).

MURDER (1918–21)
Communities in highest 5 per cent of rates (78–276 murders per 100,000 of the population).
Communities in upper quartile and below highest 5 per cent (33–73 murders per 100,000 of the population).
Communities below upper quartile (less than 33 murders per 100,000 of the population).

on a map of Chicago[1] and the rates for each community figured, a startling coincidence in locus of high suicide rates and high alcoholic death-rates appeared. The Loop (1) had 57.2 deaths from alcoholism per 100,000 population; the West Madison Street area (40) stood next, with 47.8 deaths; then came the Near South Side (2), with 28.7 deaths, followed by the Lower North Side (64), with 12.5 deaths per 100,000. The next highest was the Lower West Side (42), with 11.1 deaths from alcoholism per 100,000 of the population, after which came the other communities, many with few or no deaths from alcoholism during these two years.

The use of drugs as well as of alcoholic drinks is both a habit and a means of escaping from the rigors and disappointments of waking hours. There are three "dope centers" in Chicago, places where in the night dope peddlers and craving customers meet and exchange morphine or cocaine for money. These three centers are, first, North Clark Street between the river and Chicago Avenue in the Lower North Side (64), and the exact locale of one pawnshop center; second, South State and Thirty-first and Wabash or State and Twenty-sixth, near another pawnshop center, in Douglas (3) and the Near South Side (2); and third, along Halsted Street at Madison and Harrison, a third pawnshop center, in the West Madison district.[2]

Yet a third type of activity denoting demoralization may be located: houses, hotels, and cabarets catering to those in

[1] The spot map, from which the rate map used here was made, is on file in the Sociology Department of the University of Chicago. It was constructed by L. V. Greever and Daniel Russell on the basis of records in the coroner's office of Cook County.

[2] Leonard Cline, *Chicago Daily News* (March 6, 1926), quoting L. J. Ulmer, head of the narcotic division in Chicago, and Detective Sergeant William Bowler, of the Chicago police.

MAP V

COMPARISON OF SUICIDE AND DEATHS FROM ALCOHOLISM IN CHICAGO,
BY COMMUNITIES

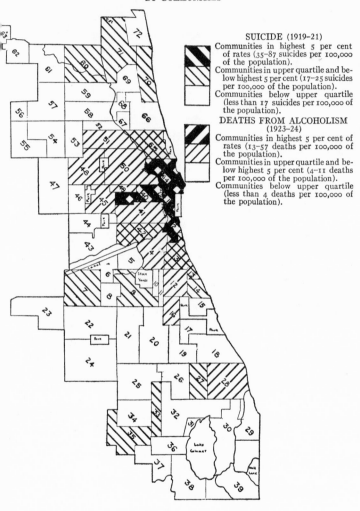

SUICIDE (1919–21)

Communities in highest 5 per cent of rates (35–87 suicides per 100,000 of the population).

Communities in upper quartile and below highest 5 per cent (17–25 suicides per 100,000 of the population).

Communities below upper quartile (less than 17 suicides per 100,000 of the population).

DEATHS FROM ALCOHOLISM
(1923–24)

Communities in highest 5 per cent of rates (13–57 deaths per 100,000 of the population).

Communities in upper quartile and below highest 5 per cent (4–11 deaths per 100,000 of the population).

Communities below upper quartile (less than 4 deaths per 100,000 of the population).

search of promiscuous sex relations. The Committee of Fifteen in 1922 investigated some three hundred buildings in which prostitution was carried on.[1] Douglas (3) and West Madison (40) each had fifty-four; in the first community, houses and cabarets; in the second, chiefly houses. The community termed Grand Boulevard (12), lying just south of Douglas, had forty-six, chiefly houses of prostitution. The Near South Side (2) had twenty-seven, mainly saloons and houses; the Lower North Side (64) had twenty-three; the Loop (1) had nineteen, chiefly hotels. The next highest was the little Negro area, numbered 49 on the map, with nineteen, chiefly hotels. The next was Oakland (13), with eleven houses of prostitution, after which came Uptown (70) with ten houses. Outside these eight communities the Committee of Fifteen found little occasion to investigate houses, hotels, or saloons in any part of Chicago.

Suicide co-incident with disorganized communities.—An adequate social organization serves two functions in society. It implies institutions—such as the family, church, school, commercial and industrial organizations, recreational facilities—sufficient to care for the varied interests of the people who live in the society or community; and it implies customs, traditions, ideals, and purposes of sufficient homogeneity throughout the group, and built up about the institutions, to control the individuals and cause them to find adequate outlet for their needs and energies in the existing institutions. In communities where there are few contacts with outsiders, and where newcomers trickle in in a slow stream or come mainly by the birth of children, the continuity and homogeneity of institutions and customs can be

[1] From a map on file in the Sociology Department, University of Chicago.

MAP VI

COMPARISON OF SUICIDE AND OTHER INDICATIONS OF DISORGANIZATION
IN CHICAGO, BY COMMUNITIES

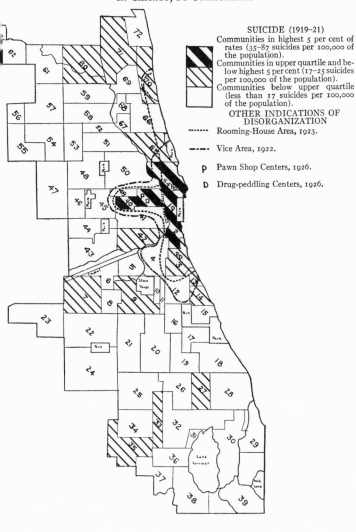

SUICIDE (1919–21)
Communities in highest 5 per cent of
rates (35–87 suicides per 100,000 of
the population).
Communities in upper quartile and below highest 5 per cent (17–25 suicides
per 100,000 of the population).
Communities below upper quartile
(less than 17 suicides per 100,000
of the population).
OTHER INDICATIONS OF
DISORGANIZATION
------ Rooming-House Area, 1923.

---- Vice Area, 1922.

P   Pawn Shop Centers, 1926.

D   Drug-peddling Centers, 1926.

assured and certain moral and ethical ideals can be maintained.

In the cities, particularly in certain sections of large cities, this community type of control breaks down. In Chicago this area includes the Loop and a great semicircle about the Loop, of land upon which industries are encroaching. This land has high value. Not many years ago it was residence property, and the homes of many wealthy Chicagoans who have long since moved to the North Shore or the suburbs still stand in decrepit condition in this area. Because of the high value of the land and the reasonable supposition that its future will be for commercial purposes, residences are not repaired; nor have new and modern houses been built. This condition alone determines to some extent the economic status of the people who come there. They are able to rent the old buildings cheaply.

Four types of people have been drawn to these communities. In the Lower North Side are young people with ambitions, ideals, and little money. This section is locally spoken of as Chicago's art colony, as Little Bohemia, as Chicago's Greenwich Village. Between Bohemia and West Madison, on both sides of the north branch of the river, are immigrant groups, Italians and Poles. West Madison is again American—hoboes, "homeless men," "migratory workers" out of a job. To the south of the West Madison area are again immigrant groups, Italians, Russians, Lithuanians, Czechoslovakians, Poles. South of the south branch of the river are more communities of these same immigrant groups, and finally, directly south of the Loop, are first more homeless men and then the Black Belt, on the border of which are more disorganized areas of white Americans, who also permeate the entire Negro section.

A glance at the maps in this chapter shows that for suicide and the types of disorganization associated with it the
immigrant areas are virtually in the same class with the
numerous communities of middle class and wealthy people
who live in the outlying communities of Chicago. It is the
three American communities and the Americans in the Loop
and in the Negro area who commit suicide, and in these
and the immediately adjacent American communities are
found those types of disorganization, both social and personal, which are associated with suicide.

It has already been pointed out that the immigrant
groups living in these compact communities are those who
have both in Europe and in America low suicide rates. The
absence of the other types of disorganization indicates, not
necessarily that they do not become disorganized, but rather
that they are not subject to the same types of disorganization as American communities. This conclusion is supported
by other evidence. The types of disorganization having to
do with children and with family life—cases of poverty,
gangs, and juvenile delinquency—tend to center in the immigrant communities. There is, then, a specialization of disorganization in the various communities which lie within the
semicircle of Chicago's disorganized area. The Loop to a
certain extent shares in the American types of disorganization; for while business there is very well organized, the few
people who live in hotels and in apartments over commercial
houses are without community life.

The low economic status and detached condition of the
Americans in these areas contribute to their restlessness and
mobility, and in the shifting population organized group life
has no place.

Whenever community organization breaks down there is

an especially good opportunity for personal disorganization to occur. Vagrant and normally inhibited impulses are permitted free reign in a way not possible in a well-integrated community where departures from the standards of conduct would bring severe criticism and social ostracism. Moreover, the community without such standards attracts those from other communities both within the city and in small towns who find themselves at odds with the restrictions of the social order and who wish to live without reference to established and conventional norms of conduct. Without the repressions of community control and with the presence of people who wish forbidden stimulations and pleasures there is a tendency for institutions to be established in these disorganized areas to cater to the peculiar demands found there. The dope peddler, the vender of alcoholic drinks, the house of prostitution, the rooming-house, and the pawnshop are such institutions the reason for whose being is both the inability of the community to oust them and the willingness of a certain portion of the community actively to support them. In other communities in Chicago the standards of conduct are more conventional, not only because the individual standards are higher, but also because there is long residence in one neighborhood and a certain amount of community consciousness and feeling of community ownership and pride.

It is not to be thought that these institutions and types of conduct typical of the highly suicidal areas cause suicide. Rather they are symptoms of a general condition of personal and social disorganization which in the end may lead to suicide. There is in these areas a concentration of unsatisfied and disorganized persons, and therefore the probability of more suicide than in communities well organized as to community life and the characters of individuals.

This analysis of the suicide rate in an urban center throws much light on the difference between rural and urban rates. In Illinois the rate for towns under 10,000 and the open country was in 1919–21, 11.7 per 100,000 population; the rate for cities between 10,000 and 100,000 was 14.1. In Chicago the rate was 15.3. But for forty-one of the seventy-three Chicago communities the rate was below the rate for the small towns and rural sections of Illinois, and for fifty-two communities it was below the rate for the secondary cities. In only certain sections of large cities, then, if Chicago is typical, is the suicide rate higher than in smaller places where disorganization is assumed to exist in lesser quantity and degree than in the city. Many communities in the city must be regarded as being as well organized and orderly in customs, morals, and conduct and with people as well adjusted as in the smaller places.

CHAPTER VI

SUICIDE AND SOCIAL DISORGANIZATION

A bird's-eye view of the very diverse data of the preceding chapters may be gained from the tabulation in Table XVII.

TABLE XVII

(Correlation of Social Factors)

The Social Situation	Type of Social Organization	Prevalent Attitudes	Amount of Suicide
Greece, before decline...	Stable	State more important than individual	Moderate
Greece, decline of power.	Confusion of customs and moral codes	Individualism	Greatly increased
Rome, before fall of the republic............	Stable	State more important than individual	Moderate
Rome, period of fall of the republic..........	Confusion of customs and moral codes	Individualism	Greatly increased
Middle Ages...........	Stable	Individual belonged to God	Very little
Temporary crises in Middle Ages, as plagues, harrassing of witches, etc................	Conflict, inability to control the situation		Increased in the groups involved
Renaissance..........	Confusion of customs and moral codes	Individualism	Greatly increased
Preliterate villages.....	Stable	Social needs supersede individual needs	Very little
Orient (until recently)...	Stable	Social needs superseded individual needs	Very little, except when dictated by social custom
Contemporary cities....	Confusion of customs and moral codes	Individualism	High suicide rates
Religious communities..	Stable	Individual belongs to God; social needs take precedence	Very little
Rural communities.....	Stable	Tendency toward attitudes of the religious community	Very little

In all cases listed in Table XVII the communities which have had stable social organization have been those which were more or less isolated and free from contacts with people of diverse customs. They have been communities, too, in which existing institutions were adequate to care for the dominant interests of the people. In such communities there is a tendency for social control to be very nearly complete, that is, the person from childhood up tends to do what is prescribed for him by customs and traditions. Whether the community is religious or merely social in organization, group needs take precedence and there is little individualism. The small amount of suicide found in these communities seems due in part to the lack of individualism and the feeling that the right to dispose of life does not lie in the hands of the individual, and in part to the way in which interests are molded to a certain pattern and then satisfied by institutions and associations already provided. The whole life of the individual is adjusted to the group where he lives. His ambitions, ideals, and interests are generated and fashioned by the group life, and they are at the same time satisfied within the group.

The communities which have had conflicts in social codes and confusion of customs have been those in which there was mobility, the going out of citizens who returned with tales of foreign lands, the incoming of foreigners with strange but fascinating habits of living. Under such conditions new interests are aroused, old institutions are found inadequate, and gradually the group unity is lost. The individual stands out as a separate entity, driven by unregulated impulses and wishes and often unable to find satisfaction for them.

The plagues and other crises of the Middle Ages and those recorded among the American Indians were temporary but sharply accentuated periods of social disorganization, times when customs and habits usually found adequate failed to regulate the situation.

In even the most stable social organization there is probably some personal disorganization, some people who cannot fit themselves wholly to the demands of customs and institutions. In times of social disorganization the difficulty is increased, and many people who would travel happily along under normal conditions find themselves unable to adjust to confused and conflicting standards. It is these people, unable, under adverse social conditions, to work out a satisfying personal life organization, who contribute to the increased suicide rates in communities where social disorganization prevails. The way in which personal disorganization develops and culminates in suicide is the subject of Part II, which thus becomes the obverse of Part I. Part I has approached the problem of suicide from the point of view of the group, of the customs and institutions which constitute the social organization and through which the individual members of the group organize their interests and wishes. Part II approaches the problem from the point of view of the individual member of the group.

PART II
SUICIDE AND PERSONAL DISORGANIZATION

CHAPTER VII

PSYCHOSES ACCOMPANYING SUICIDE

Psychoses as extreme personal disorganization.—Suicide has appeared in Part I as a function of certain social attitudes and as one resultant of a loose social organization. But suicide is more than a social phenomenon. It is also a personal experience. What groups of people are most subject to difficulties and hence tend to commit suicide most frequently? What happens to the person's emotions, ambitions, his outlook on life, before he determines to kill himself? This more personal side of suicide, the social psychology of suicide, is the subject for Part II. The approach is made through a study of adjustments which people attempt to make when obstacles appear in the on-going process of living, adjustments already shown to be more frequently demanded in an individualistic, changing social order than in a highly socialized, static social order. When adjustments fail there may occur a complete breakdown of morale, inability to satisfy fundamental interests, and consequent personal disorganization or demoralization.

The most marked type of personal disorganization is found in the various types of psychoses. The conviction is growing that psychoses are not necessarily nor wholly the result of poor heredity. True, temperaments differ and some people seem to lack resources of adjustment. Nevertheless, crises in living have much to do with the development of psychoses. Certain psychoses in which the person becomes deeply depressed tend toward suicide. These clearly marked cases in which the extreme personal disorganization of insanity and suicide are linked have received careful study, particularly at the hands of certain European investigators. An estimate can be made on the basis of various data of the proportion of suicides who are actually insane at the time of killing themselves.

Not all suicides psychotic.[1]—Of the 291 suicides which occurred in the city of Chicago in 1923, approximately 44 men and 14 women may be definitely stated to have been insane.[2] An absolute statement cannot be made on the basis of the coroner's record, and no attempt can be made to

[1] This investigation has been concerned mainly with normal persons who have committed or attempted suicide. The discussion of the relation of insanity to suicide is not, therefore, an attempt to close the subject, but merely to present current views of psychiatrists and to suggest the relation between social experiences and psychoses.

[2] There is a widespread popular notion that many suicides are due to "temporary insanity." Lack of understanding of psychological processes, inability to discover concrete causes for distress in specific cases, and the soothing effect of such a conclusion on the relatives, particularly in cases where religious condemnation of suicide exists, bolster up this conception. Temporary insanity, in the sense in which it is popularly used, does not exist. There is, on the one hand, extreme personal disorganization in which the person finds himself unable to solve his problems and may come to regard himself as a failure and thus actually become unfit to make adjustments. Such a condition might almost be regarded as "temporary insanity" were it not that it lacks certain rather common elements of insanity, such as delusions, hallucinations, degeneracy of mental capacity, uncontrollable emotional states. In disorganization the person retains his normal mental functions and perceptions and is capable of reorganizing them under changed conditions. The disorganized person is not insane. On the other hand, there are certain types of insanity which appear periodically, the person being normal during the intervals. Thus melancholia may appear and disappear, and the contrasted phases of manic depressive insanity may be separated by periods of normalcy. But the cases popularly labeled as temporary insanity are not of this type; they do not have regular appearances of the difficulty, usually unrelated to actual difficulties, and they do not evidence the abnormal mental symptoms of insanity. Cases of "temporary insanity" are in reality either cases of genuine psychoses or of personal disorganization.

classify the cases into types of insanity. Those cases have been called insane in which the inquest brought to light either a physician's diagnosis of insanity made prior to the suicide attempt or some objective evidence of insanity, such as periodic spells of melancholia, hallucinations of being pursued, delusions of grandeur, extreme fear without cause, continued "queer" actions, or confinement at some recent time to an asylum. All doubtful cases have been included among the insane. According to the figures given, about 15.8 per cent of the male and 12.5 per cent of the female suicides in Chicago for 1923 were probably insane at the time they committed suicide. It is not known how many insane people there are in the city of Chicago, but probably a smaller percentage than is found among the suicides. In other words, the insane group probably contributes more than its proportion to the suicide list, but cannot be held accountable for all of the suicides.

A slightly greater percentage of cases was found by the Metropolitan Life Insurance Company in its investigation of suicides among policyholders in its Industrial Department. Among 2,211 suicides recorded in 1923–24, in 416 cases, or 18.8 per cent, mental disease was definitely specified as a contributory factor.[1]

The estimates of psychiatrists as to the number of persons who are insane at the time of committing suicide vary greatly. Unfortunately for comparative purposes, these estimates are for the most part for Germany. Kraepelin states that "Mental derangement is the cause of at least a third of the total number of suicides."[2] Basing his conclusions on

[1] Metropolitan Life Insurance Company, *Statistical Bulletin*, VIII, No. 4 (April, 1927), p. 4.

[2] Emil Kraepelin, *Lectures on Clinical Psychiatry*, pp. 2–3.

cases of attempted suicide brought to a clinic, Gaupp reports that among 124 cases, 44 (over a third) were definitely insane, while only one person was mentally sound, the bulk of the cases being of psychopathic persons,[1] that is, persons whose assumedly innate equipment was such that they found it difficult and even impossible to make needed adjustments. Wassermeyer, with 169 cases of attempted suicides brought to a clinic, found 30 per cent of the men and 72 per cent of the women insane.[2] He called all those normal who had not previous to the suicide attempt impressed their neighbors as abnormal and who after their physical recovery from the attempt were not in need of institutional care. He further states that suicides of mentally diseased persons are more apt to end in failure than the suicides of those who are mentally sound. This conclusion would presume that data based on attempts, while based on more accurate observations than are possible for successful suicides, would show a higher percentage of insane persons than would exist among actual suicides. A third study of attempted suicides which included the investigation of two hundred women brought to the psychiatric department of the Royal Charity Hospital in Berlin gives the analysis into types shown[3] (see p. 115). According to these figures approximately two-thirds of the cases studied were insane and the remaining third was about equally divided between psychopathic persons and normal persons. The same criticism would apply here that Wassermeyer makes of his own material, namely, that the unsuccessful suicides are most apt to be those of the mentally

[1] Wassermeyer, "Ueber Selbstmord," *Arch. f. Psychiat. u. Nervenkr.*, L (1912), 255.

[2] *Ibid.*, pp. 256 ff.

[3] H. Stelzner, *Analyse von 200 Selbstmordfällen*, pp. 5–8.

diseased. It is also possible that a psychiatric clinic would have referred to it chiefly cases in which some abnormality seemed to exist.

In spite of some contradiction, the preponderance of evidence available at present indicates that the majority of actual suicides probably cannot be traced to insanity, al-

	Number of Cases
Melancholia	64
Circular insanity (manic depressive)	1
Acute paranoia	11
Chronic paranoia	24
Dementia senilis	4
Dementia paralytica	6
Dementia praecox	7
Epilepsy	11
Imbecility	3
Alcoholism	6
With psychopathic constitution	32
Without evident symptoms of mental disease	31

though the exact number which can be is still a debatable question.

All types of insanity are not equally associated with suicide. Of Wassermeyer's 57 insane women who attempted suicide, 37 were diagnosed as suffering from melancholia. Of his 27 male cases having insanity, 5 had melancholia, 5 delirium tremens, 5 epilepsy, 4 paranoia, and the remainder are scattered. The statements of psychiatrists also link suicide of the insane with melancholia, but not with the depressive stage of manic-depressive insanity, in which periods of extreme elation and excitability alternate with periods of extreme depression.

We give the name of melancholia to this condition, in which we see the gradual development of a state of apprehensive depression, associated with more or less fully developed delusions. (Common delusions are of sin, illness, poverty, imprisonment.) . . . .

As a consequence of this mental unrest and these tormenting ideas, the wish to have done with life develops almost invariably, and patients very often become suicidal.[1]

. . . . Every case of melancholia should be considered a potential suicide. One of the principal reasons that a tendency to suicide is so dangerous a symptom here is that the carrying of suicidal tendencies into action is not interfered with by retardation in the way in which it is in manic-depressive psychosis. In manic-depressive psychosis the suicidal impulse is continuously prevented from expressing itself in action by the ever-present difficulty of the release of motor impulses, while here no such difficulty maintains, and the tendency constantly strives to find expression in appropriate action.[2]

In the depressive period of manic-depressive insanity there is a loss of will and cognition which inhibits motor action, and even though the wish for death is present, this malfunctioning of the organs tends to prevent the act.

The tendency of people with melancholia to commit suicide is emphasized by Viallon, who quotes one writer[3] who found among 730 cases of melancholia 65 per cent with suicidal tendencies; Viallon's conclusions for French data were that 40 per cent of people with melancholia tended toward suicide.[4]

The agreement on melancholia as the type of insanity which tends toward suicide throws light also on the general relation of insanity to suicide. Melancholia ordinarily ap-

[1] Kraepelin, *Lectures on Clinical Psychiatry*, p. 6; see also pp. 11–12.

[2] W. A. White, *Outlines of Psychiatry*, p. 175; see also A. R. Diefendorf, *Clinical Psychiatry*, pp. 356–57.

[3] Farghusson, *Journal of Mental Science*, quoted in *Arch. Neurol.* (1895), p. 158.

[4] Viallon, "Suicide et Folie," *Annales Medico-Psychologiques* (July-August, 1902), p. 235.

pears in men at the beginning of old age and in women at the time of the menopause, and it is more common in women than in men.[1] Yet in all of Europe and America men commit suicide at a rate three to four times higher than the rate for women, and both men and women commit suicide before old age or the menopause.

Suicide and specific psychoses.[2]—The monograph by Stelzner, to which reference has already been made, is the most complete study available on suicide among the insane.[3] Since it is not translated, a somewhat complete summary is included here, and unless otherwise indicated, all of the material in this section has been drawn from Stelzner's study.

1. *Melancholia (65 cases).*—Of these cases, eighteen were associated with the menopause. Two died as a result of the suicide attempt; of the remaining fourteen, by far the majority recovered from the melancholic condition and were discharged inside of a few months from the institutions where they were taken for treatment. In eight of the cases the menopause alone was not responsible for the suicide attempt, which followed some specific trouble, such as economic trouble or a family quarrel. In the remaining cases the immediate motive is given as "sudden anxiety," while one woman had delusions. When specific crises occurred they were superimposed upon a previously prevailing mood, incident to the menopause and existing in most cases for a

[1] Kraepelin, *Lectures on Clinical Psychiatry*, p. 9.

[2] Other studies on suicide and insanity less comprehensive than Dr. Stelzner's, are: A. H. Ring, "Factors in Suicide," *Boston Medical and Surgical Journal*, CXXCV (1921), p. 650; Viallon, "Suicide et Folie," *Annales Medico-Psychologiques*, XIV–XVII (1901–3), series of twelve articles.

[3] See p. 114 for summary of cases. Stelzner's study is confined to 200 women, attempted suicides, brought to a psychiatric clinic.

few weeks or months prior to the suicide attempt. Dr. Stelzner's conclusion was that these immediate motives were of minor importance.

> The precipitating causes often play a very subordinate rôle in the case of climacteric melancholia. The gloomy (*trüb*) undertone is produced by the feeling of insufficiency in the years of regression (*Ruckbildungsjahre*), by the onset of lack of elasticity in the case of external shock-influences, by the absence of a feeling of vitality which otherwise helps to overcome difficulties and vexations. In this way an inner mood of disharmony (*Verstimmung*) which has existed for months may be converted through insignificant external influences, such as the separation from a beloved person, a domestic quarrel, and similar events, into a genuine case of melancholia. Physical exhaustion, which is not infrequently of etiological moment (significance) for melancholia, and in cases of climacteric melancholia is brought about by excessive bleeding preceding the menopause, was observed once in the case of the only uncured patient who came to the institution in an emaciated and devitalized condition, and in the case of a second patient who had gone through thirteen confinements in sixteen years and in whom the menopause set in as early as at thirty-eight years of age.[1]

There were also eighteen cases of passive melancholia, exclusive of the climacteric cases, in which there were no hallucinations. Prior to the onset of the melancholia these women had showed a tendency toward emotional fantasies and seriousness of manner. Attenuating circumstances should be noted in several cases: one woman suffered for years from homesickness and the gruff manner of her mistress; another was a cripple and worried over her capacity for earning a living; another had made an unhappy marriage. It should be noted also that in many of the cases a crisis in living marked the suicide attempt and in several cases the appearance of the psychosis; for instance, justifiable fear of

[1] Stelzner, *Analyse von 200 Selbstmordfällen*, p. 13.

blindness, husband's illness, loss of position and family trouble, broken engagement and death of father, quarrel with fiancé. In other cases the suicide came as the culmination of a long-continued dissatisfaction, such as those first mentioned. In four cases. a period of physical exhaustion played a part: one confinement, two abortions, and one pregnancy. In one case no immediate motive could be found; in two there appeared to be no crisis; in one there was a delusion of sin; in another, an urgent idea that suicide must be committed; and in one there was sudden anxiety. The psychosis appeared very shortly before the suicide attempt in all except two cases; and in most of the cases upon which later information was obtainable the patient recovered after treatment of short duration, but retained an undue seriousness of mood. It should be noted that some of these women lived alone and hence in a condition to have the depressed mood perpetuated.[1]

In the eleven cases with hallucinations the suicide impulse came suddenly and violently, usually following anxiety caused by hallucinations of pursuers.[2] In only three cases did a concrete crisis combine with the psychosis. The psychosis had been in evidence usually several months before the suicide attempt and continued for some months or years afterward; in fact, in most cases the patient

[1] In consideration of the absence of delusions or hallucinations and the early recovery with no reappearance of the depression, the question arises whether some of these cases might not justly be considered cases of temporary disorganization related to specific crises, rather than cases of true psychoses.

[2] Here the crisis is unreal, but the psychological effect is as real as a true fright or continued persecution would be, and perhaps more real, since the persons regarded the hallucinations as inevitable and did not combat them by logical methods.

was still receiving institutional care at the time of the investigation.

In five cases the melancholic condition came after years of hypochrondriacal neurasthenia, or undue worry over physical ills, and the culmination or acute fear of illness, brought on by an operation or severe illness, is regarded by Dr. Stelzner as but the climax to a condition already operative. After the attempt, complete cure was difficult in most cases.

In the thirteen cases with periodic melancholia the suicide attempts appeared only with severe attacks of melancholia and tended to appear at the beginning of the melancholic period. Feelings of inferiority and anxiety incident to the onset of the psychosis appeared in some cases; in others, depression was deepened by some external crisis, as homesickness, the relinquishment of a long-held position as servant, fear of confinement in an institution, a lovers' quarrel. The attempts appeared suddenly and without much previous planning.

In general in the cases of melancholia the suicide attempt appears at the beginning of the psychosis and is followed by a rather complete breakdown of morale—a giving up of the struggle to appear sufficient for the burdens of living.

2. *Acute paranoia* (*11 cases*).—These cases are characterized by sudden and violent suicidal tendencies, hallucinations of persecution as the immediate motive for suicide, a short illness, and favorable prognosis for recovery. The hallucinations often followed after some actual emotional shock, such as the loss of a lover, but with the progress of the psychosis the real shock was forced into the background and the hallucinations dominated. Linked with these conditions was in almost every case a condition of physical exhaustion, such as pregnancy or malnutrition.

3. *Chronic paranoia (24 cases).*[1]—The paranoiac who attempts suicide is tired of the constant struggle against persecution and seeks relief in death, or he throws earthly things from him for a wider glorification of his person, the fulfilment of his mission, and the like. Among Dr. Stelzner's cases the patient sometimes killed her children prior to the suicide attempt, so as not to leave them for the persecutors.

4. *Senile dementia (4 cases).*—In these cases of old women the suicide attempt occurred primarily or secondarily through hallucinations or delusions. In two cases a period of depression was followed by the delusion that the police would get them and the suicide was attempted in a period of great agitation.

5. *Dementia paralytica (6 cases).*—Some of these cases approach the cases of melancholia and the suicide may be well-planned and associated with a period of depression. On the other hand, suicide may occur when the disease is further advanced and, due to the failing mentality, the attempt may be weak or even grotesque and may fail of its purpose.

6. *Dementia praecox (7 cases).*—As with the paralytic, suicide may come either with a period of depression early in the disease or later when there is more complete mental deterioration. Cases cited show that the suicides followed as the result of a mental compulsion which the patient could not afterward explain. The attempts were only half-heartedly carried out.

[1] The usual course of paranoia is that the person, unable to adjust to social conditions and life as he finds it, conceives his failure to be due, not to his inabilities, but to other people who persecute him; the logical reason he builds up to explain this persecution is a delusion of grandeur; he is greater than others and therefore they persecute him. Once the belief is established, it is almost impossible to shake the paranoiac's belief in his delusions. See White, *Outlines of Psychiatry.*

7. *Epilepsy* (*11 cases*).—In these cases suicide occurred either as the expression of an epileptic psychopathic constitution or in a period of depression following an epileptic attack or when the epileptic was in a semiconscious condition. There were few repeated attempts, in spite of the repetition of the epileptic attacks.

8. *Imbecility* (*3 cases*).[1]—In these cases no detailed analysis is given by Dr. Stelzner, the statement being made that the intellect had little control over the emotions, and the act of suicide appeared as an impulse.

9. *Chronic alcoholism* (*6 cases*).[2]

For a social psychological study of suicide the data obtained from Dr. Stelzner's study are important for two reasons. In perhaps the majority of cases the psychosis alone did not cause the suicide, but to the psychosis was added a concrete crisis which constitutes the immediate motive. In addition, the psychosis itself may have developed from some trying experience. Thus both the psychosis and the suicide are linked to the experiences the person has had, and both conceivably might have been controlled in at least some cases through control of the environment. In cases in which delusions or hallucinations constituted the critical situation or motive for seeking death, the psychological process does not seem greatly different from that found in normal life. The idea of suicide as a means of escape from a difficult situation is as evident in these cases of people who face an imagined crisis as in the cases of normal people who face a real crisis. The cases of dementia, as might be ex-

[1] It may be noticed that in 1923 among the 391 Chicago cases there appears only one suicide of a feeble-minded person and none of persons of lesser mentality.

[2] See pp. 287 ff.

pected, seem the most irrational, for here the mental capacity is not only disorganized and unable to grasp objective events in proper perspective, but is actually deteriorated.

The following case, drawn from charity records, illustrates the interlocking of experiential factors and mental abnormality in the development of a suicidal tendency.[1]

CASE I

George Rowsk, born in Austria of Polish parents, killed himself at the age of forty-five years.

FAMILY BACKGROUND

George Rowsk was born in Austria of Polish parents. His father was a heavy drinker who lived to be seventy years old; his mother died of "stomach trouble" at the age of sixty-three. He came to the United States in 1895 at the age of seventeen and to Chicago in 1905. It is not stated when he was married the first time, but at the time of his second marriage in 1906 he was a widower with one child (Anna) living, who had been born in 1904, and two children dead. His second marriage was to a woman of European birth (nationality not stated but apparently Polish) and occurred in the Roman Catholic church, although Rowsk was a Greek Catholic. This woman at the time of her marriage had an illegitimate child, Mary, who was born in 1905. Between the time of their marriage and Mr. Rowsk's suicide in 1924 eight children were born, two of whom died during the first year of life.

During all the time in Chicago the family lived in an industrial neighborhood and Mr. Rowsk worked much of the time as a carpenter in some car shops.

Anna, Mr. Rowsk's child by his first marriage, had some nervous trouble and from the time she was about twelve was cared for in

---

[1] Most of the case histories used in this study have been taken from the office of the coroner of Cook County or from the United Charity records, and are used with the permission of these agencies. In all cases the material has been abstracted by the writer, and all interpretations and analyses of causes are the writer's, for which she assumes full responsibility. Dates, names of persons and places, street addresses, and other identifying data have been changed to prevent recognition of the persons involved in the records.

institutions, as she was also feeble-minded. Mary, Mrs. Rowsk's child, lived with the family.

DOMESTIC TENSIONS

The charity was appealed to first in 1911, when Mr. Rowsk had been out of work for seven months. In 1915 aid was again asked, and from this time on the family had frequent contacts with the charity. The first difficulty in the family was mainly economic, and a few months after the charity took charge they attempted to train Mrs. Rowsk in managing her marketing. The family owed the grocer over $200, and Mr. Rowsk felt this debt was the fault of his wife's mismanagement, although he continued to turn his pay check over to her "to keep the peace." Shortly before the aid of the charity was asked he had asked the police to have his wife examined as he thought she was mentally unbalanced, and a doctor was called who said there was no need for an examination. When the social worker talked with Mrs. Rowsk about the home situation she became abusive and very angry.

In the spring of 1916 Mrs. Rowsk had her husband arrested for striking her, and at this time Mrs. Rowsk was examined at a clinic and pronounced mentally healthy.

After the arrest Mrs. Rowsk said that her husband "was a different man and never abused her and that she was perfectly happy with him."

In the summer of 1916 Mr. Rowsk again came to the charity, very much discouraged with his family situation. He stated that his wife had been very ugly and talked improperly before the children, that she deceived him in the use of money, asking for money for one thing and spending it for another, and that she whipped her three-weeks-old baby. He still thought she was abnormal mentally, and said he could not stand it there. On his last pay day he kept his check and wanted to go with his wife to the grocer or get what she wanted, but she would not have it that way and was very ugly when he bought groceries and brought them home. When Mrs. Rowsk was interviewed she said she would not continue to live with her husband much longer, that he was always complaining about her management, that he wanted plenty of food but did not want her to pay as much for it as she did, that he complained that he was the only one who worked and she did nothing at all, that he "made a terrible fuss" when she went to the neighbors and wanted her to stay home all the time.

In personal ambitions Mr. and Mrs. Rowsk also differed. Mrs. Rowsk had not been in America long at the time of her marriage and had learned only a little English. After her marriage she stopped trying to learn to speak English, although her husband bought books for her and wished her to learn. Mr. Rowsk, on the other hand, attended night school regularly and in 1917 could write fairly grammatical English.

SUGGESTED LIFE-ORGANIZATION—THE FARM

Mr. Rowsk began at this time to talk about buying a farm in Canada. He said he would like to go on a farm because his wife could not spend so much money and could not visit the neighbors so much. He refused to listen to anything which would excuse his wife, but talked steadily about how abused he was.

In the winter of 1917 Mr. Rowsk was laid off his job, took $28 with him, left $5 with his family, and started for Canada to take up a government farm. He went with some other men from Chicago; they took homesteads and lived in tents. Mr. Rowsk's plan was to obtain work and send money to his family so that they might move to Canada. His move left the full support of the family on the charity.

In July Mr. Rowsk was still in Canada, and at that time the Chicago charity got in touch with an agency in Canada, stating that unless Mr. Rowsk returned and provided for his family they would have to be placed in an institution. The Canadian agency advised that money be sent for Mr. Rowsk's return to Chicago, as he had no work and was in danger of becoming a public charge.

FAILURE TO ATTAIN DESIRED LIFE-ORGANIZATION ON CANADIAN FARM

In August Mr. Rowsk returned to Chicago. He had taken up 160 acres in Canada and had cleared enough of it to plant a garden. He wanted to return the following spring and take his children with him, but not his wife, as she had upset every venture he had made. Mrs. Rowsk was also anxious to go on a farm.

In September Mr. Rowsk found work on a farm near Chicago, but did not stay long. He exhibited the attitude that "because he had been unfortunate in business and in marriage, someone should help him."

FIRST MENTAL EXAMINATION

In October, 1917, Mr. Rowsk was examined, but the examining physician said he could not find any mental abnormality in the brief examination given.

RETENTION OF WISH TO GO TO THE CANADIAN FARM

In January, 1918, Mr. Rowsk received a letter from Canada that he must go on the farm by April 15 in order to keep it. He wrote a long letter to the charity.

I'm a man who remembers all the time to get something to support myself and my family, but at last I am broke not by my own fault. When I was myself in April, 1917, between anvil and hammer and always expecting a slack to come in America I must believe my countrymen and their promises and went with them to Canada on a homestead, ... but I'm disappointed myself, because the European war spoiled all the business for these men so few of them must come back to their families and I did too. After I returned home I looked inside then outside the city for work but it took me over three months before I started on a poor job and for poor wages. In present time I am still working but not only cannot support my family but I am sure that I will be out of work soon. Because I have a beautiful homestead in Canada on which not only I can easily support my family but in a short time I can make a fortune over there. I like to get my bread right from the ground which I am not making in Chicago in factories.

He followed this with thanks to various organizations for assistance and ended the letter by asking for a loan, stating he had been raised on a farm and would not disappoint them in repaying.

A month later he again wrote to the charity asking for money to go to Canada, suggesting that the charity publish his letter in the newspapers. He also wrote a letter to a Chicago newspaper, which was turned over to the charity.

You will excuse me for bothering although I am ashamed but have to do it. Please heartily help me if possible. In America I had hard times but this is the hardest which I cannot bear. I believe very much that you won't talk back. This same thing I sent to [two charitable institutions]. This picture represents my family except one girl 13½ years of age which is away from home is not through with school. She is working for her living.

Mr. Rowsk at this time wanted not only money to go to Canada, but also $2,000 for a complete agricultural outfit for his farm.

The charity and other organizations interested in the children warned Mr. Rowsk against going to Canada and told him that if he went his family would have to be sent to an institution; he admitted that he expected this to be done.

Early in May Mr. Rowsk wrote to the principal of the night school he attended, and others that he was going to Canada. A warrant was then sworn out on the charge of contributing to the dependency of his children. Mr. Rowsk went to court voluntarily and was put in jail for five days, then released on bond. Work was found for him and the case was discharged.

In the fall of 1918 Mr. Rowsk obtained information on unclaimed land in the United States and talked of settling on it. He resigned his work, but was taken back.

The following February (1919) Mr. Rowsk wrote to the charity again, apologizing for bothering them.

Not only my age, health and experience won't let me stay in the city, not only doctors advise me to go to the country with my family, but I can't make a living on the jobs where I'm not only working for low wages but pretty soon I'm sure will be laid off. Here is a matter where sickness tires the family, quarreling and fighting with the wife arresting me twice, first in my life, and put me in jail. I have facts about which I cannot write here but it will be necessary before judge or other commissioners so I want you to point them out and I will explain that city life is not possible for me.

He stated he had papers from Washington, evidently from the immigration department to which Mr. Rowsk applied for farm work, stating that they could not give him work as his family was too large.

Shortly after the foregoing letter Mr. Rowsk wrote again asking for work for his family and an effort was made to obtain work in the country, but the farm manager said his family was too large.

In August of 1919 he wrote another letter to the charity.

I suffered together with my family and I do suffer now worse each day. I tried many ways but could not help myself any and in the future I do not expect anything and do not see any chance of living in the city. I know that in the nearest future if I stay on the same position I will be worthless. I have tried many different people but it seems that they all push you towards you. I beg very much to examine my situation, I believe very much that you judge and decide to put me out into the country somewhere. It if is impossible to send me away on a homestead kindly let me work for somebody else on a farm in the country. I think and am sure that I will get my health back in a quiet place and will be able to work again.

PHYSICAL CONDITION POOR

During the summer of 1919 Mr. Rowsk was having medical attention at a dispensary for stomach trouble and pain all over his body which prevented him from working. The impression of the physician was that Mr. Rowsk's inability to work due to alleged weakness was posing with the idea of arousing sympathy to allow him to go on a farm. He was working only irregularly. In the spring of 1920 he was operated on for hernia, and following the operation had pneumonia and almost died. The pneumonia started a heart lesion and the physician stated he would not be able to do hard work again. In September, 1920, he was again operated on for hernia.

ECONOMIC CONDITION OF FAMILY

Most of the time Mr. Rowsk worked irregularly. Mary, his stepdaughter, worked regularly and attended night school. Anna lived away from home and was able to earn only her own support.

MR. ROWSK'S ATTITUDE

Mr. Rowsk attributed the trouble at home to the fact that his wife refused to study and learn English. He was also very bitter because he had not had a chance to get on a farm and felt that he had had a bad deal all around.

THE FARM AGAIN

In March, 1920, Mr. Rowsk again wrote to the charity.

I am a man that loves freedom, progress and right. Over twenty years ago I know that work for somebody is not profit for me. In Chicago I spent ten years working for somebody else obeying other people's command and in return all I got was all kinds of trouble and sickness. I am completely lost in the way of money and health, not able any more to work under anybody's command. I have a good piece of land among good people which will make good neighbors and on the land I must start work which I am forced to do by law on the first of April, 1920.

He then asked for help, as he had been given an extension until April 1, 1920, for settling on the Canadian land.

ALL OTHER INTERESTS SUBORDINATED

Mr. Rowsk did not seem interested in anything but his own troubles, said he was a slave and it was like poison for him to live in

Chicago. He was not interested in any plan by which Mary might continue in night school. He was determined to go to Canada and would not listen to any other plan, refused to consider moving to another part of Chicago, and said he did not wish any more aid from the charity.

THREAT TO KILL FAMILY

Mr. Rowsk in May, 1920, wrote a letter to the district attorney's office saying that he would have to do away with his family if no one would give him a farm, as he could not support them. He was arrested and his case was brought up in court, but he explained that he did not mean to kill his family, but he would have to send them somewhere where they could be looked after. He was examined by a psychiatrist who said he did not think he would harm anyone, but that he had very peculiar ideas; he was not insane enough to be committable to an institution. The case was dismissed.

DEVELOPING MENTAL DISORDER

Mr. Rowsk continued to work irregularly. Meanwhile a new baby was born and the family continued to want to go on a farm.

In August, 1921, the dispensary reported that Mr. Rowsk was developing melancholia.

He had looked for a position on a farm but could find none and was very much discouraged. He also complained that his wife, although a good woman, did not know how to manage. Early in September he was out of work, but found work one day and stayed with it an hour. He then had words with the foreman and nearly struck him, but restrained himself (his own account) and went home. His wife started to scold him and he went out with his head whirling. He said he felt like committing suicide, but jumped on a car and went to the county hospital, where he was kept for a diagnosis. When visited at the hospital he said he worried constantly because he could not support his family and had trouble with his wife on this account; he could not hold a job for long, was often transferred from one department to another, and had trouble with the foreman; he was not given sufficient work and the pay was poor. He still had the idea of solving his problems by going on a farm. In the hospital he felt that he had too much time to worry and he wanted to leave.

The diagnosis at the hospital was that the trouble was distinctly mental, and after two weeks in the hospital he was termed a borderline case, although his condition had been worse when he first came. The physician thought he could work at congenial work in sympathetic surroundings and under supervision; that if he was committed to an institution he would probably become worse; and that there was some chance to save him if he could be placed in proper surroundings, but otherwise he might develop manic depressive insanity.

EFFORTS TO PLACE ROWSK ON A FARM

The company for which he worked had tried to get Mr. Rowsk farm work and secured for him a position on a farm for $45 a month and free rent. He went out, but returned in a week and said he could not work as fast as the farmer and his sons. He refused to work on the farms south of Chicago where men were needed.

SUICIDE DESIRE

The latter part of December, 1921, he wrote to the charity.

I am very sorry that I have to return and bother you again. But I hope that you will excuse me after you read this letter. Not long ago I was sick at the hospital the cause being laid off and again I have the same trouble which makes me a wild idiot. It is this morning I got lay off and have nothing to do. I think that the last time you did not understand me. I suffer troubles and sickness about which I can explain only before the man. Please send me to some doctor or judge before whom I will be able to tell about my suffering. I think it is only way for you to find out the matter and I am sure as you will try together with the other to do best you can until it will bring some result for me. I beg you and all interested to take care of this case because otherwise I don't see anything else but kill myself. For some answer I am waiting right here in your office.

The first of January, 1922, he impressed the social worker as being in a better frame of mind, spoke no longer of the farm project, and seemed more resigned. He was working in a specially supervised occupational department for mentally abnormal people, earning $8 a week.

DOMESTIC TENSION CONTINUED

Mrs. Rowsk objected to the $8 job and could not be made to understand that her husband was ill, saying that his only trouble was that he did not have a decent job.

In the spring Mr. Rowsk again began to talk of a farm and wanted a box car provided for his family to leave the city. In an effort to force him to work the charity withdrew the money it had provided for the rent and had no contact for fourteen months.

INSANITY AND SUICIDE

In July, 1923, Mr. Rowsk appeared before the board of health and stated that the world was against him and that he was going to kill himself and his family. The case was investigated and he was sent to an insane asylum in August with a diagnosis of dementia praecox. In December he was paroled but obtained no work, and four months later, in the spring of 1924, he was again writing to various agencies for help to get on a farm either in Canada or the United States. He asked the charity for a definite "yes" or "no" answer about help to go on a farm. Help was not given. At this time Mary was the only one working and earned about $25 a week.

In June, 1924, Mr. Rowsk hanged himself.[1]

ANALYSIS OF CASE I

PERSONALITY

Mr. Rowsk was apparently normal when the charity first had contacts with the family in 1911. Thirteen years later he was definitely insane. There is a suggestion of a congenital condition in the fact that his daughter by his first marriage was not normal mentally and also had some nervous trouble which required special institutional care; but not enough is known of this child's heritage on her mother's side nor of Mr. Rowsk's family to base any conclusion on this fact.

The first indications of abnormality were the fixation of attention on the farm project and the differences with foremen and fellow-workmen, which signify irritability and emotional instability, and also the feeling of abuse and threats to kill his family.

[1] Abstracted from records of United Charities, Chicago.

The reports of mental disorder as given were: 1917, no abnormality observable on brief examination; 1921, developing melancholia; 1921, manic depressive insanity indicated; 1923, dementia praecox. This array of different diagnoses from different physicians seems to indicate that the disorder was not distinctly marked in character, although there was general agreement of abnormality.

WISHES AND SATISFACTION

Mr. Rowsk developed a "fixed idea," to go on a farm. Gradually the attitude grew that he could not work except on a farm, that all of his difficulties were due to working in a city under someone's direction, that farm life would solve all his domestic difficulties. This conception was illogical, since most of his troubles did not arise directly out of factory work, although they were all somewhat connected to his economic condition, which made it possible for him to imagine a connection. His difficulty with his wife was due on the one hand to her failure to keep pace with his interest in self-education and on the other to her inability to manage expenditures. The increasing size of the family added to the economic strain. His difficulties with factory work were largely due to his growing belief that he could not adjust himself to it (although he had previously been successful with it) and the irritability that accompanied his psychosis.

He was never able to satisfy his wish to go on a farm— to try out the one type of life-organization which he thought would satisfy all his desires and solve all his problems. At the same time he was constantly being tantalized by offers. The Canadian land was held open for him for several years and other opportunities seemed about to open. He was not, when given an opportunity for farm work, able to adjust himself to it. The farm became an idealized utopia to him and he could no longer adjust to actual conditions (the basis, no doubt, of the dementia praecox diagnosis). His poor physical condition after 1920 only added to his belief that city life was not for him.

CRISIS

No definite crisis is apparent. Mr. Rowsk had been asking for help again and for a definite answer from the charity. The suicide was apparently the culmination of the long-developing hopelessness of getting on a farm, which represented for him the adjustment of all his problems, personal, economic, and domestic.

DEVELOPMENT OF THE SUICIDE WISH

The tendency to commit suicide was preceded by one vague threat (which he repudiated) to do away with his family, which was one factor in preventing the farm project reaching completion. The first mention of suicide appeared three years before he actually killed himself and came after a conflict with a foreman and after his psychosis had begun to develop. He later in the same year stated in a letter that if he could not get on a farm he saw nothing to do but kill himself; he still had hope at this time of obtaining a farm. Two years later he made a public announcement that the world was against him and he was going to kill himself and his family; this statement indicates hopelessness and also desire to coerce officials to help him obtain his wish. The result was confinement in an institution. The actual suicide came a year later, after definite refusal of help for the farm project by the charity and other agencies.

The interrelation of the social situation, the peculiar

attitudes of an abnormal mind, and the desire for death are clearly indicated in this case history.

Psychopathic personality.—Midway between the definitely insane and the normal are the psychopathic persons. While these people do not have the irrational mental processes of the insane, they find adjustment to anything but the most simple and pleasant environment difficult and even impossible. The characteristics which Stelzner emphasizes for this class of persons are a tendency to hysterical and emotional behavior, extreme moods, suggestibility, egocentrism, and fluctuating moral standards. The cases given by Stelzner show that adjustment to life is very difficult, and out of the continued maladjustment developed acute situations for which the person was unable to find any solution and which led to attempts at suicide, often poorly planned. In many of the cases the early training and home surroundings had been deficient and undoubtedly contributed to the unresourceful and vacillating personality which is assumed to have an underlying constitutional basis. The reaction of these people to institutional care emphasizes their weaknesses. They adapt themselves readily to the attention and care bestowed upon them and give up all effort to adjust to the outside world. A prolonged treatment in the institution not only does not cure them but makes them totally unfit to combat the difficulties in the outside world which a normal person finds himself able to adjust to—such as meeting and working with other people, distractions of office or schoolroom, change of location, and temporary friendlessness.

The case histories upon which this study is based are not of the type to bring out exact reactions and to make possible a statement of the prevalence of psychopathic personalities among the suicides in Chicago. Logically, it seems that they would probably number fewer among actual suicides than among attempts. Their characteristic handling of life is ineffectual and unsuccessful, and it is probable that many of their suicide attempts are also unsuccessful. Nevertheless their inability places them in a position to undergo many and severe crises which might lead them to become discouraged and to attempt escape by way of suicide. While a numerical statement is not possible, the type can be illustrated by the following case of a psychopathic person of rather extreme type.

CASE II

Nellie Mensch, born in South Carolina of American-born parents, attempted suicide when she was thirty-three years old and later made many threats of suicide.

CHILDHOOD

Mrs. Mensch was an illegitimate child. She told the social worker who handled her case that even as a child she felt the disgrace keenly; other children were not allowed to play with her.

According to a report from her mother, she finished the seventh or eighth grade, was hard to control, did not get along well with her mother, and had a love affair with a man in the South Carolina town where she was reared. The mother lived in a one-room house.

At the age of fifteen or sixteen Nellie left home and began to work. She said she was in debt all the time but managed to live somehow by "hook or crook."

MARRIAGE

When Nellie was thirty she met Mr. Mensch, a man of thirty-eight, in a rooming-house in southern Illinois. They knew each other from occasional meetings in the hall, later corresponded and became engaged by letter. She knew very little about him except that he was born in Germany. She stated that she "saw others were being married and getting homes of their own and decided that she wanted to do likewise." Mr. Mensch asked her to come to an Ohio town where his sister lived. She made part of the trip alone, met Mr. Mensch, was married and went to Cleveland, where $600 was paid on a $2,500 home. This house was lost later when Mr. Mensch deserted.

Two years after the marriage a child, Dorothy, was born. Mrs. Mensch became pregnant a second time almost immediately after the birth of Dorothy. Her husband left her when Dorothy was a few months old. Later he sent for her to come to Gary, Indiana, where the second child was born. Mr. Mensch again deserted but returned when his wife took a position as housekeeper for a man, and moved his family to Chicago. When the second child was about a year old he deserted for the third time, leaving his family in Chicago.

At each period of desertion Mrs. Mensch came to the attention of welfare agencies.

BEHAVIOR OF MRS. MENSCH IN CLEVELAND AS REPORTED BY WELFARE AGENCY

Mrs. Mensch was "very excitable and unreasonable and did very foolish things." On one occasion she was given $1 to buy milk for Dorothy and she said she was going to buy socks for the baby instead of milk. She loved Dorothy passionately but said she would hate the new baby and that she had taken everything she knew about before its birth to cause its death. She stated that it would be a crime to breed a child for the insane asylum, which she thought would be the inevitable result of her troubled state of mind. She insisted on keeping a very expensive baby carriage on which only $10 had been paid. At the same time she objected to receiving assistance from the charities, saying that it would "choke" her to "eat charity food." When her mother sent her $12, instead of applying it on the house she spent it for pictures of Dorothy. Mrs. Mensch wept a great deal and was also very profuse in profanity during interviews. Any little thing would start her off. At the same time she was very appealing in her attitude.

During this first desertion and while she was pregnant with the second child she talked of suicide and on one occasion attempted suicide by drowning, but was stopped. She was then taken to a hospital for a long stay, which improved her mental condition.

Before Mr. Mensch's desertion in Cleveland he swore at his wife in an offensive and obscene manner. He threatened to throw the baby in the heater or take it away from Mrs. Mensch when she was asleep.

As a consequence of this she slept with the baby pinned to her night-gown. He frequently suggested to his wife that she had been immoral and described to her her condition after he had taken the baby and left her and the difficulties she would have in obtaining work with her name smirched. When she "cut up" he threatened to have her put in an insane asylum.

REPORT OF WELFARE AGENCY IN GARY

Mr. and Mrs. Mensch had trouble in Gary, and when Mrs. Mensch pawned her husband's trousers to buy milk he deserted. Juvenile court authorities were called in by the police because Mrs. Mensch threatened to commit suicide. She also threatened suicide if something was not done to prevent the juvenile court from taking her children from her.

IN CHICAGO

Mrs. Mensch was in contact with the Chicago welfare agencies for about fourteen months. During the first part of this period she made many threats of suicide. On one occasion she stated that in Gary she had been forced to go into a "sporting house," but that she was not a streetwalker or trashy and would turn on the gas and throw her children out of the house as corpses rather than take them to live in the slums, by which she meant the Jewish section near which she lived. Another time she beat an old woman who had cared for her children while she worked and who had said she neglected them; after the beating Mrs. Mensch was very much afraid she would be arrested and told a minister to whom she appealed for aid that she would take her children's lives if she was not helped. She also said that she would do anything for the sake of her "poor babies" and would commit suicide rather than be separated from them. She wrote her mother that she was dying and had no one to care for her children and asked her mother to come to them; she wanted her mother to live with her, care for the children, and give financial support, although she would not go to her mother's home. She said if her mother did not come she would jump in the lake. She was persuaded by the social worker to look for work again. She had to move because she could not pay the rent, and wrote her mother for money with which to buy furniture. The social worker suggested second-hand furniture, but Mrs. Mensch became angry and shouted that no matter how poor she was she was still a lady and did not want other people's cast-off furniture. She said she would rather put her babies out for "nigger adoption" and kill herself.

EXPERIENCE AT WORKING

In five months Mrs. Mensch worked at nine different jobs, mostly in cafeterias. She had one job in a cutlery company which she left because the grinding and occasional breaking of a knife made her nervous. From some of the places she was dismissed because she could not handle the work. She became discouraged after the eighth job and spoke of drowning herself and also threatened to sell herself to any man who would have her.

SEXUAL LIFE DISLIKED

Mrs. Mensch said that sexual relationship was a part of married life she had most disliked. She could remember only one time that she enjoyed intimacy with her husband, and that was when he kissed her good-by before she came to Chicago. She had no men friends for about a year after her husband deserted her in Chicago, but finally had two men friends who came to see her at her home. She said she would be scared to have anything to do with them for fear of pregnancy. She said she would never "sell her body" for physical pleasure, but would do it if she could receive enough money, because of her craving for the "riches of life."

About fourteen months after the desertion of her husband she had a man roomer who paid most of her expenses and it was suspected that she had sexual relations with him, although she stated that he paid the expenses in return for her housekeeping. Her conversation at this time pertained to sexual matters.

Shortly after this her mother sent her money with which she paid her own and her children's expenses to South Carolina.

PERSONALITY TYPE

She was examined by a competent agency which reported that she had no psychosis but was a constitutional psychopathic type of personality, emotionally unstable in that she was easily made tearful, was flighty, talkative, noisy, swore easily, and would perhaps never be able to apply herself continuously to work. Her display of affection for her children and suicide threats were regarded as devices to obtain sympathy and help.[1]

ANALYSIS OF CASE II
PERSONALITY

She is charactized as being constitutionally psychopathic. There is no doubt as to her emotional instability and inability to apply herself continuously to work, but some account should be taken of (1) the ostracism bestowed upon her as an illegitimate child; (2) her inability to maintain herself adequately before marriage, which might or might not have been due to native inadequacy; (3) the treatment by her husband who threatened to take her babies from her, lock her up, etc. Any of these would contribute to her feeling of inferiority and insufficiency.

WISHES AND THEIR SATISFACTION

Her wishes were extremely simple and centered about the maintenance of herself and her children and her desire to keep her children with her. She was never, however, able to acquire for herself the satisfaction of these needs.

CRISES

Her first attempt at suicide came after her husband's first desertion when she was left without support, pregnant and with a small child. This attempt, however, did not occur immediately after the desertion, but while she was receiving assistance from the welfare agency. Desertion has more than an economic aspect in this case. It meant the break-up of one system of life-organization and the need to establish another; it meant, too, direction by the charity as to how to spend her money and criticism of her method of managing;

[1] Abstracted from records of the United Charities, Chicago.

so that while under the guidance of the charity she was not able to satisfy her dominant wishes which centered around her affection for, and a desire to "show off," the baby. There was also a psychological factor, for she had undergone what amounted to mental torture at the hands of her husband and at the same time was pregnant with a child which she did not desire.

This attempt brought a marked change in her condition. She was placed in a hospital for a fairly long period of time and given rest and care. This hospital care was followed by a return to her husband, so that the condition she was in before the attempt was not repeated.

The later talk of suicide was for the most part in the nature of genuine threats, that is, to coerce someone into doing something to help her. She did not threaten suicide to avoid a bad situation, but to get someone to help her out of it, e.g., she threatened suicide unless something was done to prevent the court from taking the children from her, unless someone saved her from arrest after she beat a woman, if her mother did not come, etc.

The last threat (after the eighth unsuccessful job) was more in the nature of a contemplated attempt; she specified the method, was discouraged, and saw no hope of going on. Soon after this threat she made the alliance with a man who paid her expenses, and when this arrangement was questioned she went to her mother and thus avoided the situation which called forth the threats.

CHAPTER VIII

SUICIDE AMONG NORMAL PEOPLE

There has been all too great a tendency to explain suicide as the result of a diseased mind. Studies made of psychotic people who have attempted or committed suicide show (1) that a large group of suicides are not insane, and (2) that even among the insane and psychopathic the suicide is usually precipitated by some real or imagined crisis.

The crucial situation.[1]—Crises may be regarded as a part of normal living. Even in static societies there are the crises of birth, death, catastrophies of nature, wars, and the like. In a changing social order crises are multiplied and the process of living must be regarded as the process of solving problems, of facing new situations and finding satisfactory ways of meeting them. The problems may be very trivial: what shoes to wear today, or whether to have eggs or steak for breakfast; or they may involve wider interests and entail serious consequences, as the problem of investment of a sum of money, whether to propose to a certain girl, or how to adjust a serious quarrel. Problems which are recurrent may become routinized and habitual, and thus require a minimum of reasoning. Europeans have standardized their breakfasts—they do not have to think about what to eat; military, police, and other official forms of dress are standardized; men of wealth often have financial advisers to re-

[1] For the theoretical background, see W. I. Thomas and Florian Znaniecki, *The Polish Peasant in Europe and America;* John Dewey, *Human Nature and Conduct;* Ellsworth Faris, "Social Psychology" (MS); Florian Znaniecki, *The Laws of Social Psychology;* L. L. Thurstone, *The Nature of Intelligence.*

lieve them of the worry of investments; in certain groups, for instance, the Jewish, courtship and marriage are carried on in routine and formal manner.

But before the solution of a problem has become routinized and during those situations which may occur only once or at most a few times during an entire lifetime—such as severe illness, falling in love, or removal from one type of community to another—the person finds himself with very urgent interests for which he can find no satisfaction. Even a trivial interest unsatisfied may lead to disturbance and discontent.

　　. . . . Tonight I was in *extremis*. . . . . First I read the paper; then I finished the book I was reading, *Thus Spake Zarathustra*. Not knowing quite what to do next, I took off my boots, and poured out another cup of coffee. But these manoeuvers were only the feeble attempts of a cowardly wretch to evade the main issue, which was:

　　How to occupy myself and keep myself sane during the hour and a half before bedtime.

　　Before now I have tried going to bed. But that does not work— I don't sleep. Moreover, I have been in the grip of a horrible mental unrest. To sit still in my chair, much less to lie in bed doing nothing, seemed ghastly. I experienced all the cravings of a dissolute neurotic for a stimulant, but what stimulus I wanted, I did not know. Had I known, I should have gone and got it.[1]

　　During my first three months in boarding school when I was seventeen I wished many times that I had never been born, for I was very homesick, very unhappy and not particularly congenial with my roommate. I am the youngest of three children in a none too wealthy home if you compare my home with a city home, but it is exceedingly comfortable as compared with homes in a small town. In this school most of the girls were very wealthy, wore clothes that I could not afford, shocked me because they smoked and drank. I became very self-conscious and began to feel inferior and was utterly miserable. I don't remember what was said to me or what I read when I was at home at

　　　[1] W. N. P. Barbellion, *The Journal of a Disappointed Man*, pp. 148–49.

Christmas time, but I decided that I wasn't going to let myself be unhappy the rest of the year, so I gathered up all my sister's clothes that I could use, learned to smoke and went back and broke every rule that I could and ended up the year by being sent home.[1]

In analyzing these situations two phases are apparent. On the one hand is the personality of the individual—his wishes, interests, longings, and the attitudes, standards, and codes which limit and define them, and which in well-integrated personalities are fairly stable and harmonious. The formulation of these interests and the types of attitudes he has are dependent upon the group experiences he has had, but they may be considered as individual, for to the person and in the way in which they function in his life they are a personal possession and the origin of their force is within himself rather than in the social group. On the other hand there is the objective world in which the person lives—the world of food, of houses, of friends, clubs, institutions, which come to have meaning and value to him and which, taken together, constitute his life-organization or social world.

The solving of problems is the process of adjustment, first between interests, attitudes, and wishes as the person attempts to integrate them into a harmonious whole which constitutes his personality, and second, between these interests and the external world in which most if not all of them normally find expression and fulfilment. Personality and life-organization then become respectively subjective and objective aspects of the process of living.

When the personality or interests and the life-organization or means of fulfilling the interests complement each other, life tends to go on in a more or less habitual manner. But when for any reason there is a break in the reciprocal

[1] From a university student.

relation of subjective interests and external world, a crisis or crucial situation exists and old habits and attitudes are no longer adequate to the situation. If an adjustment cannot readily be made the person finds himself dissatisfied, restless, unhappy, and in time unable efficiently to order his life. He is then personally disorganized. Personal disorganization may be of many degrees of intensity and may arise in numerous ways.

When a crucial situation arises there is a very definite tendency for adjustment to occur. The interests which have been aroused demand fulfilment. Unless they are fulfilled or are weak enough to be discarded they continue very near the surface of consciousness and, constantly coming to the surface, prevent the functioning of other interests. After a short period an actual adjustment may be brought about. It often happens, however, that actual readjustment seems impossible to the person. There are then a number of ways in which the force of the interest may be assuaged and an adjustment made which permits the person to continue a normal life. Substitution of some other interest or object of attention may be made, and the sentiments and energy organized about the original object may be transferred almost intact to the new interest. This new object may be merely a symbol of the old, as when a mother preserves and cherishes the clothing and toys of her dead child. Or it may be an object of the same kind, as when a young man, disappointed in love, finds immediate solace in another woman. Methods of adjustment found effective by persons who had in times of difficulty wished for death or thought of suicide and abandoned the idea include the following: occupation or residence was changed, thus affording a new social group and life organization; new interests were consciously or unconsciously acquired; day dreaming occurred, in which the wishes were fulfilled in the imagination; prayer and confessional (among Catholics) relieved the tension of worries and brought new strength and counsel. The development of a philosophy of resignation ("God would make it work out for the best"; "we must not expect everything our own way") and the development of an objective and rational attitude or of a sense of humor were also found effective.[1]

When the crucial situation cannot be resolved in some way which permits the person to continue to lead an efficient, normal life, the force of the thwarted interests may lead to types of behavior which are injurious to the person's physical, mental, or social welfare and which are usually labeled pathological. It is well recognized that, once aroused, a strong interest cannot lightly be laid aside, and that if given no outlet it will usually accumulate emotional tension until an expression of some sort is forced. Various types of pathological expressions discovered by experts working in the various fields of pathological behavior are pertinent.

ALCOHOLISM AND DRUGS

There are relatively normal types of the heavy drinker—the socially minded and the hard manual worker. But there is a large group of those who find in alcohol a relief from the burden of their moods, who find in its real effect, the release from inhibitions, a reason for drinking beyond the reach of reason. Do you feel that the endless monotone of your existence can no longer be borne—drink deep and you color your life to suit yourself. . . . . And so men of certain types of temperament, or with unhappy experiences, form the alcoholic habit because it gives them surcease from pain; it deals out to them, temporarily, a new world with happier mood, lessened tension and greater success. . . . .

[1] From data supplied on questionnaires by university students. See footnote, p. 179.

The feeling of inferiority, one of the most painful of mental conditions, is responsible for the use not only of alcohol but also of other drugs, such as cocaine, heroin, morphine, etc. . . . . Similarly a shameful position, such as that of the prostitute or the chronic criminal, is "relieved" by alcohol and drugs, so that the majority of these types of unfortunates are either drunkards or "dopes." Too often have reformers reversed the relationship, believing that alcohol caused prostitution and crime. Of course that relationship exists, but more often, in my experience, the alcohol is used to keep up the "ego" feeling, without which few can bear life.[1]

SEXUAL PERVERSION

Curiously enough, one of the sex perversions, masturbation, has in a few cases a similar genesis [to alcoholism and drug addiction, just quoted]. I have known patients who, when under the influence of depression, or humiliated in some way or other, found a compensating pleasure in the act . . . . face to face with mental pain, men seek relief or pleasure or both by alcohol, drugs, sensual pleasures of all kinds, and . . . . the secret explanation of all such habits is that they offer compensation for some pain and are turned to at such times. What one man seeks in work, another seeks in religion, another finds in self-flagellation, and still others seek in alcohol, morphine, sexual excesses, etc.[2]

DELINQUENCY

In his study of 2,000 cases of delinquent children, Dr. William Healy found that in at least 7 per cent of the cases the misconduct was directly traceable to a mental conflict. The child had undergone some experience—in a number of cases, the crude and sudden acquisition of sexual knowledge or habits—which acted as an emotional shock and which the child could not assimilate into his previous stock of attitudes and experiences. Repressed, the inharmonious memories and emotions tended to reappear in forms

[1] Abraham Myerson, *The Foundations of Personality*, pp. 62 ff.
[2] *Ibid.*, p. 64.

of misconduct, such as stealing, which were in some way associated with the original disconcerting experience and to which the child was impelled almost against his will.[1]

INSANITY

One current view of insanity is that it is the result not invariably of inheritance, but of unfortunate social experiences. The person has found a conflict between his dominating complexes or associated interests and the world in which he is compelled to live. In seeking a way of escape he represses and puts out of mind the unpleasant part of his experiences. This repressed experience becomes dissociated from his total accumulation of memories and experiences, but does not disappear. In the cases which Healy studied, such a repressed portion of experience led to delinquency. In other cases it leads to delusions, hallucinations, and other phenomena of insanity.[2]

Finally come the cases in which the struggle for adjustment has ceased, in which the person "gives up," and suicide is the result.

Suicide a double problem.—When suicide is viewed as one of a series of possible adjustments, two distinct phases of the problem appear: one, the problem of personal disorganization; the other, a consideration of why suicide rather than some other adjustment is used.

[1] William Healy, *Mental Conflicts and Misconduct.*

[2] For a clear statement of this view of insanity, see Bernard Hart, *The Psychology of Insanity*, 1922.

CHAPTER IX
THE SUICIDE PROCESS

The task still remains to present in detail by means of cases the various kinds of crises which end in suicide. For while all personal disorganization may be regarded essentially as a lack of adjustment and harmony between the interests which constitute personality and the external world in which life must be lived, this disorganization is of several types. It may arise in different ways, it involves different emotions, and is subject to different personal interpretations.

In addition to a short discussion, cases are given for each type. While these cases are all in some sense individual, they have been carefully chosen as representative of types actually found to exist in a large number of suicide cases. A transcript of the inquest records for all cases of suicide in Chicago in 1923 gave 391 unselected cases from one urban community. In addition, cases from other years in Chicago and newspaper accounts of cases numbered approximately a hundred, while from the records of charities in Chicago came case histories of some two dozen cases, some of actual, others of attempted, suicides. It is obviously impossible to give a record of all the cases. They have been studied and classified and illustrative examples chosen. While the classification is based in the main on the unselected cases for 1923, the examples are in some cases from other sources which provided more detailed case histories.

No. 1. The unidentified craving.—Most vague of disorganizations leading to a suicidal tendency are general dissatisfactions with life. Fairly common among people who wish for death,[1] this type can only occasionally be identified in the actual suicide cases. This is probably because, so long as the craving is vague and not attached to any particular object, it may be satisfied in any one of a number of ways. Merely to be hungry is an easier craving to satisfy than to be hungry for clams when one lives in an inland town. Usually the restlessness generated by the craving, vague though it is, leads to experimental attempts to satisfy it. Once it has been satisfied, the craving when it again arises is recognized as a wish for some particular thing and plans can be made to obtain that thing directly. But before the craving has been defined in terms of some definite wish, it may upon occasion become so insistent and uncontrollable that it may lead the person to commit suicide. The emotional tone in these cases is not high; there is no sharp crisis, no mourning for something lost, no resentment toward anyone, no impassioned emotions, no self-judgment, but a strong desire to stop living, since life is flavorless.

CASE III

J. was a young married woman of twenty-five, with two children whom she killed at the time she committed suicide. Born and reared in Kentucky, she had lived in Chicago seven years with her husband, There she found it necessary to work and had a mediocre job at night work in a factory. The letter which she left at the time of her death indicates the vague dissatisfaction under discussion, and the inquest revealed nothing more definite. The letter follows: "I am going to hunt my cloud with the silver lining if there is one. There is none on this earth so maybe there is on the next, and the kiddies will find their's quicker if there is any. Bob [her husband] please pay Jennie the money we owe her. Be good and don't ever do anything I would not do."[2]

[1] See chap. x.

[2] Coroner's inquest record, Cook County, Illinois, 1923.

Cases in which no crisis is apparent and the person says that he is "disgusted with life" or that life is useless doubtless fall into this class of undefined dissatisfactions. In some cases there is the possibility that the dissatisfaction appears vague simply because the information about the case is fragmentary; yet certain cases seem clearly to imply a general dissatisfaction and that the person was not able to specify the types of satisfaction which would bring contentment.

No. 2. The recognized wish.—Somewhat more tangible than the preceding type is the dissatisfaction which has become clear to the person as the need for some particular thing or type of thing. Psychologically, these cases may be described as those in which the craving or impulse, at first vague, has through experience become defined for the person into a wish for a specific activity, but in which the circumstances of his environment are such that he cannot discover appropriate stimuli which would permit him to find in reality fulfilment for the defined wish. Among the 1923 Chicago cases, four very similar cases of this type occur. Two widows forty-five and fifty-five years old, and two widowers, sixty-five and eighty-two years old, left notes stating (or had constantly reiterated before others) that they were alone and lonely. The sixty-five-year-old man stated his need specifically as the need for a home and a wife. In these cases there is no vague search for a cloud with a silver lining, no nameless disgust with life, but a specific need. What there is not, however, is the stimuli—the external objects—through which the desire may meet fulfilment. The man wanted a wife, but he had not been able to find a particular woman whom he wished to wed.

These four cases carry the implication of a crisis through

which the intimacy desired was lost. It is to be assumed that before the husbands or wives died, these widows and widowers were satisfied. But in these cases the period of grief has passed and the wish is apparently not for the departed one, but has become generalized into a feeling of loneliness without fixation upon any one person who might assuage the loneliness.

The cases before cited give the impression of a gradual wearing down of resistance. The experience may, however, assume more of the character of a crisis and entail a determined seeking for means of fulfilment, as in the following case of threatened suicide.

CASE IV

Ellen Barnes, a deaf mute of twenty, married, with one illegitimate child (whose father was presumably Ellen's stepfather) and one legitimate child, gave out her children for adoption following conflict with her husband and her father. She came to Chicago, but failed to find adequate work and appealed to the charity for aid. Her previous experiences had developed the dominant wish to be independent, not only economically but in her choice of work and conduct. She left a home for the deaf because she did not wish to come in at the required time at night. She refused even to consider a number of jobs which the charity found for her. Her first threat to kill herself was stated as a preference for death rather than return as a dependent to her father's care. Her second threat, in a note, followed her complete failure to find work and a short period as a prostitute which resulted when she voluntarily left the home for the deaf, without any place to go. It is not known whether she actually attempted to kill herself. Her attempts at independence ended when she was discovered to have contracted venereal disease and was sent to a hospital for treatment.[1]

In this case the difficulty centered about the inability to establish the independence so ardently desired.[2]

[1] United Charities of Chicago.

[2] The case entitled "The Youth Who Was Prematurely Tired," in chap. xi, is of this type, No. 2.

No. 3. The specific wish.—The more specifically a wish or interest becomes defined in the mind of the person who holds it, the less possibility there is for variation in the type of fulfilment which will satisfy the wish, and hence the more probability of disappointment in fulfilment. So long as a man is merely lonely, he may find numerous ways to gain companionship: he may join a club, go to room at a friendly boarding house, elevate his dog to the rank of a pal, adopt a youngster, marry, keep a mistress, and so on. Hence he is in less danger of failing to find satisfaction and of becoming disorganized than is the man who in the course of his experience has come to feel that his loneliness can be alleviated by one person and one person only. The definition of his wish is no longer, "I am lonely, I want to find someone to talk with," but, "I must have this one particular girl or I shall be forever lonely."

Once aroused, there is a tendency for an impulse to fulfil itself. If the impulse or wish in which the impulse is embodied is thwarted in some way, several things may happen. The wish may be abandoned and other interests rise to the foreground of attention; the original plan of fulfilment may be abandoned and another object substituted for it; day dreaming may take the place of actual fulfilment. But it may happen that the wish continues in full force, gaining in emotional intensity as the fulfilment seems more remote and usurping gradually the entire field of attention until nothing else in life matters save this one wish in its one specific form.

These cases may appear as conflicts between two persons, since the thwarting often is not of the impersonal sort, but occurs at the hands of some other person who seemingly has it in his power to grant the wish. The suicide does not define his failure to obtain fulfilment in terms of any inability on his part, but wholly in terms of an unjustified, or at least inexplicable, contrariness or wilfulness on the part of the other person. The situation appears to him entirely in personal terms, and the accompanying emotion is one of resentment more than of disappointment.

It is characteristic of this type of case that a further degree of fulfilment is wished and denied. If the girl is a friend, the man wishes her for a sweetheart; if a sweetheart, he desires her for a wife.

In some cases of this type the whole wish becomes symbolized, as it were, in some one particular or little act. A man whose love affair had not been going well asked the girl for a dance at a public dance hall. She replied that the dance had been taken and that she would never dance with him again. His response was to fire at her and then at himself, with the remark, "If I can't have her, nobody else can."[1] In another case a girl had demanded that her lover choose between her and another girl, and that he call her at a certain time. No telephone call came, so she attempted to commit suicide.[2] Suicide cases are often misunderstood because of this tendency for small acts and occurrences to have portentous significance to the person who experiences them. The girl who commits suicide because she is scolded for bobbing her hair—a number of such cases have appeared from time to time in the newspapers—sees in the disapproval of her bobbed hair the disapproval of her entire range of ambitions and ideals. The event which causes the suicide is the climax of a train of preceding and gradually culminating circumstances which have already created a frame of mind

[1] *Chicago Tribune*, February 25, 1924.
[2] *Chicago Tribune*, May 1, 1924.

requiring only one added bit of pressure to reach the break-
ing-point.

Cases of this type occur in which the person with the unfulfilled wish apparently never had any degree of satisfaction.

CASE V

In the 1923 series appears the case of L., a man of thirty-three,
unmarried, born in Hungary, in the United States for sixteen years.
Before he killed himself he shot at Mrs. M., wounding her. The inquest developed the fact that L. had been known to Mrs. M. and her
parents for years, and that Mr. M. met L. at the parents' home. In
Chicago the friendship between Mr. and Mrs. M. and L. was renewed,
and L. was at the M.'s house frequently. One evening L. invited both
Mr. and Mrs. M. out with him. Mr. M. stayed home with a sick
child and Mrs. M. went with L. to a café where he had some whiskey.
On the way home in a cab L. said to Mrs. M., "Tonight is the last night
you will ever see me. I have known you since you were a little girl
and I have loved you dearly, but have never told you so." He asked
her to leave her husband. She told him he must be crazy to talk in
that way. He then took a pistol from his pocket and said he would
unload it before it went off. Instead he pressed it against her breast.
At this point the cabman stopped the cab to investigate and Mrs. M.
was given an opportunity to get out of the cab. L. fired after her,
wounding her, and then shot and killed himself.[1]

In some cases a certain degree of satisfaction has been
attained, expectation runs high, and then thwarting occurs.
Of this type is the case of a woman of thirty-six who, having
a love affair with a married man, found it impossible to
relinquish their plans for divorce and marriage when the
man decided to abandon the plans and to return to his wife.
Her wish here was not to return to the *status quo* (compare
with No. 5, Broken Life Organization), but to go forward
and have more complete fulfilment than had ever been

[1] Coroner's inquest records, Cook County, 1923.

granted her. As the case is rather complete in detail it is given in full, together with an analysis.

Elizabeth Walters, thirty-six years old, in July shot and seriously injured John Brooks and then shot and killed herself.

Nothing is known of the family prior to four years previous. At that time the mother, Mrs. Walters, and her two daughters, Anne and Elizabeth, lived in Detroit.

Mr. Brooks had known the family for twelve years. He went to Detroit to seek work, but found none. When his finances grew low he called on Mrs. Walters, and because of the long friendship she rented him a room for which he paid irregularly until he had secured work. After he found work he continued to stay in their home, although his wife, to whom he had been married twenty-five years, lived in Chicago and was supported by him. For almost a year he was there, and during this time Elizabeth typed and kept books for him. They became attached to each other and went through what Brooks termed "an infatuation."

Anne then married, moving to Chicago. Soon Mrs. Walters and Elizabeth followed, and they took an apartment. Brooks also returned to Chicago, where he found work with an insurance company which frequently called him out of the city.

Brooks continued to see Elizabeth from time to time and escorted her to many places; but the relationship seemed to remain on a basis no more intimate than that of friendship.

A divorce for Brooks was talked of. He finally packed his trunks and moved them to the Walters', where he was given a room. Meanwhile his wife filed suit for separate maintenance.

The mother and sister of Elizabeth knew that she and Brooks were attracted to each other. Although they did not wholly approve, they made little protest, except that the sister advised her to drop the affair. Brooks told them that he would get a divorce (instead of separate maintenance) and marry Elizabeth, while Elizabeth maintained that she would go with him, in case he could not secure a divorce. He, however, did not urge this, but said he would do everything to make a marriage lawful; that he would go to jail before he would give her up. He was jealous, disliked having her go out with other men, and even forbade her to do so.

But before the separate maintenance was granted Brooks "made up" with his wife and returned to her, as he discovered that after all she meant more to him than Elizabeth did—so he testified at the inquest. He did not, however, at once remove his trunks from the Walters' and still nominally had a room in their apartment, although he at once broke off relations with Elizabeth. This direct move on Brooks' part followed on a period of uncertainty about the divorce during which Elizabeth talked of "finishing the affair soon" and "going through with it, since he had gone that far."

Brooks' decision to return to his wife came in January. Mrs. Walters and Anne were pleased with this move, but Elizabeth would not agree. She called Brooks on the telephone at his home, wrote to him, and insisted that he must leave his home and come to her. threatening to kill herself if he did not do this.

One of her letters to him follows:

January 24. The end of the world. My heavenly John; help me, John, help me now. No, no, you cannot do as you say; it is impossible. I am dying, John, I cannot live. I will give you time to reply to this. You must do as I say and stick to me, and anything else is impossible. I cannot live without you. You know it, lover, you know it. I cannot. I must hear from you and see you my love. I love you forever. Please and please, my angel, please. I adore you, John. Mother couldn't believe you could leave me, honey dear. I am helpless, and whatever they threaten, you must take your chances for my sake now, there is no going back to that life again for you, no dear, no dear. I tell you once more, before it is too late. Don't be a coward, honey dear. My John, my John, where are you this minute. I am waiting now for you to call me, as always. You know it will be dreadful to say the least to pay no attention to me now at this hour, as I now love you, love you, love you—do anything but leave me—anything, now—for, my pet, how could you, how could you? Lover, lover, lover, what can I say to you? Send for me, darling, send for me, dearest. If you don't, lover sweetheart, think what you are doing to me. If I don't hear from you with instructions to meet you by long distance telephone by Saturday morning, a terrible tragedy will occur. John, I love you—if you know the meaning of the word which you have so often used to me. Lover, there is no alternative. You are my life—how can you say you will not write or talk to me? How can you? Think what you are doing, sweetheart of sweethearts. Do you think you can leave me at this hour? Does your heart permit you to do this? And therefore, lover, I will do anything you say.

ELIZABETH

Brooks finally wrote to her in June, sending $50. In reply he received more letters.

One evening in July Elizabeth walked past his house, and to prevent her entrance he followed her and walked with her. After an emotional scene on the street he promised to arrange to see her soon, as she insisted on an interview "to straighten the matter out." By telling his wife that he must leave town one day earlier than was really necessary he arranged to meet her at a hotel, where they talked in the hotel parlors. Elizabeth was excited; she trembled, and her conversation was distracted. Apparently no decision that pleased Elizabeth was reached.

About midnight they went to the Walters' apartment. Elizabeth went to her own room, and Brooks to the one which was still held there for his use. About six the following morning, Brooks was awakened by Elizabeth entering his room. She shouted something to him which he could not understand, then shot him and herself. Brooks recovered and testified at the inquest.[1]

ANALYSIS OF CASE VI

In this case a woman past thirty had a fundamental impulse, the desire for love and personal response, fully aroused, and defined or particularized the impulse with reference to one person, John Brooks. A definite type of adjustment had been planned—Brooks' divorce from his wife and subsequent marriage to Elizabeth. Pending the completion of this act, she received partial satisfaction through his affection and the anticipation of the divorce and their marriage. At this stage in the process two things may be noted:

[1] Coroner's inquest records, Cook County, 1923. Much of the evidence at the inquest was furnished by Brooks, who, in an apparent effort to defend himself, testified freely.

(1) Elizabeth apparently was not disorganized; her family knew of her friendship, and it therefore lacked many of the elements of a clandestine and unapproved love affair; (2) she was subordinate to the man she loved (gave up her other friends at his jealous demand).

Brooks' determination to return to his wife provided the cause of Elizabeth's disorganization. Her demand for affection had now no outlet. It is conceivable that an outlet might have been provided, either through some other friend or through a continued friendship with Brooks after his return to his wife. But the previous fixation of affection on Brooks, plus his evident desire to make his unions lawful, prevented this. The strength of Elizabeth's wish and her subordination to Brooks caused her to suggest an unlawful union, but he did not accept this offer.

This situation continued for six months. During this time Elizabeth used suicide as a threat to force Brooks to return to her. She also refused to recognize the fact that he no longer loved her, but chose to interpret the situation as fear and lack of courage on his part rather than lack of love for her. Hence she was enabled to cling to the thought of her original adjustment (their marriage) as still possible. The situation had changed radically, but Elizabeth made no new definition of it, and hence no attempt to adjust to it.

It must be assumed that in the course of the six months Elizabeth realized that her interpretation of the situation was inaccurate and that her plan of adjustment would not work. Thus even her partial satisfaction in Brooks' affection and her anticipated happiness were denied. Yet her wish for his love was no less strong than originally, and, because of the complete thwarting, no doubt more urgent.

Yet she was not able to plan another line of satisfaction in action, nor did any form of compensation come to her.

Suicide ceased to be a threat to force Brooks to comply with her wishes and became an active means of adjustment. Her attempted murder of Brooks may have been due either to hatred and revenge or to the desire to keep him away from his wife, or it may have been a mixture of both.

It is not only in regard to love that wishes and interests and plans may be thwarted. Any wish, if thwarted, may assume the characteristic of a "fixed idea" and become dominant. Nevertheless, a love relation, which is in its normal state emotional and at times disorganizing, becomes highly disconcerting when any blocking occurs in the course of its fulfilment.

No. 4. Mental conflicts.—In the preceding cases the conflict which occurred was between one certain wish or plan of a person and some element in the social environment. In other cases, fewer in number perhaps, and often less detectable, the conflict is entirely mental and rages within the mind of the suicide. The conflict here is often between two sets of attitudes, both of which the person holds and which he cannot adjust to each other. So long as the conflict is unadjusted, the act or enterprise cannot proceed, and is as definitely blocked as though the obstruction came from some outside agency. The following case of day dreams of death is illustrative of this type.

CASE VII

A Jewish man in the early thirties with two years of high school and proficient in a good trade for some time found himself with conflicting desires to assist his widowed mother and marry his sweetheart. He writes that he has wished he were dead intermittently for the last two years, but has had no definite plan of death. "I have to help at home. We are paying off a house and my mother objects strenuously to the marriage. My sweetheart will not live in a small flat, and until I can give her the flat and furnishings she desires she will not marry me. I also finished paying off the expensive diamond she wanted. So I thought I was doing well. I can't see my way clear to furnish an elaborate flat, keep the car, and still help mother pay off the house. I owe my mother the duty of paying off the house. I also owe my sweetheart something but my mother must come first. I can't see any reason for not wanting to start in small and work up, but Ethel says, 'If you start low down, you will always be low down.' So torn between the two my life is miserable. I work at as many jobs as I can, make good money and am dissatisfied and many times despondent, wondering how it will all end. I like to see myself dead and wonder just how much they'll grieve over and miss me, and if they'll realize my situation then."[1]

In this case, as often in mental conflicts, the conflict is not merely between two individual desires, but between two sets of social codes or mores held by two different groups in both of which the person has membership. As a Jew the man has acquired the belief that parents should be honored, cared for, and obeyed. As an American, he feels that his married life should be given precedence over other considerations. He is both Jew and American; he shares both attitudes and he cannot reconcile them. The situation is complicated because he has emotional attachments to members of each group. The Jewish group is personified in his mother; the American, in his fiancée. He desires the affection and respect of both. He is experiencing not merely a contest between the attachment to his mother and to his sweetheart, but a genuine conflict between two sets of attitudes regarding his "duty," both of which he has accepted and in both of which he believes. It is possible for a person to subscribe to several moral codes so long as they are not brought into

[1] Questionnaire No. 107.

conflict with each other. This man probably found nothing incongruous in the ideas that a man owes a duty to his parents and also owes a duty to his wife until the two came into sharp conflict in his own experience. When such a conflict does occur there is often involved not only a moral decision as to which set of attitudes shall take precedence over the other, but consideration of the losses and gains involved in accepting wholeheartedly the creed of one social group and discarding the creed of, and with it membership in, another social group. In this case, if the man decides in favor of his fiancée he will undoubtedly lose the respect of his mother and her Jewish friends; if he clings to his mother, the American girl and her friends will scorn him.[1]

But the conflict is not always between the simultaneously accepted but conflicting creeds of social groups. It may be between an ideal and reality. Such a conflict is not unusual in the latter years of adolescence when the youth measures his conceptions of life gained from books and the sheltered circle of family and friends against people as he meets them in a new environment in his first independent plunge into college or business. Usually ideals change or by some process of rationalization an adjustment is made between what the person expects of other people and what he finds them actually doing. Such a conflict is intensified when it occurs in an intimate situation, when, for instance, a man finds the woman he loves does not reach his ideal conception of what a woman should be.

The following case shows the disappointment of a person in someone he loves and the impossibility of reconciling the

[1] The case quoted on p. 187 involves a mental conflict between the girl's own wishes and attitude, that she should love the man she marries, and the pressure of social opinion, that she should carry her engagement through.

actions of the loved one with the ideal conception held. There is a sharp conflict between what the man thinks is right and good, and hence wishes to experience, and what actually is happening.

CASE VIII

Oscar D., aged fifty, born in Austria-Hungary, had been in the United States eight years and in Chicago two years. He killed himself by gas. At the inquest his brother testified that Oscar had married a woman with an illegitimate son, and that the marriage had been followed by difficulties and frequent separations. At the time of his death they had been separated for a month. Before dying, and apparently while the gas was taking effect, Oscar D. wrote a series of short notes.[1]

Wifie dear, I thank you very much for everything which was good. I am not responsible for this trouble. But between us there were men who caused us a lot of trouble. So forgive me, that I must leave this world. Your husband, Oscar D. Live as long as you can.

This is what the wives in America can do. This is all your fault. On account of all my trouble. You led me to perform this act. Do whatever you please. Later, let God pay you for this.

Here is an address I found in your sweater.

With these words I separate with you. You made me do this. But it is so in America, wives like to fool around with other men and then pull their own husbands into court, so he would be locked up and then give her a better chance to stay with another man. You were away from me with other men in the west for one year and three months, and after all I took you back. Now let God help you, Amen.

What she done to me God help her as she knows nothing. Forgive me God for my sins. I am not such kind as to have relations with other women.[2]

In some instances these cases approach the thwarted-wish type, in which the conflict is between two persons. But in the thwarted-wish type the person wants some definite thing to happen; he may be completely satisfied with the

[1] There is occasionally some question as to whether the farewell notes of suicides are valid in giving the psychological state, but in cases similar to this one there seems little question that the emotions expressed in the notes are genuine. They seem an uninhibited expulsion of feeling.

[2] Coroner's inquest records, Cook County, 1923.

other person's attitudes, general behavior, and moral standards, resenting only the refusal of the other to satisfy some specific wish. In the type under discussion here, while there may be conflict between two persons, this conflict does not center around the gratifying of some wish, but around the efforts of one person to make the other conform to some preconceived ideal. These efforts to change the other person may touch many phases of life.

In the case which follows the wife had instituted divorce proceedings; hence the husband was free from her presence. Still, her failure to meet his ideal conception of a wife harrassed him and blotted out all other considerations.

CASE IX

Ernest King, a man of thirty-six, of German parentage, a carpenter by trade, a Catholic, who earned $55 a week and owned real estate, killed himself after some five years of married life. He was separated from his wife, who had started divorce proceedings. The five years of their married life had been a series of quarrels, and several times his wife had threatened to commit suicide and also to kill him. The final straw was added when he met his wife at her lawyer's. After writing a history of his married life he went to his wife's home, killed his sister-in-law, wounded his wife, and killed himself.

HISTORY OF MY MARRIED LIFE

I was married five years ago and have been living in hell ever since. My wife was nagging me from the first day until this day. The first Thanksgiving day after we were married she threatened to kill me. She was never satisfied. She was always complaining about money. She wanted to go to work and I did not want her to. Well, she went to work in January and worked three weeks. I was working then, bringing her home $55.00 a week ever since we were married. She was in a family way then. She was not a good housekeeper. She never dusted or cleaned the furniture; all she did was lie in bed all day or went over to her mother's house and all I got when I got home from work was a fried supper. She thought more of her mother and money than of me. . . . .

Then our baby was born and I had more trouble. She cursed me and cursed the baby, she did not want him. She said she would rather work hard all day than take care of him. So I worked and paid the bills and was nagged. She wanted a home of her own and I tried to satisfy her. We saved money and I wanted to buy old houses, fix them up and sell again, but she would not do that. She wanted a new house or none. Well, we bought a lot and built a garage on it and lived in that.

[Twice his wife turned the gas on when he and the baby were in bed and he turned it off.]

Always a fight over money and she wanted to go to work. She did not want to take care of the baby. I stayed home because I could not get work. Well, I took the baby to my mother's house and she took care of him. My wife never was a mother to him. She threatened to kill him several times. I was afraid of her. She took the gun out of the drawer once in one of her fits and I thought sure she would shoot me. Well, she was as dirty as any woman could be and she left her dirty clothes around the house. It was terrible. I told her to be clean, but she would not. She left dishes dirty from one end of the week to the other. I always had to wash them. All she wanted to do was go out and have a good time, go to dances, but did not think of her baby. I never had a happy day with my wife. My mother has taken care of my baby since he was nineteen months old and has him yet. I hope she keeps him. . . . . I have not much longer to live. My heart is bad tonight. I do not know what will happen.

MY WILL AND TESTAMENT

I am alone in my flat. My wife left me and left our child without a cent. [Ten days ago] she started suit for divorce without reason. I am a sick man with heart trouble. My wife is responsible for my condition. She just nagged me to death. She did not believe I was a sick man and claims everything I earned, worked and paid for as hers. . . . . I made as high as $160 a week. I gave her all I earned and still she was not satisfied, she wanted more. And I tried to earn more. In the summer I was hurt internally. . . . . I went to a doctor and he told me . . . . that I should rest for one year and I would be well again. My wife did not believe it and I went to work anyhow. . . . . My wife said I was too lazy to work and she drove me on until I am a physical wreck today. . . . . I have not long to live so I must write this to let people know my side of things in general. I met my wife at her lawyer's office today and she laughed at me and sneered at me and said all kind of mean things to me, showing that she has no sympathy for anything. When my wife saw me she just laughed at me. She never asked how the baby was. She did not think that much of him. . . . . All she had in her mind was money and the property. And that she earned it all and I did nothing. Well, I am so sick I do not know what to do; she hounds me to death.[1]

[1] Coroner's inquest records, Cook County, 1925.

Although this man was separated from his wife and a divorce was soon to sever all relations, he could not mentally release himself from her. He apparently had the old-fashioned German idea of a wife: a mother and housekeeper, content to look after the needs of her family and follow her husband's advice. His wife, on the other hand, preferred a business position and dancing to housekeeping, and wished the money earned to be spent in material pleasures. At the time of the suicide his actual conflict with his wife was almost completed, but her actions and his memory of her still conflicted with his ideal conception of a wife to such an extent that his grievance led him to attempt her life and to take his own.

No. 5. The broken life-organization.—In a large number of cases persons who had previously been happily adjusted had the experience of having some factor entirely outside of their control disturb the habits of life and the contacts they had established to care for their various interests. Sometimes even the threat of some such disturbing factor is sufficient to cause great emotional disturbance and suicide. In several cases the fear of blindness with its attendant discomforts led to suicide. Arrests, illness, the breaking up of a home, change of residence—anything, in fact, which changes the external relationships to which one is accustomed may lead to severe emotional disturbance and eventually to suicide.

This type of suicide differs from the preceding in that the new element which comes in to cause a crisis has a different origin. In the case of a wish or interest which is blocked in the process of fulfilment the new element is subjective; it is a new wish or plan or interest. The disorganization is initiated within the personality. In the broken life-organization the new element which enters in to cause a crisis is in the external, objective world in which the person lives.

This objective world, while it has its physical elements, is most significant in its social aspects and may be thought of as a series of relationships. Each wish or interest is satisfied through relationships with certain persons and institutions. If the person lives in a small community and his contacts are few, the same people and institutions may give him response for many or even all his interests. Under other circumstances the systems of relationships do not overlap. Thus, a man may look to his wife and children for love, to his golf and business associates for admiration, to his club friends for intellectual stimulus, and so forth. When these systems of relationships are separated it is possible for disorganization to occur in one of them while the others remain unaffected. In other cases, when many interests are interwoven with one group of people, disorganization in one type of relationship may lead to complete disorganization and a collapse of the person's entire life-organization.

Disorganization of the objective social relations may concern any important interest. In the following case the authority and status of the husband in his family have been threatened. There is no change in the husband's wishes; the change is entirely in the social world in which the man was accustomed to have his unusually dominant desire for prestige and authority satisfied.

CASE X

Joseph Borowski had served seven years in the Austrian army before he came to Chicago and married a countrywoman. He told his wife that in the army the officers beat and shot the soldiers who would not obey. In his home he was the officer, his wife and children the soldiers. At one time he became so angry with his wife that he shot at her. He beat her and also his children. He believed that the youngest child was not his. At the time of his marriage his wife had an illegitimate daughter who lived with them. When this girl, Rose, was about fourteen, and at a time when Borowski had been particularly abusive following the birth of the child whom he disclaimed, at the instigation of the midwife, the man was arrested on a warrant signed by Rose. From then on he disliked Rose, threatened not to live at home while Rose was there. Rose's mother, however, preferred her daughter to her husband and the entire family continued to live together. Six years passed during which Rose became an independent earner but still lived at home. The crisis came when Mr. Borowski demanded that his wife obtain more board money from Rose. The mother refused. The result was an attempt on the part of Mr. Borowski to kill Rose and her mother, followed by his own suicide.[1]

This suicide can be understood only in the light of Mr. Borowski's wish to dominate his family completely. Most of the difficulty with his wife arose from the fact that he was jealous and suspected her of having sexual relations with other men rather than confining all of her attention to him. His animosity toward his stepdaughter dated from the time when she signed the warrant for his arrest for abusing the family—a direct assault upon his authority and dignity. The crisis did not come, however, until the wife, on her own initiative, opposed her husband. The life-organization by which Borowski's authority, his prestige, his conception of himself as the indomitable head of the family found expression, threatened for six years, was gone, and his emotion found outlet in an attempt to kill those who opposed him and in his own suicide.

While the external agencies which may cause a broken life-organization are many, they fall in the main into two general classes: those in which, as in the case quoted, the

[1] Coroner's inquest record, Cook County, and records of the United Charities of Chicago.

disturbing element is another person, someone who can be blamed and against whom emotion can flame,[1] and those in which the agency of disorganization is impersonal, such as illness, or disease, or discovery of a crime.[2]

The psychological process.—Suicide relates to no one type of disturbance of habits and interests, but to all kinds. The types of disturbance just listed are not peculiar to suicide; they may be found with many other endings than suicide. Hence this presentation of suicide cases becomes, psychologically, simply a study of personal disorganization in its various manifestations.

The types of disorganization, while they seem diverse, are related and harmonious. Theoretically, they are examples of blocking at different stages of an act, usually a complex act or enterprise. In general, the "life-history" of a successfully completed enterprise moves from the general to the particular; from the vague to the definite. The initial stage of any plan or activity is a more or less vague impulse, craving, or longing which manifests itself in restless trial-and-error seeking. In this stage the possibilities of fulfilment are manifold, and a tentative response is made to many different stimuli in the effort to find the one particular type of stimulus which gives maximum satisfaction to the need felt. To take a simple example, a child may be hungry without even knowing that he is hungry. He becomes restless and "fussy." This state is recognized by his mother or nurse and he is fed. In time the child associates his hunger-feeling with food and knows that he is hungry. His impulse has become defined for him and the second stage of the completed act has been reached. The next time he feels hungry he

[1] See p. 198 for a case of this type.

[2] See p. 282 for a case in which illness provides the disorganizing element.

seeks food. In the case of food, it is usually easy to find. But in more complicated acts, such as the attempt to establish satisfactory intimate relations to satisfy a craving for companionship, while the need may be recognized, the specific activity may be difficult to find. At this stage the act is defined but not particularized, that is, no one person is thought of as necessary to satisfy the need. In time, however, contacts with different people lead one to prefer the company of some one person. The craving has now become particularized with reference to one object; only one stimulus will now call forth the satisfactory response and bring contentment. If this stimulus is found promptly, and, in the case of companionship, if the person responds to overtures for friendship, the act may go on to completion and satisfaction result. If the act is repeated, it may become habitual, and become a part of the accustomed life-organization of the person.

Unless the act has become habitual, there is nowhere any assurance that it will proceed smoothly. At almost every stage there may be inability to find the proper stimulus to carry it on to the next stage, for every act is an affair both of the person who is seeking and of the social and physical environment in which he expects to find satisfaction for his need. In the very first stage the person may not find the necessary stimulus to help him define his craving. He wants, but he does not know clearly what he wants. This state is characterized by Type 1 of the suicides. In this vague and early stage of the act there is little emotion. The tension accompanying such a blocking of the act is not high, and seems to lead to relatively few suicides. This is the state usually called restlessness.

After the craving has become defined, either in general

terms or in particular terms of one object, blocking of several kinds may occur. The stimulus may not appear even though definitely sought (Type 2); or, if found, may not give the required response to the person (Type 3); or a mental conflict may occur between the defined wish and some other attitude which opposes and contradicts the defined wish (Type 4).

If it is assumed that the act has been completed and a routinized way established for obtaining satisfaction, difficulty may still arise through some later interruption. The person has built up a life-organization, but it may collapse through no activity on his part. Cases under Type 5 of the suicides belong here.

Hence the different types of suicide are really but interruptions which occur at different stages in some definite, ongoing enterprise, whether this be the enterprise of earning money, of securing a wife, or striving for less important things.

The statement as given is of course very much simplified. Life is made up of innumerable acts, some of which have become habitual and are carried out almost automatically. Others are very brief and require only a moment's thought. Others extend over weeks, even months, and involve many intermediate stages, plans, successes, and failures. So long as these long and complicated acts or enterprises seem to the person to be going along advantageously there is little emotion, although there may be temporary blocking and the necessity for new plans.

But when an act at any stage, especially toward the latter part, when particular objects are desired, is blocked and no plan can be formulated to carry it forward, there is an accumulation of emotion. It may be anger, it may be depression, depending somewhat on the type of act and blocking and in part on the interpretation put upon the blocking by the person. Unless some solution is found the emotion tends to force some sort of action.

Traits of acts ending in suicide.—As has been shown, these blocked acts sometimes end in suicide. There are special traits of the acts which so end, although it cannot be asserted that they are peculiar only to suicide, for at present the exact combination of factors which would invariably lead to suicide is not known.

The interest involved becomes dominant.—"Nothing seems to matter now except that I love you. Everything else is so futile, meaningless, fruitless, and blank," wrote a girl to her indifferent lover, before she attempted to kill herself. Another girl in love said if she could not have the man she wanted she would just as soon be dead. There are numerous cases in which the wife left her husband due to his drunkenness, quarrels, or disagreements, against the husband's wishes, and in which the husband, after statements that he could not live without his wife, killed himself. In these cases one interest has been disturbed and has become dominant. Employment, amusement, ambitions, all other interests are forgotten. In other cases the intimate family relations are intact but loss of position or of status due to quarrels at the place of work is the dominant interest involved. It is a normal psychological process that interests or acts which are being carried out in habitual and uninterrupted fashion arouse no emotion and often little attention. They may lie almost beneath the surface of consciousness. Any act which is disturbed comes into consciousness and receives the major portion of attention and interest. In many suicide cases this normal process goes to extremes and the interrupted interest becomes an obsession. Nothing else counts. The girl who is jilted forgets at least temporarily about her parents, her friends, her career, her pleasures. "If I cannot have this one thing which is denied me, I do not want anything," is the attitude.

The interesting speculation arises whether certain needs are inherent in human nature and so insistent that denial of satisfaction leads to personal disorganization. Such a hypothesis has been held by many students of human nature, who have posited lists of inborn instincts, desires, wishes, dispositions, and the like to account for human activity.[1] It is possible to group the situations leading to suicide and to make generalizations as to the interests involved. Such an analysis has been made for the Chicago suicides for 1923, resulting in the list which follows. It is not asserted, however, that these needs are innate human needs. They may simply be the acquired needs of people living in Chicago in the year 1923.

1. The desire to continue in the routine of the past when that routine has been interrupted.

2. The desire to avoid pain.

3. The desire for response, varying from loneliness to the active wish for the love of one specific person.

4. The desire for social prestige or recognition, including both the wish for the respect of some particular person and instances in which there is a general feeling of disgrace and humiliation.

Fixity of idea.—Related to the dominance of the thwarted interest over all other interests is the fixity of any plan by which the interest may be fulfilled. In many cases suicide

[1] See Ruth Shonle, "Social Psychologists and the Method of the Instinctivists," *Social Forces*, V (June, 1927), 597.

could undoubtedly be averted were it possible for the person, thwarted in one plan of fulfilment, to adopt another plan by which the same interest might become satisfied. But with his interests once defined in terms of some person or group of persons, or in terms of some activity or profession, it is difficult for the human being to wrench himself loose and seek new attachments. In the suicide, this non-adaptability seems unusually prominent. If he has determined upon a certain way to satisfy an interest he can consider no alternative way. If a system of relationships once found satisfactory is for any reason broken, he can conceive of no new system doing the work of the old.

Lack of objectivity.—There is often a striking lack of objectivity among those who commit suicide. This is particularly true in cases in which the disorganization involves a social relationship. When the agency of blocking or disorganization is another person the situation often takes the form of conflict between two persons. In such cases the one who commits suicide often blames the other for his death, failing utterly to see that his own conduct may have contributed to the disharmony or that the situation is largely a matter of his own point of view rather than that it is inherent in any external object or person.

Types of crisis.—The ordinary notion of crisis as a sudden catastrophe should be extended. Psychologically, a crisis is any situation into which some new element enters which cannot be readily grappled with and adjusted to. In some cases of suicide these crises are of the sudden, cataclysmic sort.

CASE XI

Adam Woods, a street-car conductor, twenty-seven years old, had for three years successfully played the part of husband to a wife with three children and at the same time the part of lover to another young woman. Finally his wife learned of the girl and called her on the telephone. The girl denied knowing Adam Woods was married and insisted that she was engaged to him. For some time the man retained the loyalty of both women, his wife throwing the blame for the difficulty on the girl. Finally the girl came to Woods' home to see for herself whether he had a wife, taking with her two detectives, since Mrs. Woods had threatened her and she was afraid to go alone. Just after they came into the house Mr. Woods came in with a bucket of coal. He faced his wife, the girl, and two detectives. Turning, he ran out. The detectives went out to bring him back and found him dying in the alley. After leaving the house he had gone to a drug store, bought poison, and taken it. He refused to take an antidote, saying he wanted to die. At the time he was on parole (for what offense is not known), and it was assumed that the sudden appearance of the girl with the detectives in his own home caused him to think he was to be arrested.[1]

So long as this man succeeded in keeping his wife and the girl in ignorance of each other he was not apparently disturbed. Their knowledge of each other placed him in an unhappy position, and the appearance of detectives, the thought of arrest, came as an unforeseen crisis.

In other cases the crisis is prolonged, that is, following the initial disturbance no adjustment is found, and, the important point for suicide, the emotional tension generated by the initial stage of the crisis is prolonged, perhaps for years. A surface equilibrium may develop, but the emotion is apt at any time to come to the surface and the crisis situation to be reinstated.

CASE XII

Anton Zukov, a Polish immigrant who had lived some 23 years in Chicago, had a family consisting of seven children by his first wife, one stepdaughter, and two children by his second wife. Except for a temporary period when Mr. Zukov was ill, the family had sufficient

[1] Coroner's inquest records, Cook County, 1922.

economic resources and owned a small amount of property. In 1921 discord arose between Mr. and Mrs. Zukov regarding the children. Mrs. Zukov objected to her daughter by her first marriage working in the soft-drink parlor run by her husband, although Mr. Zukov's older daughters worked there; jealousy also existed between the children. Mr. Zukov attempted to beat his wife, but was stopped by a policeman. He finally drove his stepdaughter out of the house and refused admittance to his wife's relatives. Mrs. Zukov soon followed her daughter, taking her children by her second marriage with her. Mr. Zukov's younger children were placed in an orphanage and he was lost sight of for some time, living under an assumed name. Mrs. Zukov moved to another part of the city and through a court order obtained $20 a week from her husband. After a time Mr. Zukov began to make weekly calls on his wife and to give her money. One day he came partially intoxicated, and after an argument shot at her and then killed himself.[1]

In this case the crisis came at the time of the separation. Mr. Zukov found himself unable to force his wife and stepdaughter to submit to his dictation, which, according to his Old-World traditions, they should have done. His position as the head of the family was attacked and his wife's desertion was the final affront. Two years later, after a partial reconciliation with his wife, under the influence of alcohol he became subject to the old emotions and the situation of the crisis, two years old, was reinstated.

In still other cases there is no sudden or sharp crisis, even in the beginning, but a cumulative increase of tension. Illness is particularly apt to cause such a condition. Gradually the illness interferes with first one, then another, interest or plan. Or a series of minor difficulties may have the same effect, perhaps no one of which alone would have been sufficient to cause the thought of suicide.

[1] Coroner's inquest record, Cook County, 1923, and records of the United Charities of Chicago.

The emotions attending suicide.—From the point of view of the emotions involved, suicides are of two general types: those in which resentment, anger, hate, dominate, and those in which the depressive emotions dominate—grief, despair, melancholia. The emotion which is aroused is closely related to other factors in the situation. Resentment, hate, anger require an object toward which they may be directed. Hence these emotions are most apt to appear in cases in which the agency of disorganization is some other person, particularly some other person who has been in a relation of intimacy and from whom the suicide has expected better treatment than he received.

Grief centers about the loss of some cherished plan or beloved person in cases in which no personal blame is attached to anyone for the loss. Despair and melancholia are typical of situations in which the person feels the need for some immediate change or help and knows no way of obtaining it.

The interpretation of the difficulty.—The essence of the suicide situation lies in the meaning which it has for the person who experiences it. It is for this reason that classifications of suicide made on the basis of external situations, such as economic failures or domestic difficulties, have little value, except for indicating in a general way the social relationships in which disorganization may arise. Economic failure does not mean the same thing to everyone, and a domestic difficulty is capable of a dozen interpretations.

Disorganization occurs only when the region of life which has become chaotic is regarded as essential and necessary for the person's happiness. If a man cares little for his home and finds his pleasures elsewhere, he may suffer little, if any, disturbance when his wife dies or divorces him. In the practical handling of possible suicide cases it is essential to know how deeply into the organized life of a person any instance of disorganization cuts.

The situation is also defined as intolerable, irremediable, hopeless. There is here a true psychological crisis. The man who kills himself is through with life; he has literally died psychologically before he kills his body. Over and over again in the notes left by suicides appears the phrase, "I can't stand it any longer." It is a crisis which cannot be adjusted to—which ends in defeat. Externally, there may be little or even no evidence of the difficulty, but in his subjective life the person is enduring doubts, unsatisfied longings, and finally hopelessness and inability to struggle longer.

CHAPTER X
INCIPIENT SUICIDES

Why do people when disorganized commit suicide rather than make some type of adjustment which would permit living to continue? There is in the United States a widespread tendency to regard suicide as a justifiable and desirable means of solving difficulties. To say that half the people in the United States have at some time or other actively wished for death or thought of suicide as a desirable end is a conservative statement, if data presented in this chapter are at all typical. Since only a few of the people who die in the United States each year die by suicide, it is evident that for most people the wish for death does not progress into the overt act of suicide. Nevertheless, day dreams of death and wishes for death reveal attitudes favorable to suicide, and people who hold such attitudes may be thought of as potential suicides and the occasions upon which the wish becomes evident may be regarded as incipient suicide situations. These incipient suicides appear to differ from actual suicides in degree rather than in kind, and are related to the overt act of suicide as the beginning of any act is related to the completion.

The suicide attitude may make itself evident in numerous ways. Having appeared, it has several possible lines of procedure. It may appear in the form of a day dream of a gorgeous funeral and mourning friends, as a wish never to have been born, as a threat, as a conscious plan for suicide, and in other ways. And it may be dispelled by an actual resolution of the difficulty, by a stronger, conflicting attitude, or by some alternative solution.

The material quoted in this chapter, gathered from students and young professional people, represents a wide variety of experiences. It could no doubt be supplemented and conclusions might perhaps need some modification were material added from other occupational and age groups.[1] It seems sufficient, however, to support the hypothesis that suicide is partially dependent upon the existence of attitudes favorable to the act of suicide which show themselves in the form of wishes, day dreams, and vague plans, and that such attitudes are extremely widespread in the United States today.

The wish never to have been born.—Most vague of all death wishes is that never to have been born. It can never be anything more than a wish. While it implies dissatisfaction with life and perhaps at least a temporary willingness to stop living, it implies also that self-inflicted death as a means of release is not a harmonious suggestion, and may even be disagreeable.

CASE XIII

K is an American girl, an undergraduate in a university. She has several brothers and sisters, lives at home, and is a Christian Scientist. She has recurrent, rather vague wishes that she had never been born. She places the first occurrence of these wishes at about the age of fifteen or sixteen, but does not recall what called it out. At the times

[1] Unless otherwise stated, all material in this chapter has been taken from 201 questionnaires filled out by students in sociology classes at the University of Chicago and at Ohio State University, by teachers in Chicago schools, and a few persons miscellaneously selected. A number of the questionnaires were used in the University of Chicago summer school and hence reached an older age group than the usual university student group. Professionally, these summer students were in the main teachers or ministers. For copy of the questionnaire used, see Appendix A.

when she has this wish her emotions are those of despair and hopelessness. She writes:

I cannot remember specific times when I have wished that I had not been born or that I would have been better off dead. The times when it has occurred have always been when I was alone. No one else ever knew what my desire or feelings were. The thought usually came as a culmination of many disturbances. For example, if I had made a mistake which was comparatively serious and had my attention called to it, it stayed in my mind for a long time, growing larger and more significant with every thought until finally there would be an outbreak of feelings and emotions which accompanied the thought, "Why was I born if I am always to be making clumsy mistakes?" I could see then in my past life a series of somewhat similar mistakes which made the thought more prominent. The idea was always passing and I soon forgot about it.[1]

Three points should be noted: the outbreak occurred as a result of K.'s particular definition of something which had occurred, her feeling that she had failed to reach standards accepted by herself and her friends; it was attended by definite emotions (despair and hopelessness); it was related to a mood and passed when her mood changed. In other words, her wish not to have been born, vague though it was, was definitely related to a certain type of (to her) disagreeable experience and was expressive of an emotional attitude toward it and toward herself.

The next statement shows the antipathy between the wish never to have been born and actual suicide.

CASE XIV

W. is a Protestant American boy, an undergraduate living in a fraternity house. He writes, "I have never had even the slightest impulse or desire to commit suicide. Sometimes when I am very tired I wish I had never been born because I long for the blissful state of nonexistence. But never do I have this desire for long."[2]

In the following case the wish never to have been born

---

[1] Questionnaire No. 131.   [2] Questionnaire No. 123.

has become a somewhat habitual expression, and hence is lacking in emotional quality.

CASE XV

B. is an Irish Protestant girl of twenty-two, a high-school graduate, who lives with her parents and large family of brothers and sisters. In reply to the question whether she had ever wished she had not been born she states, "Always wished it when I couldn't get my own way." The wish lasted from several minutes to some hours and was accompanied by anger against her family, whom she wished to make sorry. Her parents disliked the expression and punished her for using it, but when she continued to use it they decided she had a "wicked temper" and she usually got her own way. "How or when I acquired the habit of using this expression," she writes," I do not know, nor can any of the family remember, although I used the expression when I was very young. I use it now, diplomatically, and always when I have the proper background (neighbors or somebody around), so that I can be sure to get my wish."[1]

Having found her wish not to have been born effective in obtaining more possible and immediate desires, she used the expression consciously as a threat.

Day dreams of death.—Day dreams of death have one notable quality which the wish never to have been born lacks. The day dream brings a certain satisfaction which not even suicide itself can afford, since suicide places the person beyond participation in the after-effect on relatives and friends. In the day dream the person not only sees himself as dead and beyond his difficulty, but also enjoys the grief and remorse of those who have caused his distress. The day dream of death may be of any degree of definiteness: the person may have an image of himself as dead, without an image of the way he dies; or he may think vaguely of suicide as

[1] Questionnaire No. 101.

the method; or he may think definitely of the means and even contemplate the actual committing of suicide.

Day dreams of death seem particularly prevalent among children, but are found also among adults. As with the wish never to have been born, they arise at times when there has been some thwarting or blocking of interests.

CASE XVI

H. is a young man of twenty-five, unmarried, a teacher and a Protestant. He writes:

Due to an unhappy love affair which terminated some time back, I had for a brief moment when in intense emotional excitement an idea that to "get even" with my friend I might go out and get drunk and disgrace her, or better still, commit suicide (preferably by turning on the gas in my room). A wish for revenge dominated me at the time and I gained a slight amount of pleasure out of thinking how mortifying the situation would be to her when she knew that she was the cause of it all—especially when I had been right and she was wrong. After my action she would discover that she had been wrong and this, I knew, would increase her sorrow. But I didn't even get drunk over it—the worst I did was to chew a cigar a bit to quiet my nerves![1]

CASE XVII

A young teacher writes that during the time she was away from home in a training school she had a definite wish for death lasting over a period of six or eight months.

I was engaged to a jealous man before I went away to school. A friend of his came to the city where I was studying and I was asked to entertain him. I did—took him to a school dance, and the boys, knowing that I was engaged, told him how popular I was, just to pass off the usual "applesauce." I really wasn't, and he found out before he left. But he told tales back home and my sweetheart without writing came to the city and proceeded to play detective. He must have learned that his friend fooled him, for he called on me and confessed the reason for his visit. I was astounded and told my room-mate and the girls that night. The next day I broke my engagement and had a terrific quarrel. I loved him and yet I would not trust my future happiness in his hands. I grieved and fretted for months. I missed him and thought of answering "yes" to his many pleas for renewal. At one time I was so lonely

[1] Questionnaire No. 67.

up there; all the girls were at a dance (could only go with a man escort), the maids were out, and I missed him and thought of all the good times we had had and how unhappy I was without him and I actually thought of death. I played with the thought, picturing the results and seeing what happened. I visioned how it would be to die by gas, even pictured what I would wear and the position I would lie in. But this would disgrace the family. Then I thought of the gun—I always have a gun in my room. Those things go off accidentally. I could fix it so that it would look as if I were cleaning it. Perfectly natural, my roommate would say; she always was afraid I would let it go off. But the vision of a bullet wound, painful, maybe not effective the first time, and all the blood was too gruesome. Natural, but not agreeable Also water was out of the question—my natural instinct would be to swim and save myself. Besides, it would look like suicide and that was impossible. Throwing myself under an automobile led me into all kinds of fancies. I dreamt I would be only half dead and would be rescued by a handsome young man who would fall in love with me. This led to other dreams, mostly romantic, and I forgot how fast the time went. The girls were home from the dance and had made a date for me for the next one. The girls took me under their care and the tragedy gradually wore off.[1]

In these cases, which seem typical of the adult day-dream type, there is a true crisis of some continuation. The wish never to have been born accompanies a mood and passes when the mood wears off; it is a fragile wish and easily dispelled. The day dream, on the other hand, while it may characterize certain moods, is also the result of a thwarting or denial of some deeply seated interest or plan. Day dreams of any kind are characteristic of such a situation of thwarting; denied the actual fulfilment of some wish, the person lives out the desired end in his imagination. The suicide day dream is peculiar perhaps in that it partially accepts the thwarting—acknowledges rather than avoids the dissatisfaction—and centers around a secondary wish, to make sorry the person who has caused the thwarting. The jilted lover does not day dream of the life he might have lived with her, but rather of the sorrow which his suicide, caused by her, will

[1] Questionnaire No. 177.

bring to her. There is an element of self-pity on the one hand and of retaliation on the other in the suicide day dream. These elements distinguish it to some extent from the genuine plan for death, which, while it may have these characteristics, often represents an intense desire to gain release.

The planless wish for death.—A wish for death without a definite plan may be very similar to the passing wish never to have been born, or it may tend toward the day-dream type. Thus one girl, who found her task as a supervisor-teacher over older teachers very disagreeable and yet was unable to break her contract and leave, says that on especially hard days she would wish she were dead, but the thought of taking her own life never occurred to her, and she speaks of suicide as a "disagreeable subject." When letters came to her from home her wish for death passed. Another woman, married to a man whom she had come to hate, prayed for death. "It seemed as though God had the power to take me," she writes. But she never thought of death by her own hand.

Suicide by subterfuge.—It is impossible to determine the extent of suicide by such indirect means that the death appears as accidental. Several of the cases quoted elsewhere indicate that the person thought of ways of suicide which would appear accidental.

Contingent suicide wishes.—A little more near to the definite act than most of the foregoing cases is the man who says, "If this thing happens, I will commit suicide."

CASE XVIII

A young college man contemplated suicide in a situation which, he says, "grew out of the reflection upon what might have resulted in an illicit relation between engaged sweethearts. The relation never took place. Looking back upon the nearness to a moral lapse, the man (referring to himself) wondered what he would have done should all have gone to the worst. Suicide was thought of as the solution, that is, it was thought of as a solution of the terrible consequences of a moral lapse with a sweetheart, which, though it never occurred, might have happened in a particular case."[1]

CASE XIX

A young colored man states that as a young boy living in a southern city he became involved in a rock fight with white boys in which he inflicted a dangerous scalp wound on one of the boys. He had read the horrible details of a Tennessee lynching, where Negroes were roasted to death, and thought of shooting himself if attacked by a mob. The motive and desire were very definite and he says he did not do it because the mob did not materialize. His emotion at the time was that of hate.[2]

The contingent suicide plan is related to a crisis just as definitely as are other types of death wishes, but it precedes and anticipates rather than follows the crisis. It is a possible solution decided upon ahead of time, and if the crisis occurs may follow with rapidity. Undoubtedly some of the apparently impulsive suicides which occur have been preceded by a psychological experience of the type of the contingent suicide.

Threats of suicide.—Threats of suicide may be used consciously and deliberately as a technique of coercion, or they may be a part of a truly emotional situation. In the latter case they are the reverse of the contingent plan for suicide. The threat occurs when a wish is thwarted; the person's life is already partially disorganized and he threatens suicide unless it is reorganized for him. The contingent plan occurs when a satisfactory organization is on the verge of disintegration.

[1] Questionnaire No. 64.   [2] Questionnaire No. 118.

From the cases at hand the deliberate threat appears as a later stage of the emotional threat.

CASE XX

S. relates that as the youngest child she had every wish satisfied until her parents were criticized for "spoiling" her. Subsequently they refused to grant some desire, whereupon she said, "I wish I were dead"—an expression which she had heard her mother use—and hid herself in a closet, where she cried herself to sleep because no one came for her. Meantime her family tried without success to find her. When she finally awoke and came out she found no one in the house and went into the yard. There her father met her, much agitated. "My father grabbed me up into his arms and started to cry and talk so fast and brokenly that I didn't know what he was saying." Other members of the family were equally disturbed, and she says, "I thought this would be a good time to get my wish. It was granted so fast that I learned that lesson well. So whenever I wanted something very much and saw no hope of getting it, I would wish for death and after a while I would get my wish. No fright like that for mother and dad again!"

But if the threat is not effective in securing the desired result, and the crisis is of long duration, actual suicide may follow.

Definitely planned suicide.—Threats are always verbally expressed and communicated to others. But suicide may be planned and thought of without oral expression. The crisis which produces the wish for death may exist in the experience of but one person and be known to no other. Hence it is that suicides which appear to happen without due cause may actually follow a critical experience and a period of wavering between life and death.

Even definitely planned suicide may belong wholly to the incipient class. If the original cause of difficulty is removed, or if an alternative solution is found, or if some at-

¹ Questionnaire No. 71.

titude exists which opposes suicide, the actual killing of one's self may not occur. Suicide is in the nature of a last resort.

The case which follows is of the kind which might have passed over into actual suicide had not an almost accidental solution been found. Had it occurred, it would beyond doubt have been incomprehensible, for to all appearances this girl was at a very happy period of life.

CASE XXI

Q. is a university student who was born, reared, and lived with her mother and brother in the city in which she attends college. She writes:

Last winter, while visiting a cousin in Philadelphia, I became engaged to a young man about five years my senior. This step had been planned to some extent by both families, as it was to unite the last living unmarried member of each family, and the two families had been related distantly some years before. Having never been in love, I was greatly influenced by other people's opinions of an "ideal marriage."

When I came home I gave up school and to some extent all other dates (after my fiancé returned to Philadelphia). I spent all of my time preparing for the wedding to take place in a few months. At first I lost interest in my plans, then I felt "out of things" with the crowd I had formerly played around with in school. I began to worry about the interest I had in other men, especially those more nearly my own age and interests than was my fiancé.

At first I thought if the wedding date were postponed I would in time feel differently about it. Finally, I realized that I could never enter into this arrangement wholeheartedly. The thought of marriage became repulsive and unbearable. Yet I could not think of breaking the engagement when it had been publicly announced both in Philadelphia and my home city. All of my friends and immediate family thought we were properly suited to each other, innumerable plans had been made, and I had received many gifts from both my friends and those of my fiancé. I could find no fault with this man—nothing I would desire changed, only that he was not the fulfilment of my ideals, and I did not consider myself in love.

At this time I much preferred to die than to go on with the marriage, or to break the engagement.

My family knew nothing of this feeling or even that I had lost interest in the affair except that I was constantly being restrained in my desires to go out with the old crowd of boys and girls with whom I had formerly spent much of my time.

The desire to attempt suicide occurred many times, almost daily, for the five or six weeks that I was in this mental condition. Sometimes when driving a car I had the desire to drive over an embankment, and other occasions when driving I had impulses to allow an accident to occur. I think the thought which always suppressed this desire was the thought that I might maim myself in some way which would not result in death. The thought of poison or gas seemed so disgraceful to my family that I never made any definite attempts in this way. My whole attitude toward life became changed to one of carefree existence, trying to get all the enjoyment and pleasure out of life in any way until I made the final decision.

Up to this time my mother and brother were unaware of my ideas on the matter. My brother, catching a slip in my conversation, began to see more and more into the whole state of affairs and finally influenced me to tell him the whole thing. Of course he insisted that I break the engagement, and after talking along this line for several weeks I was influenced to try this way out of the situation. Up until the time the engagement was broken, about four weeks later, when my fiancé came to be best man at my brother's wedding, I still had the desire many times to attempt suicide. The three days before my brother's wedding, when my fiancé was visiting at my home (I did not intend to tell him of my wish to break the engagement until he had participated in the wedding), were a million times harder than even I had expected and if I had had an opportunity to be alone I am sure I would have attempted suicide, probably with poison.

This feeling has never occurred since then.[1]

Another case brings the series to the attempted but frustrated suicide.

CASE XXII

A young woman of twenty-eight, of English parentage, who has been in this country for ten years, just before leaving England had very definite plans for suicide by drowning, which lasted over a period of several months. By killing herself she thought she would meet her sweetheart who had killed himself and left her a farewell note. She still regards his death as her fault: "Unhappy love affair—false pride on my part. By the time I realized the seriousness of the situation it was too late." She also says:

[1] Questionnaire No. 300.

I thought I would go insane and did run a high temperature—developed a fever and went into what the doctor in England said was a decline. This was the cause of our coming to America. The doctor said it was absolutely necessary if my family expected to pull me through. My brothers saw me through the worst spell and saved me several times when I was bound and determined to do away with myself. It is forgotten now. I have never prayed since the time when I prayed for God to take me and he didn't.[1]

Prevalence of suicide attitudes.—The prevalence of an attitude favorable to death in some form as a means of release is little short of astounding. Two hundred and one questionnaires were returned, approximately two-thirds of those given out. Five of these were from oriental students and have been omitted from further discussion since they represent a foreign social background. The great majority of the others are from American-born children, although a small proportion are from European-born persons, now Americanized. Regardless of the relative cultural homogeneity of the persons (students and teachers) at the time of answering the questionnaires, the various homes and communities in which their attitudes were formed represent a diversity of cultural backgrounds. Some of these people came from homes of wealth, others from homes of poverty; some had a high, others a mediocre, social position; some had long-standing American traditions, others were from immigrant homes. Fully four-fifths of the persons replying to the questionnaires had at some time wished for death. Only thirty-eight, or 18.9 per cent, stated definitely that no thought of suicide or wish for death had ever come. This prevalence of a suicide attitude is especially remarkable in view of the fact that the people answering the questionnaires were for the most part in their twenties, and hence not yet in the period of life when suicide is most commonly found. Their statements are

[1] Questionnaire No. 105.

expressions of attitudes pre-existing that age period when actual suicide might be expected of them.

In practically all of the questionnaire cases the wish for death is recalled in connection with some definite and disturbing occurrence. In many instances this disturbing element is inherent in the social situation and hence is repeated time after time, each time calling forth the wish for death. Such a circumstance is particularly true of children who are unable to choose or alter their objective life-organization, who may experience the wish for death recurrently over a long period of time, and have the wish altered only when the life-organization is changed, usually when the boy or girl leaves home to attend school or begin work.

CASE XXIII

A young woman, teaching dramatic art, writes that as a child she recurrently wished for over a year that she had not been born. "I was the homely one in the family and all the 'pass me downs' were passed to me. As I was the last one, anything I got was sure to be no good. Also being homely I attracted a good deal of unwelcome attention. I never dreamt of anything but how homely, how lonesome, how alone I would always be." Such was her attitude in the family. In a different situation her attitude changed entirely. "I coaxed the family to let me go to the convent day school for my high school work with a girl I had become chummy with. The nuns found out my good points and taught me self-confidence and all my dramatic ability. The desire never to have been born was with me constantly, sometimes more definitely than at other times, until I received my B.A. Now I never think of it. I must say I owe everything in my life to the nuns."[1]

CASE XXIV

Another young woman teacher intermittently during her adolescent years wished she had not been born whenever her brothers "tattled" on her for being a "tom-boy." She rather naïvely thought that

[1] Questionnaire No. 97.

had she not been born she would have caused sorrow to her brothers who told on her when she excelled them at their own sports. She is now a physical education teacher, and thus in organized fashion indulges in the activities she likes and says that although the wish not to have been born recurred many times until she started to teach, it has not occurred since.[1]

In other cases the wish for death relates, not to irritating elements inherent in the social situation, but occurs at the time of some crisis which breaks up the accustomed round of life, and when this crisis has been adjusted the wish does not recur, although it may have been more or less a permanent attitude for some months or even years. The death of parents, husband or wife, transition from home to boarding school, a long illness, are typical situations.

On the other hand, the wish for death may become a "habit" and recur upon the occasion of any kind of difficulty which may arise.

CASE XXV

A teacher records three times within five years when she wished for death. At the age of seventeen, when her parents refused to permit her to go to the school of her choice, to which her chums were also going, she wished she were dead over a period of six months. Then, in the school to which her parents sent her she became adjusted and happy. During the period of adjustment, however, she did such poor work that it seemed doubtful at the end of her course whether she could graduate. She was "ashamed"—a very different type of situation from the first one when a definite wish was thwarted—and "kept wishing" she would die. She graduated, however, and obtained a very good position. Here she was homesick and found older teachers jealous of her authority as supervisor. She tried to resign, but the school board refused to accept her resignation. She describes her unhappiness and says she wished many times that she were dead.[2]

[1] Questionnaire No. 70.

[2] Questionnaire No. 77.

There are other, similar, case histories in which at every difficulty the wish for death arises. This recurrence is an indication of a latent attitude which requires only the external stimulus to call it forth.

There is one further degree to which the latent attitude may go. It may become incorporated into a philosophy of life and consciously be accepted and stated as a part of one's code or creed of life.

An unmarried man of thirty says, "If I ever come to a time when the prospect of happiness seems overshadowed by the probability of gloom, I expect to settle up my affairs and quit. The sight of old people clinging to life when joy is gone, and usefulness, often causes a feeling of mild disgust. Perhaps, if I reach that stage, I'll see the situation in a different light—one can't tell what his future consciousness will be or contain—but if one may project his future self by his present, then I'll cause my own death."[1]

CASE XXVI

A woman of thirty who as a child wished she were dead that her parents might be sorry, says, "I never have contemplated suicide for myself, but I see no reason why if persons have reached the point, as some people do, when they are a burden to themselves and other people, when their continued existence means the hampering of lives that without them would be much happier, they are not perfectly justified in putting an end to themselves.[2]"

The existence of an attitude favorable to death as a means of release, or even of the approval of suicide as a part of one's philosophy of life, does not mean that the person will necessarily actually commit suicide. The utterly intolerable situation may never arise. Or there may be other

---

[1] Questionnaire No. 65. [2] Questionnaire No. 34.

attitudes which inhibit the overt act of killing one's self, although not the thought of how pleasant death would be could it but come in some natural form.

Inhibiting factors.—A distinction should be made between inhibiting factors to the actual act of suicide once the wish for death is aroused, and the means by which the wish for death itself is dissolved. Thus the arousal of some new interest may cause the wish for death to disappear, but it is not an inhibiting factor to the act of suicide. The inhibiting factor must be another attitude which conflicts with·the still active wish for death, and, because it is the stronger, prohibits the wish for death from progressing into the act of suicide. Such conflicting attitudes as revealed by some of the questionnaires include: religious teachings that suicide is self-murder; the belief that suicide is the act of a coward; repulsion aroused by the thought of actual methods of killing one's self; fear of death or of the grave.

People who have never wished they were dead.—Forty people answering the questionnaire asserted they had never wished for death. Thirty of these gave an unqualified "no" to the questions. While the evidence of the remaining ten cases is not conclusive as to factors which prohibit the wish for death, it reveals several definite types of experience and of life philosophy which militate against the wish for death even in the face of difficulties.

In two cases religious teachings early in life built up an attitude which made the wish for death an impossibility.

CASE XXVII

A Catholic man of maturity writes:

I have never looked upon suicide with anything but the greatest revulsion. In early life such an act was thought of as self-murder; in more mature years I have felt most definitely that it is cowardly. Sometimes when very tired and confronted with disappointments I have looked forward with a thought of satisfaction to what the end would bring, but even then the thought of death has been only of its coming in old age and in the natural way, never as by my own hand.[1]

Social as well as religious experiences may make suicide repulsive.

CASE XXVIII

A man of thirty writes:

In so far as I can remember I have never thought of suicide as a way out of troubles. Nor can I remember any time when I have longed for death, or wished I had never been born. I can remember hearing of the suicide of a neighbor when I was about six or seven years old, and recall vividly how shocked my parents were. I have more or less retained the feeling which I experienced then, although it has become modified. I have never had any serious trouble in my family or in my circle of immediate associates.[2]

In other cases the attitude is not one of revulsion toward the thought of death or suicide, but a positive attitude toward living and its purposes. "I figure there is a work here for me or I would not be here; that the Power-that-is knows much more about it than I do, consequently any such thing as suicide is entirely wrong for me," writes one woman. "I have always enjoyed life too much, with all its troubles, to desire death. I want to live to enjoy life and will fight to the last ditch for it," writes a man who relates two experiences in which he almost met death accidentally, and states further that for several years his work led him into constant danger of losing his life. The remaining cases, all of young people in the twenties, express an eagerness to experience whatever life brings, or a contentment with life.

Only one case suggests what is probably common to many of the negative cases—a habitual type of adjustment to difficulties. A girl who says she has always been im-

---

[1] Questionnaire No. 137.　　　　　　[2] Questionnaire No. 137.

pressed with the shortness of life states that anger, disgust, and depression have never excited a wish to be dead, but rather a wish to get away from present surroundings and begin over.

Fragmentary as this group of negative cases is, it suggests that the wish for death or thought of suicide does not occur when such a thought has a connotation of repulsiveness to the person, either through positive teaching or through social experience; that one's attitude toward life in general and its purpose may make the thought of voluntary death incompatible with one's conception of one's self as a worthy adventurer ready to meet any hardships; or some habitual mode of adjustment may have been found satisfactory for difficulties; and finally, life itself may have been smooth and happy, and difficulties few and trivial. "I have always lived at home and have been happy. Of course this is one reason why I wish to remain alive," writes one girl.

The suicide attitude among actual suicides.—The material discussed thus far on the suicide attitude has been, with few exceptions, of people who had not actually attempted suicide. But there is evidence to show that the thought of death and suicide had a place in the attitudes of those who actually killed themselves long before the act itself occurred.

Of the 391 Chicago suicides for 1923, it was testified at the inquests that 11 had made one previous attempt at suicide; 10 had made more than one previous attempt; 49 had talked of suicide; and 9 had talked of not caring to live—a total of 79, or 20.4 per cent, who had in some overt or audible manner expressed a suicidal tendency. One can only surmise the number of others who had thought of suicide but who had not expressed the thought. The condemnation of suicide would tend to prohibit an expression of this wish.

The fact that it was expressed indicates that it lay very near the surface of consciousness.

In some cases the expressed wish for death was a part of the same situation which led eventually to suicide, but in many cases talk of death and of suicide extended over a period of years, even as many as ten or twelve years, and clearly shows a latent attitude requiring only the appropriate, particularly difficult situation to call it forth.

The social genesis of the suicide attitude.—The attitudes of repulsion toward suicide have appeared as social attitudes, that is, they were developed as the result of definite social experiences. The attitudes favorable to suicide as a means of solution to problems are also social in origin. In several of the questionnaire cases accounts of elaborate funerals or of suicides in newspapers led to the thought that death would be desirable. Funerals in the family and the sight of sorrowing relatives led some children to regard death as a means of obtaining sympathetic attention. Cases in which suggestion operated as an automatic and abnormal phenomenon were not found. When the suggestion of suicide came from some such source as a previous suicide in the family or neighborhood, or from newspaper accounts, it was superimposed upon an already active trouble.

More important than these specific suggestions of suicide is the prevalent attitude toward life and death, especially in many Protestant and non-religious circles in America. The old religious attitude that life belonged to a divine creator has broken down. The newly advocated attitude that the individual owes a duty to society is not widespread. The widely accepted and highly individualistic attitude that life is an individual possession to be disposed of as one chooses opens the way for suicide, which is, from this point of view, neither a sin nor a lapse from civic duty. It is a private affair, similar to eating, or refusing to eat, raw oysters. Additional light on the social aspect of attitudes toward suicide and their reflection in the number of suicides which occur is given by the data presented in the section on religious groups in chapter iii and the historical data in chapter ii.

CHAPTER XI
THE DIARIES OF TWO SUICIDES

In addition to the brief cases already quoted, the series used in this study contained a number of lengthy cases which contributed materially to the analysis of the suicide process. Two of these cases, both consisting of long diaries, have been reduced to convenient length and are presented here with detailed analyses. The first case contains a crisis in which the complete life-organization of the suicide was on the verge of destruction (Type 5 in chap. ix); the second has a crisis of Type 2, in which definite interests and wishes have been developed, but no means can be found for their fulfilment.

It is hoped that these cases will not only make more clear the theoretical aspects of suicide discussed in the preceding chapters, but that they will also contribute to an understanding and appreciation of the manner in which one or two interests may come to have supreme value for a person, without which life has no meaning.

CASE XXIX. MARION BLAKE AND HER LOVES[1]

One spring morning when Albert Cummings failed to keep a business appointment, his friends traced his whereabouts to an apartment in a white district on the edge of the Black Belt—a district at that time a veritable hotbed of suicides. In this apartment his body was found. He had

---

[1] This same case is discussed from the point of view of the family disorganization involved in Mowrer, *Family Disorganization*, chap. xi, under the name of Miriam Donaven.

been shot and killed while asleep, apparently by the girl who lay beside him, dead by her own hand. Marion Blake left behind her a detailed and uninhibited diary covering the seven years prior to her death. Through the almost daily entries of this diary the periods of storm may be selected, Marion's characteristic reactions to disturbances discovered, her personality clearly identified, and the growing resolution to commit suicide traced.[1]

From material not contained in the diary the following background has been obtained. Marion was a high-school graduate, the daughter of a well-to-do tradesman who was divorced from her mother. Marion apparently lived with her mother and sister until the time of her marriage, and also maintained a correspondence with her father. Her home before her marriage was in a middle-class residential neighborhood in Chicago.

Marion met a young clerical worker, Thomas Whitford, at a high-school dance one spring, and five months later was married to him. She was nineteen at the time of their marriage. They moved into a neighborhood very different in character from the well-organized communities in which both had lived. Their apartment near Forty-fifth street and Wabash Avenue was in a mobile neighborhood where roomers were common, and the South Side vice district with its cabarets and dance halls was near.

The first entry in the diary is about two months after Marion's marriage. The diary may be divided roughly into three parts: Marion's married life, a section ending with

[1] The propriety of publishing a diary of a personal nature is of little concern in this instance. Marion Blake wrote for others to read, according to certain entries. Moreover, many portions of the diary were published in the newspapers at the time. In this record all names, dates, street addresses and other identifying data have been disguised.

mental distress and a permanent separation; an unsettled period of temporary friendships with a number of men; and a longer period as the sweetheart of Albert Cummings, a period at least as settled for Marion as her marriage had been, lacking, however, the certainty of marriage. Since the diary is some 50,000 words long, much of it has been summarized here, with emphasis on the particular traits of importance for the final act of suicide.

The first few entries in the latter part of 1912 are concerned with Marion's craving to be loved, with the need of herself and Tom for money, and with their quarrels. Typical sentences follow, repeated often with slight variations of phrasing. "Oh, I wish my husband knew how much I want to be loved. I tell him, but he does not realize that I mean all the time, every minute he is with me." "This A.M. we had words about money. Oh, how I wish we could live together and not have cross words every day."

He is just breaking my heart with his cross words and indifference. Every time it simply widens the gulf between us. I don't love my boy less, but I cannot love him more, as I should. Oh, God, wake him up, make him kind and considerate all the time. Is it because he is ill that makes him so fierce tempered sometimes, or am I really to blame? I remember, I always said that if I could not get along with my husband I would partly blame my mother for the quarrels we used to have, and that I consider myself all wrong. Oh, I know I must be wrong, but if so, why does God let me live? Life is unbearable to me now, and if things don't get better, something happens.

Some of the quarrels concerned Marion's conduct, especially before her husband's family. When some of Tom's relatives came, whom Marion liked, but whom Tom's mother disliked,

we all had drinks and drinks, and Tom said I was drunk; but I wasn't. I was just feeling good. I wish his mother could have seen me. It would do her good. . . . . I am tired of acting like an angel around his folks. I told him a lot of things that I have only been thinking so far. He ought to know how I feel, anyway, about these things. Anyway, I wish we were out of town, so that all we could do was write to our relations. That's enough for me, thank you.

Interspersed with the quarrels and discontent are entries concerning the trifling events of the passing days and expressing loving satisfaction with Tom.

In the early part of 1913 Marion had an abortion, accepted in a very matter-of-fact manner both by herself and by Tom. A period of tenderness from Tom, and happiness, followed. The pressure of economic needs and Tom's inability to find satisfactory work brought some assistance from the families of both, and also the theft of small articles from restaurants and stores. Marion found it necessary to obtain work and secured a position in a men's clothing store, where she found it possible to purloin many articles of clothing for Tom.

As the year continued the difficulty between the two because of Marion's inability to "get on" with Tom's parents continued.

Tom and I have decided we are altogether indifferent toward one another. I wonder just how my life with him will end. Ever since Saturday eve about seven there has been something missing, when he spoke to me of his dad and mother the way he did, making me feel like a thief, which I am, or a convict, or most anything that is not good enough for his father and mother.

And a few days later, in the midst of perplexity:

I asked Tom what he wished to do, if we could go on, and he suggested separation. All of a sudden I seemed really to know what that would mean for me and I thought I would go mad. I certainly am an unhappy woman with him now sometimes; how should I feel without him?

With regard to Marion's working: "Way down in his heart I know he thinks I am selfish because I don't help. I guess I am too, but I do love to roam around all day in my comfy little home, this dear place that is Home to both of us now."

1913–14. A year married. Marion wrote:

Tom and I seem to be growing farther apart day by day. Whose fault is it? I am always ready to love and be loved and Tom is so busy with cutting articles from newspapers concerning baseball and the president, that he does not care to spend his precious time kissing me. I just wonder a year from now what I will be writing in this book or if I shall be here to write at all.

The tensions already outlined continued. The second year of marriage brought infrequent expeditions to shows by Marion with men she "picked up," and also occasional brutality on the part of Tom. But at times the difficulties were forgotten and they were happy together.

1914–15. On her birthday in February, 1915, married about two and a half years, Marion wrote, "I hope that next year I won't be here to write."

Toward the end of her third year of marriage, Tom left and went to his parents, a separation lasting for only a few days. While he was gone Marion had a "date" with another man. A man roomer had also added to the estrangement between Marion and Tom. Shortly after Tom returned to her Marion learned to smoke, another bone of contention between the two.

Early in January, 1916, came a period of particular difficulty for Marion, with many death wishes. Tom confessed to her that he had spent a certain night with another woman.

The unjustness of everything is all I can think of. I don't believe I can live and bear it much longer. I wish I could get away from it.

No one phones me any more, and I am playing square with Tom. . . . . Last night we walked to Wilson Avenue [they had moved to the north side] and back and all the way talked of but one thing, our ideas of each other, the one moral standard, which is the only one for me, and about the night Tom saw me in the ———— restaurant. He said he was with a woman that night. . . . . Tom went the limit that night, but I did not, thank God. . . . . For the first time in my life I had the desire to kill, to plunge a dagger in her [the other woman's] heart. She's innocent. She didn't know he was married, and even so, she is not to blame. He is all wrong. I wonder if what I feel is jealousy. I think not. It is simply repugnance for the whole human race and their ideas, their unjustness. This is a man's world, ruled by men because they made it. Woman simply fits in for man's convenience. . . . . Why cannot a woman do all a man does? Because she is supported by him. If she rebels she is put out of her home and her children are taken away from her. . . . . My God, a woman is a fool and a coward, and by God, sometimes I do believe these puppets of women who bow down to their lord and master ought to be treated as they are. If they don't know enough to stand up for their rights. But how can they stand up for their rights? They have none, or only those men give them. . . . . Oh, God, why can't these things be made clear to me? Why cannot woman do as man does, or rather man do as woman does? How can the world go on? Oh, God, tell me. Let someone explain. . . . . Is there any answer but the one, "Man makes it so?" Doesn't a woman count for anything? Is she nothing? What is there a woman can do that a man cannot do? Bearing a child is the only thing I can think of. All this is killing me, but thank God, I want to go. I want and beg to go home, to drop out of this earth where there is no place for me—where I don't want a place. . . . . I wish to God I could drop off the earth and just end my life, but it is not so.

Two days later: "Bichloride of mercury, cyanide of potassium, either will kill a dog." Tom tells her that he cares for the other girl. Marion wrote:

I am not jealous. I am tired of living, of fighting and arguing. . . . . Oh, God, if anyone needed me, was dependent upon me, if even I had work to do, I would never think of death. But I have always thought of that since I've been ten or twelve, and I certainly am not made to be happy. If I had anything to do, I'd leave here and get a room and if I could I'd live decently, and if not, I'd go the limit or jump in the lake. Which is the worse? I prefer the lake. Tom said let's try once more. And I told him that when I wanted to smoke he would be angry. All he said was try again, so I promised. . . . . If I had not promised I would have been happy now, happy and beyond all recovery to pain and sorrow and despair. . . . . They say it is only a coward who commits suicide. There once was a race in Julius Caesar's time, the Romans, his race, who thought it honorable death. I think it is not cowardly, and I know many people who have not nerve or bravery to do it. Myself is one, otherwise I would have been dead long ago, long ago. I lack either courage or despair. I believe it is the former, which will show to what extent I pity myself.

Several weeks later her mind was still in a turmoil:

I have just crawled out of bed. Can't sleep. . . . . The last rest is all I pray for now. Oh, God, how many times have I asked you to take me, take me, take me. Either I shall go mad from the thought I have, or I shall change my mind when I find an answer to the question I ask. Why should I be made to suffer for what Tom does? Before we were married he lied to me about himself. Simply because he knew I would believe him. Now that I am awake and know what he is, I suffer. Oh, God, the pain. I loved Tom with the tenderest love in the world, the almost tender mother-love, and then to have my little god broken.

Twice during this period of disturbance she wrote of wishing to kill Tom, and almost every entry is filled with questions regarding the inequality of standards of morality between the sexes and requests to God to take her. They decided to separate in May and Marion asked God to take her before she should sink into the mire.

May passed without a separation and there were again happy times when Marion admitted that she was happy; but she also recorded that sometimes when Tom touched her she thought of the other women with whom he had been intimate, and her comments on him became critical. She no longer blamed herself for their difficulties. "He is so discourteous that I feel I hate him. He is so small and mean. A man with a big heart would never act as he does."

More than a year passed, until November, 1917, before a final separation came. During this year relations between Marion and Tom became more and more strained, and over and over appeared the wish for death.

I looked around at my pretty things and longed for someone to appreciate them with me. Tom never has—he is not the kind who can, but if I were to tell him he doesn't love them as I do, he would be angry. There is nothing left to me but to read, draw, or strum on the piano of evenings. I am sad and lonely. Oh, God, how lonely. I am starving. Oh, God, I am ready for the last, last chance. I have taken two already, and they are not right. Life was the first chance, marriage the second, and now I am ready for death, the last chance. It cannot be any worse than it is here.

After a quarrel involving the throwing of an eggnog, "I wish to God there was some way for Tom to get rid of me, marry some other dupe, and try his insults on her. I wonder if another year will see us together. Would to God I could die first. I am too great a coward to kill myself."

A few months before the final separation she wrote:

Oh, God, what a night I am having and no sympathy. No understanding, no words of approval. . . . . This A.M. when I came home from swimming I had a queer idea, I burned. I know I would be happier with Tom off the earth. I don't know if mere separation would bring any feeling near content. . . . . I had my hand gripped around a $40 roll, God how I would love to have one loaded. Now just as I write this I wonder if this book will be found some day *after* and used against me? . . . . Have heard time is the healer of all wounds; it is not, it is a lie; the more time passes the more outraged I feel. Oh, God, I am crazy to feel as I do. I would like to know what Tom is doing with his money. . . . . I just wrote a letter to my mother. I give her everything. If I go it will be most interesting for these people near me. I can almost hear Tom saying to himself that he never thought it was as bad as that. Well, it is; it is unbearable. I must go, I want to go, and by God, I shall go, I shall go; I will thrust myself upon him. I want to be in peace, to rest quietly, and I have no words for Tom but these: Make yourself a worthy man before you marry again, and watch her heart so you will not break it unknowingly or wilfully. . . . .

October 7, 6 P.M. Alone all day, sick in mind and body. The day is dying, I wish I was, and I am sad, lonesome, and forgotten. . . . . Tom will not be home to dine. I told him if he would not pay for a washwoman and phone I would not cook. Then it is he tells me to go. Oh, if I only had someone to love and think of me, even yet I should be happy.

On November 13 Marion found herself alone in a rented room, finally separated from her husband. Two problems occupied her mind: "I have spent twenty cents for phone, how long will my little $60 last?" and "I want to be loved and taken care of."

For ten months Marion lived a hand-to-mouth existence, dependent upon the bounty of several men with whom she became intimate. New men friends, cabarets, shows filled her time. Always short of money, she expressed during this period no wishes for death. The entries are filled with the trivialities of uneventful days. Several times Tom visited her, and on his last departure in June an entry similar to those of her married life with him appears:

Only trouble, only heartaches. Tom's trunk is on the back porch, waiting to be taken away. He left this A.M. without a word, and don't know where he is going or anything. . . . . After Tom left it seemed as though the world would end, or as though there would be no end to my pain. Do I want him? Do I want Roy [her most constant man friend]? Do I want both or either? Or am I crazy or am I unhappy simply because I don't love either one? Sometimes I believe that is it. My mind tells me I must love Roy, he is so good.

Two months later, of Roy she wrote that he "does so many things I don't like, and never will learn." Then Marion met Albert Cummings, a married man, and soon her old friends had been discarded in his exclusive favor.

Bert told me tonight that everyone has the impression that I'm promiscuous—anybody's girl. . . . . It is just up to me to show him I'm straight, before he and I get an apartment. I'm so perfectly happy with Bert. . . . . Bert is so wonderful and I feel so insignificant. . . . . Bert does like me a little or he would not spend so much time with me. Then his voice is as kind and gentle when he says, "My little Kitten, Kitten." Oh. Bert, Bert. Poor Roy was here yesterday morning. . . . . I want only Bert.

The latter part of October Marion took an apartment, which Bert visited frequently.

I'll be happy to have my things out of storage, and Bert and I will have such a lovely little home. Oh, God, I wonder what I'll be writing about Bert a year from now. Tom's "little girl" is surely having her fling. God help me, I am weak and contemptible, but I'm so alone. Bert does not care for me enough, it is lightly, passionlessly, it is not enough. I must make him care more or be utterly miserable. I long for companionship, love, and tenderness, and someone to help me live outside of myself. By what Bert does for me, it would seem he cared a lot. But he does not. He cannot—I'm not interesting to him—I am simply a little plaything, and what is so despicable is that I'm willing to be that or anything so that he is with me. I am waiting here tonight alone—waiting for him—and knowing he won't come to me. Oh, God, have mercy, comfort me. Take me—and keep me.

November 9. . . . . I leave in a few minutes now to meet him. Suffered dreadfully from despondency, ennui, and loneliness. Oh, I long to throw myself into some sort of dissipation, something to make me forget—forget myself, my troubles, my very life. Why can't it end—am I so unfit that God can't take me?

November 16, Sunday, 11 A.M. . . . . No word from Bert yesterday. I hardly thought he would come. It's all right if I never hear from him. My heart can't break any more. But the pieces left will drop out. They must. Again I am beginning to wish I was dead—through, put away—it must be a fall disease. It is a dreadful one, more agonizing than any physical ill. Life is a burden. I was born in vain, a restless one.

November 26. Waiting for Bert, that is all I've been doing for three weeks. I'm a fool. . . . . Bert said he'd be here at seven at the very latest. Piffle. He came this A.M. long enough for me to get breakfast for him—then left quickly. Oh, God, I am so miserable. I am on my fifth bottle of beer, but can't get drunk, or even feel happy or forget. Saw Tom day before yesterday, asked me where I am living. I told him, which he may not remember, and then said he sent me a letter, which came back. Oh, God, I can't help but think I am playing the fool with Bert. He surely does not care, and I do. That's what makes me so miserable. If I could only be indifferent. . . . .

December 17. Another anniversary. I'm a little drunk and very tired—dead. Am waiting for Bert to come on home. It seems I am always waiting. I sure am. Tom spent the night and today with me till four. When I left him he had ten cents, went to see his dad to get more. . . . .

December 21, Sunday A.M. Last night when I returned late because I had been told Bert was out of town, I found the key and a note, had phoned me at 4, 5, 8, 8:30, 9, why not at Joe's restaurant at seven? Can't Bert ever do what is right? I am all broken up. I'll crawl on my knees to him.

Bert returns to her and soon is called for war service.

January 17, 1 P.M. Bert is going! Bert is going! That is all I can think of now. My heart hurts. I am miserable. Nothing is right. I don't wish to live longer. There is nothing to live for. Everything—every object in the house—makes me think of Bert, his little dog on the table, the dear violets in the living-room that I wouldn't allow my mother to touch. Oh, God, I just want Bert, my Bert. I am only fooling myself when I think of him as mine. He is not nor does he wish to be, but he is good and kind to me, and I love him. Last night in the restaurant with Mamma and Bert I had a lot of cocktails after he told me he was accepted. It was better to drink than sit and cry. Oh, God, I am crazy. Bert wants me to live with my mother. He said last night that if I don't after he is gone (how it hurts to write those words) I will be staying with everyone. Does he care? If only I could believe that he does. In two or three weeks he goes to Fort ——— and may be placed in the administration section here. I pray to God he is here. It is only a poor little chance but I can live on that now, and if he goes away, there is nothing left for me—nothing, nothing! This has proven to me that I do love Bert. I wonder what will happen to me when he is away. I'll be straight for him—but how to live—how to keep up—to keep sane. . . . .

January 21, 11 P.M. Dined with Bert last night. . . . . Every other word is "My sweetheart," or "My precious," or "Dear." Oh, God, I do love Bert. If only I would not. Why is he so kind to me? Laughingly, I said to him, it is because you are going to leave me soon, and feel sorry for me. Bert endears himself to everyone, he is so lovely, so sweet and kind. He said tonight that when he was gone he will send me some money every month, even though it will be very little. God bless him for even thinking of me. All my thoughts are of Bert, Bert, Bert.

[In her diary, Bert wrote:] Something in my Kitten's diary? What shall I write? I want to write something that will last, but all my words seem just like an ill wind that chills—I can't tell her I love her. She never believes me. . . . . Can I go on my knees to her—as I am always —figuratively? Can I sit at her feet, and kiss her knees and tell her how I worship her? No, one cannot do that—one can only think it, feel it, know it, believe it. To me she is all that is perfect and good and beautiful in the world. To me she is all that I have dreamed of, wanted, longed for, all my life. . . . . I close my eyes in a sort of ecstasy, just watching her—God! If I could only kiss her everywhere at once, her eyes, her lips, her knees. . . . . I love her—I love her more than all the world, and yet I must not tell her so, because I am going away, really far away, and it would only make it harder for us both. . . . . Goodbye, sweetheart. I say "sweetheart" because you are sweetest—to me, who loves you so, who loves you, only you.

In the next few days came trouble, for Bert was suspicious of Marion, whether with justice or not Marion does not state. Then again she is happy, planning to study nursing and go to France when Bert goes in the army.

March 8, 10:30 P.M. Bert has been with me most of every day for three weeks. He is so good. I am becoming so used to having him here that I feel as though I'm married again. . . . . I have become a home body—wash, work, sew, cook, wash dishes—and Bert likes it. It's a pity I have to make a servant of myself to hold him, to make him really care, to raise myself in his esteem. My nails are ruined again for the present. Bert admires faithfulness.

Bert brings his little daughter, Janet, to see Marion, and Marion calls her "adorable."

March 22, 9:00 P.M. Bert just left. Angry because when he went into the bedroom after dinner I did not follow him. Not once today has he kissed me first. He always waits till I kiss him. I am so unhappy. Bert knows just how unfair he is. Last night or night before he was drunk, and told me how he used to keep Ethel afraid of him all of the time. I suppose he is playing the same game with me. He wants me to be on my knees to him all the time, and I am, but such humiliation as he seems to wish is more than I can bear. He left saying, in a most unconvincing way, that he would see me tomorrow. *What I will do* is phone him; *what I should do*, is to wait for him to come to me. What I want, is to follow him home, to see that he really goes home. . . . .

April 24, Sunday, 1 A.M. . . . . Money, of course, is the all-important thing. I have got to have it. Things are not running smoothly. I don't know how I am going to make enough to keep me, and I can't do what I have done, to love Bert and give myself, or rather sell myself, to someone else whom I loathe. I do all men, but my Bert would kill me. I couldn't get drunk enough ever to slip, thank God; and I won't drink without him. The past few days I have been ready to cry any time.

May 4, Bert left for the East for war service. The entries in the diary alternate between "insane happiness" on days when Marion hears from Bert, and "terrible times" when no letters came. In June Bert was back in Chicago.

I am so happy that he is here, but I am still the same unhappy [person] when he is not with me. I thought this separation would have broken the spell, but it has not. I am still his slave, as I always have been, still foolishly in love with him.

May 24. . . . . Bert is in bed, sleeping the sleep of the just. He threw me down about one and a half hours ago in Michigan boulevard. Why don't I get a divorce, and here I sit writing while he sleeps peacefully in bed. . . . . God damn Bert for the abuse he has give me.

May 27, 1 P.M., Sunday. . . . . Every day I love my Bert more, if possible, and when he is away from me, I feel miserable. Bert is my whole life. All I want is to know that he cares for me.

September 25. . . . . I'm fooling myself into believing that Bert is in love with me. He is not the kind to love anyone. He is fond of me, that is all. But God knows how all this will end. If my Bert goes "over there" he will put me out of his life forever; he will leave me behind, as he will leave his civilian clothes.

October 4, she records that she is studying typing.

Nov. 7, Saturday, 5 P.M. No letter from my Bert today. Jim told me that the night last week that Bert was drunk, he said he had been trying to break off with me for some time. Oh, God, what awful thoughts to have. What can I think—Bert does so many things to make me think he cares, and so many, God help me, to make me think he doesn't. If only my body would die as the rest of me has. I seek oblivion. If only I could drink. I think I would if I was unemployed. This position has saved me, in a way. I am at the office, and when busy I cannot think.

December found Bert in the East on war service and Marion with him, living in a small cottage and working as filing clerk.

February 5. I hate working. My God, how I loathe going there and reading and writing for seven hours each day, when the sun is shining on the beautiful world outside my window.

February 11: The cottage had been exchanged for rooms and a quarrel had led to Marion's striking Bert, which resulted in his beating her. For three days in her diary she wondered whether he would return to her; then she called him on the phone and he met her for dinner. In March they returned to Chicago.

April 8. It's nine, Sunday night, and I have not seen Bert since yesterday at 9 A.M. Knowing that he cares so little, that he doesn't want to see me, breaks my heart. It is a mystery how I stand it. I have been busy working in the new flat, and got the furniture arranged the last week. The place is cold and dirty and old. I hope I am not here long. Am I weak, that I cry continually? I am miserable. I have the utmost contempt for myself, I pity myself. But the lake is near, and soon it will be warm. Oh, God, to rest in your arms—to rest and have peace.

April 27. Last night Bert and Ma were here to dine. After Mother left, Bert acted so badly and drank. Broke candlestick and dish in bedroom, and swore and started to dress twice to go.

May 7, 10 A.M. . . . . I lose all self-respect living the way I am. I guess I mean I want to be married and have someone with me all the time. I have sinned a lot, and am being paid too much in return. What's the use of being straight with Bert? He doesn't give me enough money to even pay the milk bill, or anything. What little he does give me I do not spend on myself, because things are always needed here, but there is always money for whiskey.

May 21. At breakfast alone—always alone. . . . . Bert said he had no money and that is why he had not been to see me for so long. He gave me two. I asked about the rest, and he said he could do nothing, so there I am. I'm sure I don't know what to make of it. So far this month he has given me $23.00. My common sense tells me Bert is through, and my heart will not listen to my mind. I want Bert just as I have always wanted him. My Bert! I have never yet had from Bert what I want—love and caresses lavished on me, and yet I keep hoping that some day he will care enough to embrace me first.

May 26. Bert keeps saying he has no money, so I suppose he is through. He has lived here and never paid any rent. Fine stuff!

The first week in June, Marion made a trip to Ohio with another man, named Stout. The nature of the trip is not clearly stated. While she was away Bert had been to the apartment and burned his photograph.

Bert left after half an hour of abuse, and then returned shortly, and was here all night, drinking, abusing me, and crying. I did not think Bert cared so much. He said he will see me once a week or so. I protested my innocence, but he does not believe me, and I can hardly blame him. My Bert, my poor Bert, what have I done, or undone? He said he wished I would starve to death. I wish it also, and will if I can, but it is so slow."

June 8. Bert here last night and Sunday with me a great deal. Bless his heart. He seems very miserable, and I wish I could help him. He is very good, and loves me a lot, more than he has for so long.

[Bert continued to "rage" about Stout.] June 10. . . . . Bert swears he will find out if I have lied about the past and if I have, all will be over. He has a presentiment that the end is near, and I, oh God, I see only death or life without my Bert ahead of me. So many things are preying on my mind, destroying my peace—killing me slowly.

June 14. Bert and I are getting along without one cross word. I thank God for my wonderful happiness, for which I have long waited. Bert comes home sober every night for supper. God bless him.

Until August the entries indicate harmony between Marion and Bert. Then a telephone call to Marion from another man again aroused Bert's suspicions.

Bert was drunk with one bottle of wine with dinner. He insulted me, as usual. It seems there is no happiness for me, but to have Bert leave me alone for so many hours when I am unwell. Last night he said I might as well not be straight, because I got no credit for it. He doesn't believe me. He never cared much. I know—but now he doesn't cover. He never has cared much. He is with me simply because I do everything for him. This week and last I had a woman do washing and cleaning, and he said it cost too much. . . . . I just want to die, and to rest, rest forever in peace. Friday night, Bert brought me orchids and tube roses, beautiful—first for a long time.

The latter part of August a quarrel in a cabaret over Bert's drinking led to Bert's knocking Marion over, and her comment is that he is "insulting and unbearable." She wrote that she loathed the touch of his hands, that the Bert she loved was dead or never had lived and her dream had turned out to be a nightmare. Her refusal to submit to his caresses and her lateness in meeting him brought an ultimatum from him.

He laid down the law—said I'd jump through as long as he wants me to, and if I am tired doing it, he will get out.

[A few days later:] He pulled me over on his lap, and said he had been cross, and that he was sorry. That was what I had waited to hear. Everything now is O.K. He said he was going to believe me, but that I have to make good. Well, I sure am good.

September 11. I've been reading all the foolish things I have been writing for the last two years about Bert. This book is filled with moans—just one moan after another. It is surprising how I can remain untired of it all. I have written many times that I cried because Bert did not kiss me good night. I don't cry now. That's something, anyway. Does it show that I care less? Or what? It hurts me to drop into the rut of regular married people who show very little enthusiasm or happiness when they meet at night after having been separated the whole day. If I did not run and jump and kiss Bert when he comes home for dinner he would never make a move toward me. On the surface everything is smooth, never a cross word; he calls me kitten, and once or twice comes up to me and says "eenie Weenie" in a very soft, tender voice. No, there is no one like Bert, though sometimes I think I would be happier could I forget him, but in those few moments when he is so kind and tender, I live my whole life, and try to forget the other times, or to put them from my mind, when he is contemptuous of my sex and of me in particular. Underneath his sweetness he feels that loathing that can never be overcome for the woman who has given herself to more than one man, and the woman has only a heartache and the realization that others have known him first. Having Bert go to the suburb to see "that child" [Bert's daughter] is not pleasant to me. But what can only a mistress expect?

October 11. . . . . Bert informed me again he will spend part of the time "at home." God knows how long I can stand it. He is going to give me $200 a month. . . . . Marjorie [Bert's wife] gets $300 and rent and other things paid. . . . . I wish I could put Bert out of my heart and life, but I fear I should be more miserable *never* seeing him than I am at present. He loathes me for having no ambition, but for what or whom should I struggle? I'm ill, thin, worn out—how can I even hope for any future life with Bert? It is all that keeps me from taking the last final leap into darkness, just the thought, not even hope, that some day maybe something will happen that will bring us together never to be separated. And so I go on, existing from day to day, that sole thought keeping me from the arms of God.

October 26. Four days ago Bert held me in his arms close, close, as I always want to be. He is working hard, too hard. Said the other night he can't go along living with me this way the rest of his life and that as Janet gets older he will spend more and more time with her, so that I will be alone more and more and have time to see other people, and that he will probably catch me out with someone, and that will end it between us. He insists that I learn to be a copy writer, so that I can be independent.

She hoped to be able to rise to his ambition for her as an independent business woman.

November 2. . . . . Oh, God, help me to do the work that is necessary to keep Bert with me. . . . . He seems to think money and clothes are enough to make me happy. It is strange how little I care for anything. It is only Bert, Bert. My love for him oppresses me. It is consuming me. And the few happy moments I have are terrible ones in their emptiness, for I know that Bert does not care. I have work to do. Oh, God, I must make him care, or at least have some interest in me, and it is only by being able to talk business with him that I can do it. Business! He is bristling with business, and I—I am melting away with love. I must rise to his plane. I must be cold, cruel, calculating, and I must use people to gain success for myself. Truly, I have much to do to be successful, in his eyes. Today I fixed the shirt I bought Bert two years ago, and he wore the green tie I just got.

November 15 she refused to submit to his caresses, whereupon he started to leave until she begged him to stay with her.

I thought the end had come last night, and if he had gone, so would I have gone, but never to return. Bert is driving me crazy. He will kill me yet. I have done my best to please. I am ill, I think, worn out, and he cares not at all for me. . . . . I've gone the limit. I see there is no use trying to gain Bert's affection, and I may as well go now, or very soon. He is giving me much courage.

December 10, while Marion was away from the apartment, Bert packed his clothes and left, but returned after a few hours.

The next time he goes like that, I won't be alive when he returns, if he ever does. What is the use of being unhappy? He hardly spoke this morning, never touched me, just nothing. If only I had the ambition to take care of myself, or eat, but I can do nothing.

December 12, Sunday, 1 P.M. Bert left an hour ago to go north. He kissed me last night in a spasm of passion. . . . . I am ready to collapse. Sometimes I think I can go on, but always in my mind is the thought of going, of leaving this world. Just two days ago I thought of taking Bert with me. I am writing this deliberately, while my colored Fanny is near me, cleaning the floors. I am conscious of the terrible madness of such a plan, but I cannot go on. Bert still has a few shirts and shaving things at the Club, in the satchel he took Thursday night, ready to take to his wife's apartment, and this morning I said he'd better bring that suit of underwear back, and he told me he had already mentioned staying out there some "two or three or four nights a week, to see that child." I cannot have him all to myself. He sees that Marjorie has everything, and if there is anything left, I can have it. I got my hats on Mother's charge account. They are not paid for yet. Nothing said except once about winter clothes for me. I'm the goat and I'm tired. This is all written for others to read after—I wonder if I will do it. [The foregoing entry is the first mention of killing Bert.]

January 3. . . . . We were talking about orange marmalade. I said I could make it, everything but one thing. I said I can't make you love me, and my Bert said, "I love my little kitten. I love my kitten in my own way." It was good to hear him say that, even if he does not mean it.

January 16. . . . . We had a talk this morning and Friday night and he said he'd rather be here all the time, but has a duty to perform. . . . . He said . . . . he does not intend to spend the rest of his life with me. I told him he would be very sorry when he gives me up. Oh, God, the end seems very near.

January 21. [Marion caught Bert in a lie about his whereabouts on a certain night and she suspected that he was with another woman.] He lay on the lounge, and I sat and looked at him. He told me it was none of my business what he does. Oh, God, I'm miserable. This is the last straw, to have him untrue, and to lie about it. . . . . . I told Bert he is playing with fire, but he will not take seriously anything I say. . . . . I know now that Bert has been untrue right along.

A few days later she again wrote of her "wonderful Bert." Throughout February the entries are short, commonplace, with occasional references to her suspicions of him or to quarrels or love-making.

March 14. Did not see my Bert yesterday at all. . . . . I'm a mighty lonely Kitten, but somehow I stand it, and have not gone mad or torn my hair for a month. It is the decision I have come to that is keeping me from such madness. That Bert is the last man in my life. I will never know another, never! I told Bert that, but he thinks I'm only "talking." Bert just phoned me . . . . he is not coming home to me tonight. Oh, God, is it any wonder I nearly go mad? How long, how long when he just coolly lets me go like this? I think of everything—everything wicked.

March 15. Bert just phoned and is not coming tonight either. He is going to B's to board. Have a care, Bert. I am mad, mad. I have held myself in for so long. Not a tear, not a sigh, not a spark of anger—only quiet despair, and madness. I can feel myself slipping— my mind is—is going. It is blank, except for the tormenting thoughts I have. If only I could forget—complete oblivion would be a blessing.

March 17, 9:45 A.M. Well, I didn't. I had a sleepless night. Watched Bert, and tried to, but somehow I just couldn't.

April 16. Just talked to Bert; did not see him Saturday or Sunday, and told me to come to office at six to get some money. Said nothing about being with me. I am crushed and broken.

His coolness and the long intervals between visits caused her to think he was visiting another woman. The entries which follow are uneventful: telephone calls to and from Bert, visits from him, her birthday present to him, and the like. Then, following a day when she tried to locate him by telephone and failed:

May 6, Saturday, 9:40 A.M. Thursday A.M. Bert phoned, swore at me furiously about phoning the night before. Marjorie raised Cain, he said. I listened to nothing but oaths and hung up. I did not phone yesterday, nor did he. I thought I'd let him cool down, and he knew I had only $6 Tuesday night. Just now he phoned and said he wanted to send me some money, and I said I was going downtown and would meet him for lunch. I'm glad I didn't phone first. I am all broken up about Bert. My sense of honor (Oh, God, how ridiculous that sounds, for me) tells me to leave my Bert, who belongs to another. Some day I will have the strength.

The foregoing is the last entry in the diary. What happened between Marion and Bert when they met is not known, but Bert stayed with her the night of May 6 and sometime while he slept Marion shot and killed him and then killed herself.

ANALYSIS OF CASE XXIX

PERSONALITY

The keynote to Marion Blake's personality is her absolute dependence on someone—some man—stronger and more mature than herself. This dependence is very obvious in economic affairs, but has its real significance in her emotional life. Her entire personality was organized around the need for constant and intensive response and love from someone. She liked to vision herself as small, defenseless, protected, and beloved. She could be happy with almost anyone who would give her the kind of response she craved, and, since she wanted affection, tended to cling closely to whoever gave it to her.

Another characteristic which explains much of her conduct is her lack of conventional moral standards. Stealing of small articles, the abortion, promiscuous relations on her part, even killing another person aroused in her no repulsion or disapproval. Everything was interpreted in relation to her own interests and needs, rather than in relation to the moral norms of the American community where she lived. It is true, of course, that after her marriage she lived in parts of Chicago where moral standards are disintegrated and where life is carried on in reference to individual sensations and impulses rather than to conventional standards. It is evident, however, that she could never have had a very stable or well-integrated personality or she would not so easily have adjusted herself to the easy moral code of the cabaret communities.

DOMINANT INTERESTS

Marion wished to have a certain amount of individual freedom. She was irked and exasperated by Tom's efforts to remake her in the image of his conventional and old-fashioned mother. At the same time she craved the complete devotion of one man—first, Tom; for an interval, Roy; and finally, Bert. Without such devotion life had little value for her; and when, having tasted the satisfaction of the love of a man, she felt herself losing it, death seemed the only relief.

A secondary interest, which in the case of Bert came to be a criterion of his devotion, was the economic one—the simple need for necessities and a few luxuries.

POSSIBILITIES FOR ATTAINING HER INTERESTS

Two of Marion's interests—the desire for great freedom and the desire to be loved intensively—conflicted. While she lived with Tom she sought both, and as she lost Tom's regard, she indulged the other wish—to have freedom, excitement, and stimulation. After Tom left her, excitement and promiscuous relations became almost a complete substitute for the intimacy of one man. With Bert she repressed her desire for diversified stimulation in order to retain his affection. Nevertheless she found it difficult to hold Bert. The limit of her appeal to any man was her capacity to provide certain physical comforts of a home and to love him. She had no intellectual interests and none that could be termed cultural. She was never a companion, but always a sweetheart.

Tom, being himself young, selfish, and intolerant, could not inspire in her for long the admiration with which she wished to regard her husband, and could not mold himself to meet her needs. Bert was more mature, more fatherly in his attitude toward her; he brought her flowers, and admired and appreciated her. He created for her, at least in their happiest moments, the atmosphere of tenderness and appreciation which she craved.

Marion's constant demand to be loved—her feeling that if a man read the newspaper in her presence instead of caressing her it was a personal insult—became after a time tiresome to the man and created friction between them. Her economic dependence was also a source of friction, particularly with the men who followed Tom. She seemed totally unable to provide for herself, and had built up an attitude of indolence which made any steady occupation tiresome to her.

CRISES

Two crises are apparent in the diary, to both of which she reacted in the same way. When her marriage with Tom was on the verge of breaking down, the wish to die was dominant and she also experienced a desire to kill Tom. As soon as Tom was gone, and the suspense ended, she recovered her equilibrium and adjusted herself to the situation in which she found herself. Her relation with Bert gradually came to a crisis situation. She knew from Bert's actions and statements that he was preparing to withdraw from her—that he no longer loved her. She faced again the loss of the man she loved along with the need to establish new emotional bonds and new means of support. In the second case the strain was too great and the needed adjustment seemed beyond her capacity.

THE SUICIDE ATTITUDE

The suicide of Marion Blake was not a thing of impulse. Since the age of ten or twelve, she states, death had seemed desirable to her. Every violent quarrel brought the longing for death. Her idea of death was rest, peace, happiness. At first she sought only a normal death, and in a naïve manner called upon God to take her. Prior to her separation from Tom she came very near to suicide, even going so far as to write a letter leaving her possessions to her mother. During the interval between Tom and Bert she had little desire for death. It is evident that she had difficulties during this period, but they were mainly financial and scarcely at all emotional. The distress which made her long for death was the threatened loss of someone she loved and had incorporated into her life. When she realized that Bert's departure from her was imminent, the attitude which had been evident during her last days with Tom revived and grew in strength until actual suicide occurred.

Nor was her killing of Bert an impulsive act. She speaks in the diary of wishing to kill the girl for whom Tom was unfaithful to her, the girl of whom she was jealous; she wished also to kill Tom when she knew she was no longer highly esteemed by him; she planned to kill Bert and herself months before the act occurred, and at one time contemplated the act while he slept, but was unable to bring herself to do it.

Neither suicide nor the murder of one who had injured and hurt her had any moral connotation to her. She had no religion in the ordinary sense of the word, no ethical restraining attitudes to conflict with her own desires and emotions.

CASE XXX. "A YOUTH WHO WAS PREMATURELY TIRED"

The following pages are excerpts from a diary written by a young man who committed suicide at the age of twenty-three. The diary covers one year and seven months prior to the death of the writer, the last entry having been made on the day of his death. Before he drowned himself off Manhattan Beach he mailed the diary to Mr. B. Russell Herts, of the *International Magazine*, with the following letter.

DEAR MR. HERTS: Under separate cover I am sending you a record of a young man who is about to commit suicide. My only object is that it may help, if published in part or whole, to ease the way for some who come after.

If you will kindly read it through, especially the latter part, you will be able to judge whether you care to make any use of it. If not, kindly mail same to Mr. ———, Toronto, Ont.

I have cut out references to places and people here and there for their sake, because naturally I cannot be worried about myself after death.

Thanking you for giving this matter your attention, I remain,

---

I do not sign this, but you may verify my death by communicating with Mr. ———, whom I am writing today, so that he may look after my effects in New York.

The day after the letter was written the body of a young man was found, and through receipts for registered letters found in his pocket was identified as the writer of the diary.

The diary was published in the November, 1913, issue of *The Glebe*, a periodical edited by Alfred Kreymborg and published by Albert and Charles Boni.[1] The publication has long been out of print and is exceedingly difficult to obtain; hence it has been quoted with a generosity not justifiable in the case of a published document easily obtainable.

January 26, 1912. It is with mingled feelings of hope, discouragement, joy and pain that I begin the second book of my diary.

My hope springs from the fact that my outlook seems to be clearer ahead, the old uncertainty is more in the background, but there is another side to it all. My discouragement comes from my constant feeling of tiredness, less evident in the evening and for awhile at night, but exceedingly strong during every afternoon with few exceptions. . . . .

Havana, Cuba, February 29, 1912. Leap-year and a good opportunity to enter on a bigger fight. I must date my beginning this time as February 18, being the day after my last fall from grace. The week and a half since, however, makes me feel confident once more, despite that for three or four days I have been without a night's rest, owing to stomach trouble and the nervousness thereby engendered, but this is nothing unusual, that is, the loss of sleep, for it is long since I have had a real good night's rest, and I know a crisis is approaching and I must get rested ere I collapse. . . . .

[1] The extracts from the diary are printed here with the permission of Albert and Charles Boni, Inc.

During the last two months the first step in this attempted re-generation has been becoming more and more a determination, merging from a mere unsettled idea. Must return home for various reasons. First, I am played out physically and need rest. More important should be the fact that my mother is getting old, has been constantly calling to me to return, worries about me, needs me to put my shoulder to the wheel more than I have done. True, I have systematically put apart for my mother a certain amount every month for a long time and have sent it without fail even when only earning $10 a week back in the early part of 1910. This at least has kept me in constant touch with my dear old home, full of strife though it was.

[He speaks of his struggle to eliminate amusements and excitement.] . . . . And the money I am saving by this closeness in everything except necessities I hope to enable me to go home, rest, think, exercise, and study calmly and sanely for a year, paying my mother a regular weekly amount; and I hope at the end of the year to have sufficiently found myself to go ahead on my work with more collected ideas as to what I want and what I should want, and all to the better interests of my mother, myself and the good of others with whom I may come in contact. By the middle of this year I hope to take the first step by returning home.

Havana, Sunday, March 17, 1912. [Writes of his earlier desire for college and the relinquishment of this desire.] The reason that the 15th of this month was an important day is that, following my decision of the previous day *re* college and subsequent weakness, I make a big step towards finding myself on the 15th. . . . . .

. . . . I realized in a flash that my temperament was more artistic than scientific. . . . . The little details of literary work do not bore me. Of course, I like the dreams best and lately find it great pleasure to sit down and write, write. I spend hours collecting scraps of books, authors, drama, and also philosophy and psychology, sociology, etc., but principally literature, drama and allied branches. . . . .

Of course, I have much to find out yet, but it was a great step to relieve myself of so many doubts and make literature my pursuit through thick and thin, as I have determined to do, knowing it is my one line. I am not sure whether I can write best short stories, novels or dramas. Short stories only appeal to me as means of expressing myself where I have not a big enough idea for something bigger and better, but I love to write them just the same. (I have only written one of 8,000 or more words, but I have taken numerous notes, written many articles of various kinds and recorded incidents and anecdotes, which I shall use fully later, and all this with an enthusiasm and pleasure not gauged by thought of profit or even publication in all cases.) . . . .

However, a sea of doubts are now behind and the vista before me is bright. . . . .

Havana, Sunday, March 24, 1912. . . . . In an endeavor to discover my feelings of a day, from the 10th to the 15th, I kept a short record by way of finding out how much I could count on myself in my struggle, and the result showed me that I lack exercise, am too nervous and overstrung to put forth my best efforts, all of which confirms the wisdom of my decision to return home to find myself after a rest.

Sunday, March 10: Fair in morning; depressed later.

Monday, March 11: Fine until middle of afternoon, then tired and nervously depressed. Night, cheerful again; bedtime, terribly nervous, depressed, wakeful, worried and despairing.

Tuesday, March 12: Tired from previous night's depths of gloom; calm later, fair night.

Wednesday, March 13: Calm and enthusiastic; tired, but not depressed, later restless in bed.

Thursday, March 14: Quiet and calm, exhausted from previous flurries; later, storm again, very bad, and depths of morbid despair.

Friday, March 15: Ambitious and determined—fine all day—restless night.

The above pretty well represents my struggle for a long time, but through it all I have had a confidence in the final triumph and a constant return to my ideals and ambition, and I am noticing a gradual elimination of some weaknesses. . . . .

March 24, 1912, 9:53 P.M. After another despicable fall following on a good and bad day. I am almost desperate and realize that the fight for life must come to a head soon. . . . .

Havana, Tuesday, April 9, 1912, 12:30 A.M. Somebody has said, "War is hell." I say, "Life is Hell," with a capital *H*. God! but I would not have believed it possible a few years ago that a man could go through such prolonged mental agony. Am I a degenerate? Is there some insidious form of insanity slowly creeping over me? Gautier has said that nothing is beyond words. I deny this—I could be as eloquent as ever man was, have as fine a command of language, be as fluent, brilliant as the best of the masters; but I could not describe the agony of the past few weeks.

It is not alone the nervousness, loneliness, and the old tired feeling; the sudden bursts of enthusiasm, followed by strange periods of peculiar calmness, now peaceful, now raging, now with an unholy joy in I know not what; then black despair seemingly without cause, it is more than this. Self-consciousness to an extreme, fight it as I will, and yet a deep absorption in anything which interests me so that I lose my identity in it. . . . . If I could always find something to interest me the solution might be at hand, but with the same dreary prospect of day after day of hell, hell (the other word for business to an artistic temperament), how can I get a night's rest? . . . .

Since I last wrote I had started afresh. I have three times lost control over myself, and but an hour ago, the last time. It is terrible. With such noble thoughts that come upon me sometimes, such beautiful ideas when I feel in tune with everything in the world, and then always the hellish reaction. Oh, God! what a sorry mess you have made of things. How could you do it? You have made a terrible mistake—to make me such a shattered wreck before I was out of my youth; to take from me everything, strip me naked, so that I can say now that I am absolutely indifferent to everything except to express myself before I die. That idea has taken possession of me. If only I can write such a book as will express all these mad imaginings, hopeless longings, the void in my life, complete absence of feminine companionship, doubly trying to one of my hot passionate moods. . . . .

April 19, 9:10 P.M. It is just ten days since my terrible night of agony, and I now hope again. . . . .

True, I have by no means found myself yet. I still am pulled in many directions, but a hopeful sign is the abhorrence nearly always with me now of the low, common and vulgar. . . . .

An idea which has gradually been forming in my mind I hope to begin to put into definite form just four weeks from tonight, and I then hope to have four clean weeks behind me as a start for my year's abstention from passion. During this time, while endeavoring to obtain a foothold in the magazine field with short stories, my big idea is to write a novel of the various struggles and emotions of an ambitious, erratic youth, with a premature weariness, and unless pre-empted by another, I shall very probably call this "A Youth Who Was Prematurely Tired," suggested by a criticism of Mademoiselle de Maupin, but this is to be altogether different, and is to touch the depths of agony and despair contrasted with the heights of ecstacy and the fierce, hungry longings, terrible disappointments, unrelieved passion, loneliness, ambition, morbidity, deep poetic feeling, and the other emotions of a sensitive, overnervous youth of artistic temperament and large insight tempered by many paradoxes in character. . . . .

Havana, Wednesday, May 1, 1912, 4:20 A.M. Slowly but surely the net is tightening. The past few months have been such a hell as I hope few young men in their bare majority have passed through. Day by day the work at the office becomes more of a burden, a yoke. Come 11:15 or time for lunch (*almuerzo* or breakfast here), and I feel as if I were leaving prison. Strive as I may to concentrate my mind on routine work I look forward to getting away soon after arrival. . . . . The weakening of my powers has been gradual and to a certain extent unnoticeable, but it has been steady, inexorable, and now I am face to face with a condition which means the end of everything if continued for too long. During these years in my heart I have protested against it all. Taken away from school when I was leading the class, without any great effort either, by circumstances, I began a business career of hope and with boundless ambition and half-formed boyish ideals. The fact that I left school of my own accord outwardly does not detract from the fact that circumstances were gradually making it more imperative and I only took the bull by the horns, as I have done many times since. . . . . In those days, after my little stories for . . . . I liked reading and probably looked forward to college at some time in the future in an indefinite way. I was very earnest and ambitious about my work, which continued more or less until some time last year, when the increasing tired feeling, nervousness, changing ideas, ideals and different outlook combined to bring on rapidly my present state, when I positively loathe my daily work. The principal reason for this, no doubt, is that I have neglected exercise almost entirely and now have reached the state where exhausted nature will not be denied.

I have at frequent intervals commented on the disturbances which haunted my bedside, and tonight, or rather today and last night (for it is now a quarter of six and the candle before me is rapidly losing its efficacy) is only an example of the recurring frequency of my nervousness at bedtime . . . . off all temptation to indulge in sexual pleasures from the first of this year, and, although I have not succeeded entirely up to the present, ... still I have radically changed from my excesses of the first few months in Havana. . . . .

This holding off naturally leaves out a vital source of relief from the all-compelling necessity of getting away from myself. Sometimes, from my twentieth year on, when the prospect of a nervous, sleepless night presented itself, sexual intercourse brought the much-needed relief, and sleep followed. And yet, such was the strength of the conventional atmosphere that I had been reared in and lived in, despite my radical views and supposed freedom of mind, I thought it was somehow or other wrong and underhand to seek relief in this way. I cussed myself for a weakling, fought, staved it off for weeks, and then succumbed again. It is only lately that I have seen a different light on the subject.

My views now are that our present system of sexual relations is absolutely false. [He expounds at some length the advantages of sexual freedom.]

Thus, now, with radical views, I am endeavoring to attain my old state as before my twentieth year, for a year at least, so as to work this out, with other problems, because in my present state of physical weakness I cannot afford to risk added weakness, and so fight this off every night, and hope soon my nature will have become resigned to this until my twenty-third birthday, when I hope to have a clearer plan of action. . . . .

Havana, Wednesday, May 22, 1912, 12:12 A.M. It is no use—I have to acknowledge defeat. . . . . It is not that I have contemplated deeds of violence, but one thing, sex, is the cause of the perfect hell my life has been. During the past year I have foolishly thought I could make myself what I willed, could be consistent and normal; vain hope, and it needed tonight to show me this. After all my noble aspirations, hopes, love of literature, and the beautiful things in life, I could not keep my resolve. . . . . Torture is the only word for it. My sexual passions, from their first awakening, have given me no rest and never will. . . . . Much of this is due to my wretched physical health, wrecked nervous force and absolute lack of any kind of love for so long that I am too selfish and self-centered ever to amount to anything.

Who is to blame? My father dead, how can I blame him for his share? My mother is the only hope left in the world. Without her, suicide would seem to be the only alternative, and I have . . . . what is this after all but the imagined courage of a weakling, my egoism the conceit of a degenerate? A month ago I would not have dared to write this, but unless this summer serves to recuperate me, I must go down rapidly. . . . .

I only write this record now for what use it may be as a human document. If it may serve as a warning to those who ignorantly bring children into the world to suffer, I shall be repaid. In case I collapse suddenly it is my express wish that such of my letters, papers, including this and any other diary, as may bear on my struggles against an inevitable fate, may be sent to . . . . so that, without using my name in such a way that the family may be involved, he may use such parts of this record and the papers as may help to show the life-story of a youth who was prematurely tired, if I do not succeed in writing this in fiction form or otherwise myself before the end. Slowly but surely I am coming to the point where nothing matters. Something always pulls me back before I go too far, but will it always? Once let me go beyond a certain point in my dark moods and shame will keep me from attempting to get up again. Deep down in my heart, however, I have had and still do have in my most despairing moment the conviction that I have in me the ability to do great things, my love of the finer things, keen appreciation of character so that I see right through many people I meet, wherefore much of my continued unpopularity, great care in small details, love of neatness, order, strong passions, enthusiasm, many other things in my good moods which I cannot quite grasp, but my physical weakness annuls everything and leaves me a hopeless weakling, vacillating and desperately unhappy.

Havana, Wednesday, June 5, 1912. . . . . I must state most emphatically that for the most part all that has gone before (during the past six months at least) is due to disease; not specific, but generally run-down, nervous, overtired condition of body and mind. . . . . Of course, everything is dependent on my recovery of health. Without this, life will indeed be not worth living, because the very things my heart and mind are set on accomplishing will be impossible, and a conventional, plodding life devoted to the accumulation of money is impossible for me. Death is much preferable. Art, philosophy, love of life in its nakedness, without false convention, must be my keyword, not for happiness, for that were impossible, but for sufficient interest to carry me through.

Havana, Saturday, June 8, 1912. I am gradually but inevitably coming to the conclusion that the only way to get along is to throw over all that I do believe and pay the price. If I had done this before I might have been saved much of this petty personal struggle and put my divine energy into bigger things. I have let false conventions battle with the natural love of freedom and radicalism of an artistic nature, frittered away life forces in unholy passions where I might have put it into the big struggle. Now I will conquer or die, victory or death. Death even by my own hand is preferable to frittering the tremendous passion and nervous and mental energy I have away in a life of conventional ease, despising myself and hating others, and being hated. Oh! if I had only conserved instead of wasted, but even now at the eleventh hour it is not too late. Now, today, I will go forward to my fate.

Havana, Wednesday, June 12, 1912. . . . . I have never for more than the briefest space of time contemplated self-destruction as I have hinted at several times. The thought has crossed my mind in my darkest moods, but I am not a coward and today must go a step further and say that I'll fight to the finish against all outside difficulties, as well as ill health and natural defects of temperament and heredity. From now on any departures from a certain standard until I have changed that standard by thought and experience, I will consider in their proper light of weaknesses to be overcome.

All of which may be what I have been reiterating over and over again, but my awakening of today is a little broader. I leave the standard fairly flexible, but strong enough to be a rock in a stormy sea until the waters are calmer, and then my mind should be clearer so that I can readjust the various uncertainties to a certain point at least. . . . .

Havana, Saturday, June 15, 1912. My contract is up today. . . . . In thinking over problems of society it has occurred to me, or the thought has come to my mind of what little use the benefactions of rich men are to really help anyone in need in a personal way. I remember how I used to have such a passion for education—I did so want to know. I wrote Carnegie, Patten, Pearsons, and E. H. R. Green, not begging for money, but telling of my great desire for an education and putting it in such a way that I asked the secretary to refer me to any board which they might have had for helping those desirous of obtaining an education. My physical weakness precluded the idea of working my way and studying at the same time. Of course, I received no replies, and I then realized that the most ambitious or deserving might be on their last legs and all this charity would ccunt for naught. . . . .

If my health permits, the necessity of making a living will cause me to write for money to a certain extent, but with a bare living income I think I should write from my heart, because of the great desire, because I look on it as an art, not a business. However, if my health continues as it is or gets worse, I will not sacrifice what little life I have left on the altar of the modern god—money. I shall write in blood the agony that has been eating into my heart and brain and give it to the world if it will take it for what it is worth. . . . .

Havana, Tuesday, June 25, 1912, 7:10 P.M. It is getting tiresome, these moral reformations and backslidings. But even now I can lay down a preliminary philosophy which I must subscribe to whether I will or not. . . . .

Life, of course, comes first. Unless a man is going to deliberately plan suicide he must live. . . . . By living I mean to touch the depths and the heights, each one according to the strength of his passions, his temperament. . . . .

For instance, if a man is of a strongly passionate sex nature he should gratify it sufficiently to save him from tremendous nervous disturbances due to holding himself back. . . . .

Life comes first, but by life I mean life with Power. Thus anything that makes for power and for a full life and healthy gratification of the senses is good. . . . .

Keeping these in view, life and power, I have something to anchor to while I am struggling towards the light, and I submit this in all seriousness as a good workable philosophy for a man who has not found himself and has hitherto been groping around blindly in the dark with very little prospect of light. . . . .

Thus, in the future, gratification may be quite consistent with my philosophy; in my present weakened state I must hold off if I am to survive. Otherwise it is a case of deliberate suicide, and the only thing to do would be to go ahead and gratify until disease and weakness made it evident that death would be the only relief. Thus I go ahead for the present. . . . .

Havana, Tuesday, July 2, 1912, 12:45 A.M. . . . . I am obliged to repudiate it all—my philosophy as outlined last week would be all right, but for two things, i.e., my absolute lack of opportunity of touching life, and my absolute lack of strength, physical, mental and moral to cultivate power. . . . . What I might have done had I not been forced to become a victim of our commercial system (so that at twenty-two I am exhausted, my enthusiasm and hope almost killed by deadly routine and no prospect of relief), I do not know, but I think I would have accomplished much under careful training or even a fair opportunity to express my individuality. Tonight everything seems hopeless—whether insanity is creeping on me I do not know. I simply must have sexual intercourse to relieve the strain, and it is the lack of it which brings on these moods. If for nothing else woman is a necessity for me to relieve the great strain when routine becomes so deadly as to tempt me to throw everything to the winds. If I could come home and have a woman, I am sure that I could be saved much if not all this. . . . . Oh! life is indeed hell—why, or wherefore, I don't know, and I am fast reaching the point where I care less. In an evil moment I consented to stay on here for a few weeks longer for a consideration of my return fare to New York. This means three more weeks before I can get away from this damnable place which has been getting on my nerves more and more so that I never hated anything as I hate this island and everything and everyone on it.

Havana, July 3, 1912. Well, despite my little outburst of early yesterday morning, I am still in the fight. After every defeat I arise, chastened, perhaps, but with a growing feeling that I will win. . . . .

. . . . I am going to disregard the foolish system of dates, time is to attain anything. I realize the folly of saying at a certain date I will stop this or that I will reform in this or that. All I can do is to attempt to live up to a certain standard as fast as I have decided it to be best and to endeavor to drop off everything that pulls me down as soon as possible.

Havana, July 20, 1912. Last day in Havana. . . . .

August 12, 1912. Since the first I have been through an intense struggle, the worst yet. Being greatly disappointed at the unfriendly attitude of the family to my ideas, disgusted and tired, day by day

I became more worried. Heated argument resulted in open charges of immorality on their part, that is, they considered my views immoral. Last night was the culmination of all this—for the first time I actually threw over all my plans and ambition and contemplated suicide. Many times the thought had crossed my mind before, but it was always as a possibility in the dim future, but yesterday the thought materialized.

I carried on a terrific mental struggle in bed and the will to live triumphed. I will fight on, but I will be more and more egotistical. I realize the vast gulf between me and the rest of my family. . . . .

Friday, August 23, 1912. . . . . I have found the family very impatient and out of accord with my views and rejecting their ideals of a man—very conventional—I must of necessity make a break, because the petty bickering engendered is bound to dissipate my energy without anything being accomplished. . . . .

Sunday, September 1, 1912. . . . . I candidly must say or write that . . . . questions are still open, but I intend to get right down to action towards a literary career, meanwhile gradually attaining the things which I have been struggling for—not peace of mind exactly, but the feeling that I am doing my best in a sincere manner under the circumstances, namely, that I must go through life with health impaired to a greater or less extent; that I am inclined to extremes, pessimistic or very cheerful, even childish, by turns; that life appeals to me when I think as terribly inevitable that I have a tendency to degeneracy at times (which I feel I can overcome to a certain extent by heroic measures); that the happiness of a home and children of my own may be denied me. With these prospects before me, my fighting blood is up and I simply have got to go on and up or disintegrate altogether—there is no halfway measure for me, and I would have it so. I write with absolute sincerity now.

October 2, 1912. Another month rolls on, despite my having written that I do not count dates now, I find it convenient to note whether or not I have made any progress in this way.

I have. . . . .

I came home, loafed around the house, read, dreamed, did nothing. Then in a burst of energy purchased a typewriter, an unabridged dictionary, supplies, taking some $70 from my scanty savings. Later I repented of this, why all this preliminary to a conventional, routine existence? Why not go away, gamble, attempt to gain all by a single throw? Why struggle to no end? But deep down something always says, "Go on, you have it in you."

Well, I recovered myself again, calling on Nietzsche as my guide, not that I had read his works, but I had read about him and his philosophy of the Superman—will to live because it is painful, and I will take a fierce joy in life. It is hard to drop those passionate dreams born of romance, but I know that happiness is not for me, not the happiness of convention or even sex conventionally, but perhaps a certain amount of intellectual satisfaction and the thrill that comes from reading the master minds which respond in me, the thrill as I feel willing to make any sacrifice for my ideals, reaffirmed by a perusal of several of Ibsen's plays within the last few days, Schopenhauer's *Studies in Pessimism*, and a part re-perusal of Haldane Macfall's book about Ibsen. . . . .

No, too long have I postponed facing the situation. No longer must I dream. I must act. I cannot fail; worldly honor is not success. If I be true to myself I succeed, the world notwithstanding. . . . .

So long as I keep unsullied by any more very bad outbursts, forward I must go and if I am carried off at any time I have not failed, the ideal still being nursed with that tender passionate regret that Emerson speaks of. A new era is dawning for me. In spite of misunderstanding, seeming selfishness on my part, sacrifice of my best nature, the spark still lives. A few more months of renunciation and I have myself in hand and then, whatever the difficulties, ever onward and upward.

December 30, 1912, 6:30 P.M. A hurried writing previous to departure for Chicago. The past three months, ones of disillusionment and blasted hopes. Future uncertain, but atmosphere cleared for anything that turns up.

Suddenly, deciding last night, Sunday, to leave for Chicago. . . . .

Chicago, January 29, 1913. . . . . I arrived in Chicago on December 31, an hour before the new year. I was met by my uncle and proceeded to his house with him. He is a vegetarian, a raw food one, an ardent and unmerciful propagandist; his wife a chronic invalid, cold and lifeless. . . . .

I have fled from one refuge to another in the hope of being free, of being able to be myself, and uncle's insistence on my not doing this and that resulted in argument but no open break.

The result was that everything seemed to fall from under my feet, and on January 10th I made up my mind to commit suicide on my twenty-third birthday, May 10th next.

Of course, this was not the result entirely, or even principally, of my trouble with uncle. That was only important in so far as it added the last straw to my . . . . [being] misunderstood and, if not persecuted, at least worried beyond endurance, by my relatives.

My reasons, in a few words, for deciding on suicide were:

Disillusionment. What had sustained me through the mental and nervous shocks, sleepless nights, ecstasies, and despair of the years, since my sixteenth (although it began before that) was the thought, which I dare not acknowledge to myself, much less express to others, that I was, if not a genius, at least a talented man, with the ability to do big things. Sometimes business success appealed to me; at other times, science or philosophy—mental and intellectual pre-eminence; then artistic effort, vaguely the idea of being an author, dramatist or literary and social reform leader.

Up to the day I left Cuba, despite reactions and pitiful weakness, I kept my faith in myself, in my mission. Reading Ibsen only served to confirm it. In . . . . I still had it. I lost it in . . . . to a great extent. After I had purchased a typewriter and sat down to work, my courage failed; I could do nothing.

Reading Bernard Shaw showed me that much that I had thought to be artistic temperament, ideals, sentiment, was plain romantic illusion, and I did not feel that I was called upon then to sacrifice myself for humanity, without the aesthetic pleasure my illusions had given me. Before this I had unwittingly cloaked my own desires and passions under the guise of doing something worth while, of uplifting and what not.

Curiously enough, all my ambition, ideas, etc., returned on further reading of Shaw in Chicago, after I had started going on the assumption of suicide on May 10th. I took them back, with the idea that now I was through with romantic illusion and prepared to face reality.

Before recurring to this, I shall go on to the other suicidal reasons.

2. The continual moving about trying to find a resting place, and

consequent disgust and quarrels with relatives, and the feeling that I was indeed alone and without a home. [In Chicago, due to his aunt, he was forced to leave his uncle's house and take a room elsewhere.] . . . . All this only added to my feeling of loneliness, of homelessness, and I took a small room, after sundry hints from my aunt.

3. Related to the above, was the deeper feeling that I had no place in the world. Forced to work myself into a nervous wreck, when I wanted to shine in intellect; laughed at by my acquaintances, for I had no friends, because of my theories, impracticality, temperament; inability to get on with people socially, due to a peculiar inherent shyness. . . . . What was the use, I said time and again, of my brilliance, of my love of study, of aesthetics, of my careful life, if it was turned on me and made into a fault, a crime.

4. Fearful of gradual approach of insanity, brought on by other causes, and degenerate stock on my father's side. I have no proof of this, except the fact that my father was small, nervous, and vacillating, and I am sure it is only my mother's blood that has saved me thus far.

5. The thought that my ideas, etc., instead of being due to higher qualities, due to this degenerate tendency or strain, in short, that I was a degenerate weakling, doomed to drift on until insanity or death ended it all. . . . .

6. Sex. I have previously gone into this at some length, so little remains to be written. To use a medical term, I presume my affliction may be called erotomania.

My passion, ungratified, except with mercenary women, has been a terrible thing. If I could have had a little satisfaction, even without actual intercourse, in my youth, as other fellows have, I might have been spared the suffering, mental and physical, caused by my random attempts to feed my insatiable hunger.

Not having anything pleasant to look back upon in an emotional way has probably contributed more than any one thing to my despair of the future.

When in desperation, just after my twentieth birthday, I first had intercourse with a prostitute, I made little distinction between moral and immoral women, that is, some women I felt naturally attracted to; others repulsed me, and this attraction, physical or mental, I was generally unable to follow up more in practically every case.

With one or two exceptions, every prostitute I had intercourse with was a source of bitter disappointment, and constant recriminations by my bitter outraged nature. I worried and worried over these downfalls, as I invariably considered them after. . . . .

As it is, I have lost something which is the cause of my condition of despair, and it will take a long, slow process of upbuilding to give me back my enthusiasm and grip on life, but events of today and yesterday give me hope and encouragement.

Denver, Colorado, February 5, 1913. To go back to my story, after deciding on January 10th to commit suicide on May 10th, my troubles became worse instead of better. The will to live rebelled against this decision, and I endeavored to drown the still small voice, and succeeded in doing so, only to have it come up again.

Only one reaction in Chicago, however, amounted to anything. In my usual impulsive, emotional manner, after reading Shaw's "Quintessence of Ibsenism," my old feelings about art and literature returned with force augmented by the depth of the preceding condition of pessimism and hopelessness. For a week I felt like a genius, went about full of aesthetic feelings, courage. . . . .

By Friday it began to peter out. Depression, unaccountable as usual, began to come over me. I shook it off, but it could not be gainsaid, and on Saturday night, January 25th, I attended a performance of Strindberg's *Creditors* and *The Stronger* at the Chicago Little Theatre. . . . .

The circumstance agreed with my mood, and in a way awakened my ambition to have my own work performed and read, but the realization after of the work, utter lack of appreciation of such work of genius by the general English and American reading public, and moreover, the ever present dislike and fear of going back to office work and working on from year to year to no purpose, until insanity or death ended it all, brought on all past forebodings, and I went down to the closed district, found a woman, more, two, and disgusted myself with life to the limit. . . . .

I might right here give the immediate supplementary cause of my suicide decision, over and above those enumerated.

As long as I was at work I still had hope. In Havana I was weaker, felt more poisoned physically and mentally than before or since, but the thought of artistic success sustained me. I looked forward to dropping the intolerable burden on finishing my work there, and going ahead and becoming a writer.

This kept me on through it all, when I worked on sheer nerve and every day was in agony. In ———— I still cherished the delusion—I was a genius, a superman, and would show them all.

When I settled down in ———— and bought a typewriter I started typewriting my shorthand notes, put down in Havana, describing my moods, passions and various mental conditions, having in mind writing a book, "The Youth Who Was Prematurely Tired." . . . .

On getting down to it, however, the thought that if I was to do anything it must be done while the money I had saved by scrimping, scraping, sacrificing social life, amusement, almost everything, lasted, which would not be any too long, and then the old agony of uncongenial hellish work—this thought took away everything.

The bottom fell out, and from that time on, last September and October, I have steadily lost all confidence and hope in myself, and my grip on life. The thought of going back to work . . . . the mental state of which it had been the product, haunted me unceasingly. . . . .

In Chicago I at first felt like making a new start, but after accepting a position, I had a foreboding I should fall down on it, and I cursed the social system and employing class for not offering me a living salary for just as much work as I could stand, and have leisure for writing, study, etc.

Death seemed preferable to working, and, dreading to go back to what it had represented in Havana and New York previous to that, I made the suicide decision. The reasons enumerated all came to me night after night as I lay awake, and I called for death . . . . it was this dread of work that finally took the ground away from under my feet. I felt in my heart that, with a weekly income of $20 to $25, I would persist and fight my mental disabilities, finding consolation in reading, studying, especially philosophy and writing. My idea would be not to write with the idea of making money, but of making literature.

I got cold feet whenever I thought of the sordid commercialism of present American authorship. My ideas and ideals, delusions, illusions, call them what you will, were too strong to face the facts.

I had wild ideas of laying my case before some rich man, or at least some institution endowed by one, seeing if they, out of pity, sympathy, or some other feeling, could be induced to allow me an income of $20 to $25 per week, and not require of me definite results. . . . .

Before the day when my last dollar is gone comes I may in desperation decide to risk this [being thought insane if he applies for charity as above] in the hope of being allowed to live in my own way rather than commit suicide, but I don't know.

Denver, Colorado, February 6, 1913. After that fall in Chicago, after Strindberg, Saturday, January 25th, hope left me until the 30th. Leaving that day for 'Frisco a certain old-time grim resolution to make another big effort took possession of me, but to no purpose as usual. [He goes to Denver as a side trip on the way to California, becomes enthusiastic about the city, decides to stay, applies for work at typewriter companies, undergoes a reaction, and prepares to leave.]

New York, Sunday, February 23, 1913. Arrived here last Tuesday night, the 18th.

New York, February 28, 1913. I leave tomorrow for ———, my last trip. On the eve of a new month I feel indifferent. Hopelessness took possession of me several days ago, and I pretty well decided to end it all as planned.

However, as my money is gone, I must work if I am to live even until May 10th, and, of course, if I work again for ever so short a time in view I cannot say how long I may keep it up, so I say nothing.

I make no grand resolutions for beginning [of the month], but the usual sexual one, having fallen again. . . . .

Sunday, March 23, 1913. . . . . For I am working again. I arrived here night of Saturday, March 1st, and on Tuesday the 4th, commenced work with ——— at the fine salary of $55 a month, with prospects. They offered $50; I suggested it . . . . and we compromised on $55. Of course, there have been openings in my line at higher salaries, but I took the first thing and will not change, as it seems good as business goes, unless the prospects do not materialize.

Though I hated to acknowledge it to myself, I needed to get back to work more than anything else to save me. I had my opportunity, or rather I saved up $400 by sacrifices in Havana, and then sat down and did nothing until half was gone, afterwards wasting the rest in a wild goose chase after my destiny.

However, I entered into my work with a spirit of hopeful resignation. . . . .

At night I sleep, but at intervals during day and evening, and in the morning I find it a great effort not to fly off the handle in protest of it all, but keep on just the same. . . . .

I still feel the call of a larger mission, but I feel more like going about it in a practical, business-like way, because I realize I must. . . . .

While I will not force it, and avoid self-pity, I cannot help feeling at bottom the tragedy of life to me. It is such an effort to live, there is so little to look back on, no youth, no sweetheart, no love except that of the children, and the mistaken love of a weak mother. . . . .

Sunday, June 1, 1913. [Records resolutions to control self, sexually in particular.] . . . . I have simply in desperation put suicide on one side and restraint on the other, and, realizing that it is impossible to go on as I have been doing, I have, with all the remaining strength, passion, love, honor, or whatever is left in me, ambition and enthusiasm, and the like, determined once and for all and for one year at least to be absolutely ascetic as the first step. . . . .

Saturday, July 26, 1913. Nearly two months passed since June 1st, and I have failed to keep my good resolutions and also to commit suicide after several failures. It seems a silly business all around, these writings included, but I must keep on for awhile in this strain.

The only thing is to try again. . . . . I hesitate to express myself so confidently as to my ability to be a superman and a genius, but I can still fight on for a time at least. The end is not yet. What it will be I don't know. The depths have been deep and the heights might have been higher, but there is a fair middle course possible and I'll try to do my best.

At twenty-three I have to go back to the self-consciousness of youth before I can cast it all off and face life as it is. I often realize the apparent priggishness and silliness of this diary, but I at least try to be sincere sometimes, and after the shocks of the realization of life I may write as a man. Things cannot go on as they have been doing. Circumstances will force me to sink or swim, either to rise from this slough and weakness or collapse utterly, and this knowledge will help me. I may be silent for a long time now, because I am about to cast off my romantic youth and be a man, and the break will appear more sudden than it is. Up to now this diary does not show the vast progress towards disillusioned manhood I have taken. In reality they are so big that I have at times bridged the gulf and said, "All is illusion."

I have felt the utter pettiness of this struggle and seen things from the impersonal and even transcendental viewpoint. The difficulty is, after making the jump, to come back to where I left off and take up the daily struggle. It is hard after realizing that finally one will say, "All is illusion, whether it be worldly success—money and honor, or artistic success and the personal satisfaction of work well done." However, I must come back in order to live at all, and if I find it too much and after repeated attempts some day give it up as hopeless, then it will be necessary to take the jump at once from youth to death and leave out what comes in between.

New York, September 27, 1913. Suicide again presenting itself as the only way out, I was prompted to read over my diaries. . . . . .

True, from my fifteenth year I have been in a bad way, but until several years ago a solution seemed bound to come. Suicide never entered my thoughts in those days.

However, as this is a sort of last testament I must not waste time on those days. I hardly know how to begin and what to say, but something seems necessary.

I could not write the greater part of this even now, because I have realized since that it is altogether foreign to the spirit prevailing among the Anglo-Saxon, so-called, at least, and I myself am sufficiently contaminated with their spirit to feel cynical about it.

If these writings do come to print I can imagine cynical and damn foolish newspapermen writing about weaklings and degenerates in line with silly editorial in *New York Times* recently about suicide and another in the *World* on occasion of suicide of a girl who was tired of 20 cent dinners, to say nothing about those arch idiots and hypocrites, the Hearst hirelings with their talks about the idle rich and the good thing it is most of us have to work for little.

Of course, I do not compare myself to the average man. If I had no sense of humor I would have persisted and made myself a genius in spite of the hell life has been. Nietzsche could never have been if he was born in England or the States.

But I only feel at home when I read men of genius. Always without a friend, the average man is a stranger to me. Women have killed me, because with all my temperament and passion I have been too shy to ever have any love or outlet to my passion.

It is hard to say that if things had been different that such and such would be the case. Sometimes I have thought absolutely sincerely that if I had had enough money to be able to dispense with the daily grind, which, with its necessity of strong excitement as a reaction, has so impaired my will-power as to bring me from supreme egoism of imagining and believing myself to be a genuis to a miserable death alone and away from home by my own hand.

At other times I have said that if I question myself honestly that with money I would have simply degenerated into a good for nothing vicious idler of the Thaw class.

Now, when about to die, I will be honest and say that the latter would have probably been the outcome, but it is by no means certain. After all I have been outraged and disgusted in the past after every fall from a certain standard and my love of books does die while I live. Who knows but that I might have got down to study and work and done something? Undoubtedly I would have had affairs with women (had time and money permitted) under any circumstances, but drink and drug has never appealed to me, even in imagination.

I have been honest and sincere, particularly to the fine points on matters of honor, at least until I began to lose my grip on life. While I never got down and faced things, it was because I was incurably romantic, and when I finally began to realize life it came to me in such a series of shocks that independence would have probably made me a Baudelaire, without his creative work to balance the scale. With such an impractical, childish mother and failure of a father, uncongenial brothers and sisters, almost hating each other, with bad heredity on both sides and a hellish environment, a shy, nervous, suspicious disposition, extremes of ecstasy and despair, ungratified passions, alone and friendless, how could I end otherwise than a suicide?

I claim that any man who commits suicide of necessity suffers more than any who continues to live. I don't want to die. I cannot make any outsider realize by anything I can write how I have tried to avoid this step. I have tried every subterfuge to fool myself, to kid myself along that life wasn't so bad after all. This record does not show up my humorous side, but I laugh as much as I feel like crying. I enjoy a comedy as well as a tragedy, am tickled by the very things that amuse the average American, and at a baseball game I actually feel like one of the boys, but where I differ is in my tragic and morbid side, and my keen sensitiveness.

Things which pass over most men afflict me with terrible force. My pride has stood in the way of my hope of success under conditions which exist in this country at present. I cannot indefinitely pretend as I apply for work that I am just like the rest. I cannot always conceal the resentment and scorn I feel as I interview business men and stand or sit before them as a mere stenographer. I, a fellow in spirit with men of genius, must show my references, call and beg and implore, for a miserable salary which I despise, must haggle for a few dollars more, the price of a meal.

The indignity of it all. I, an aristocrat at heart, of the aristocracy of brains and sentiment, must elbow with the ignorant vulgar *bourgeois* who could not for an instant understand if they would.

What is the use? Death only holds forth relief. I cannot look back on a really happy day. Light-hearted and merry have I been on occasions, but seldom a day without morbid thoughts sometime or other, generally at night. If I could have had a mistress things might have been different. When I have gone out and had sexual intercourse with a woman who pleased my imagination I have slept well—seldom otherwise.

Sex has been my Nemesis, and today if I had money I would continue to live. Without it, the whole dreary past and the prospective future is too much for me. With it, I could dispense with the grind and do work after my own heart.

Of course, others have the grind, also; but the fact that they continue to live shows that they can stand it much better, and were born to it. I wasn't. My whole nature is outraged by the life I have had to lead. Empty, cold, dismal, hellish.

Let the cynical hirelings of the newspaper whom Bernard Shaw well shows his contempt for, laugh and write editorials. The day will come when men will be allowed to live, not rot, the *New York Times* notwithstanding.

If a thousand men could be persuaded to commit suicide in protest, the powers that be would sit up and take notice.

Arise you Americans who have some blood in you and get rid of your Comstocks, Bryans, religious hypocrites and grafters, and let the so-called degenerates and insane men have a say, and if you do not live bigger and better, then you deserve what you get.

The majority is always wrong, and the minority of supermen and degenerates—Zolas, Ibsens, etc.—must band together and overthrow the whole damn system which drives the best, the most sincere and honest to suicide or starvation.

ANALYSIS OF CASE XXX
PERSONALITY TYPE

A dominant characteristic of Wallace Baker was introspection. His attention centered upon his own sensations, moods, and reactions. His whole interest lay in the development of certain ideals for his own conduct. In the entire course of the diary he mentions only one person as a friend, outside the members of the family: a girl to whom he wrote upon leaving his home to go to Chicago. His recreation had reference only to his own conception of himself; when he read or attended plays it was because he wished to become a writer of plays, not for enjoyment of the play as such.

Another outstanding trait was his egocentrism. His attitude toward himself seems typically adolescent. It is not unusual for adolescents to conceive of themselves as hidden geniuses, but usually a more objective attitude comes with maturity and contacts with the world. Wallace Baker, however, nourished his secret conviction until it embittered him against the blindness of his family and the world in general.

DOMINANT INTERESTS

Through the diary run the threads of two ambitions: to achieve a certain ideal of sexual continence and to become an author. The origins of both interests are given in the diary. His first contact with women was when he was twenty, and apparently soon afterward came the desire to resist the impulse to visit prostitutes, a desire whose roots apparently lay in his previous training which in spite of himself he could not throw off. His idea of becoming an author is set forth in the extracts quoted from the diary. Feeling himself bound for some great destiny and finding his earlier ambition for a college education out of the question, he rather deliberately considered the various possibilities for greatness and decided that authorship was the thing for which he was suited.

POSSIBILITIES FOR ATTAINING HIS INTERESTS

In themselves, his two dominant interests seem normal enough. The other half of the equation which equals satisfaction and contentment lies in the possibilities for satisfying his interests.

His preoccupation with his own minute and passing sensations made it very difficult for Wallace Baker to control his emotional nature and to resist sexual relations, while the restlessness emanating from his other unfulfilled longing added to his demand for relief from the nervous tension into which he worked himself and from which he regarded sexual relations as a relief. His egocentrism and inability to meet people and his financial poverty prohibited, apparently, any friendships with girls of his own social class, for he laments the lack of such associations. The solution for his problem would have been found either in such an association leading to marriage or in a permanent free love relation, which it seems he would have sanctioned, or in changing his ideals sufficiently to permit the promiscuous relations without the disgust and despair which inevitably followed. The diary is filled with rationalizations of his conduct; he gives in detail plans for revising the sexual relations between men and women which would provide for cases like his, but he was never able wholeheartedly to adopt the philosophy which he went to such lengths to set forth.

With regard to his second craving, to become an author, there is little evidence of any fitness for authorship. The diary itself, from a literary standpoint, is only moderately well written, and his conception of material for writing was his own struggles and mental and emotional processes. When finally, after his return from Cuba, he found leisure to write, he faced his newly bought typewriter with an empty mind. He rationalizes the situation by saying he could not bear to write for money and that the pressure of time inhibited him, but the true essence of the matter seems to be that he literally had nothing to write about. It is not shown throughout the diary that he ever finished any piece of writing and submitted it to anyone for publication. Writing remained a dream, and his grandiose statements regarding literary ideals and the horrors of writing for a paying public are more in defense of his inability to write than genuine literary standards. From his family and relatives he had no encouragement for his ambition. Nor was he ever able to arrange his employment to give him opportunity for writing. He was a stenographer and he made no effort to obtain employment which would have given him writing experience or put him in contact with literary people. The impression obtained from the diary is of a dreamy, unresourceful adolescent, whose whole life was organized about two ideals, the unattainableness of which made them all the more desirable. The dominance of thwarted interests and the fixity of plans to attain them, mentioned as traits of the suicide process, are very evident in this diary.

THE CRISIS

The crisis developed as Wallace Baker gained objectivity about himself. So long as he cloaked himself with dreams, his faith in his ultimate success remained. But gradually he gained another view of himself. The entries made while he was in Chicago give an analysis of his problem which seems quite inclusive: he states he is disillusioned, lonely, unappreciated, unable to control his sexual impulses. His explanation is not, however, in his own inability, but in the fear that he is becoming insane. At this period, while he partially acknowledges failure, he still believes the forces which hold him back are external and not at all under his control. Two months before the end he states, "I hesitate to express myself so confidently as to my ability to be a superman and a genius," and in the final entry there is evidence that he realizes his incapacities, although he still hides the full truth from himself by a series of defenses for his failure: his lack of money, of health, of appreciation. The successive attempts and failures gradually undermined his faith in himself until no further attempt seemed possible. The crisis here is not sharp and sudden; no new element entered into the situation; but the gradual accumulation of attitudes brought a psychological crisis to which he could not adjust.

There are no highly charged emotions here, such as are characteristic of cases in which the opposition to interests comes from another person. Disgust and despair are perhaps the best words to describe Wallace Baker's emotional state.

THE SUICIDE ATTITUDE

How early in life Wallace Baker first wished he were out of it is not known. He does state that in adolescent years while he had troubles a solution seemed bound to come. At least for the year and a half before his death, the period covered by his diary, suicide periodically presented itself as a solution. The setting forth of reasons for suicide and the selection of a date for it show a very definite attitude, and it remained only for the final despair and hopelessness to convert this latent attitude into the overt act.

It is probable that to his friends and family Wallace Baker was merely a restless, impractical boy, whose futile strivings were not to be taken seriously, and it is very doubtful whether anyone knew of the growing determination to kill himself when the fight should become so desperate that it would seem useless. A diary such as this is the occasional written expression of what undoubtedly goes on in the minds of many people who commit suicide but do not set down an account of their struggles in writing.

If the difficulties of this boy seem trivial, it should be remembered that to him they were intensely real; they were life itself; and in his lonely struggle against them they became magnified and intensified until they dominated his entire life and prohibited the development of any counter-interests.

CHAPTER XII
SPECIAL FORMS OF SUICIDE

Certain unusual forms of suicide require special analysis.

Suicide pacts.—Suicide pacts, or the suicide of two or more persons at or near the same time in accordance with a previous agreement, are comparatively rare. Only one was discovered among the 391 cases for Chicago in 1923. A sufficient number has been collected from other sources, however, to warrant an analysis of the peculiar conditions which eventuate in suicide pacts.

In the cases available the pacts all occur between persons having previously an intimate relation to each other: husband and wife, mother and daughter, sisters, school chums, lovers, and so forth. Not only is there a legal or biological relationship, but an emotional relationship, which often is apparent in the mutual dependence for all the varieties of response and companionship of which people weave their lives.

In one type of suicide pact the suicide is preceded by some circumstance which has threatened or destroyed this intimate relation. In these cases each person has organized his life about the other, and the loss of the relationship wrecks so large a part of the life-organization of each that an adjustment seems impossible. Hence these cases are little different from the cases already described in which a person kills himself because a loved one has died or left. In the pacts the emotion is shared by both instead of being confined to only one. Added to this shared emotion and dependence is the knowledge that the relationship is threatened. The pact is made to take care of the approaching catastrophe.

CASE XXXI

Mrs. Charles, an elderly woman, had been a morphine user for forty years. She lived with her married daughter, Mrs. Jackson, also a morphine user. Mr. Jackson, a civil engineer, had descended from his profession to very mediocre jobs on account of the too free use of alcohol. Sometime after his marriage he began to use morphine, according to two statements made by him, to counteract the alcohol habit and to relieve some difficulty with his stomach. The Jacksons had one child who was in a temporary home elsewhere.

The three morphine users at last, through poverty, came to official attention and Mr. Jackson consented to enter a hospital for treatment. Efforts were made to have Mrs. Jackson take treatments also, but after much wavering she refused to go, as she had heard that patients were strapped in bed. The mother, Mrs. Charles, was too old for a cure, and in fact was supplied with morphine under the terms of the law which provided morphine for old users.

Finally a son of Mrs. Charles and the officials of an interested agency made plans to separate the mother and daughter. Mrs. Charles was to go to live with her son, and Mrs. Jackson was to obtain work in a hospital and receive treatments. Later she and her husband were to "start over" by themselves, away from the old mother and her complete dependence upon morphine.

On the day her son was to come for her, the mother told a neighbor that if she and her daughter were to be separated then life held nothing for her. When the son came in the evening the door to the room in which mother and daughter lived was locked, and when the room was finally entered both were found dead. The daughter had killed her mother, with the mother's consent, and then herself. Several notes were found:

"We are going to die. Mrs. Charles and Mrs. Jackson."

"We are going to die of our own free will. No one is to blame. I was doing fine, but they would not give me a chance to cure myself, as I have been doing, and they would part me from my mother."

In another note Mrs. Jackson speaks of her mother and herself as "two helpless ones" and says, "There is no way out of the trouble but this."

For the complete understanding of the case it should be further noted that Mrs. Charles's husband and a second son had both committed suicide in the past, that Mrs. Charles and her daughter are reported to have attempted suicide before, and that according to a psychiatric examination Mrs. Jackson, the daughter, was of a type who found adjustments difficult.[1]

In this case the old mother was accustomed to the daughter with whom she had lived for years. The proposed change meant not only that she would lose the constant companionship of her daughter, but that she must adjust to her daughter-in-law and grandchild and fit herself into a household previously organized without consideration of her and her needs. For the daughter the separation came at a time when both husband and child were away from her. It entailed not only the loss of her mother, but also entrance upon treatments which she feared. In addition, mother and daughter were dependent upon each other for morphine, for the mother obtained a small regular supply and the daughter found ways of supplementing the amount. As to the attitudes which led to suicide, it must be remembered that two other members of the family had found suicide an appropriate solution to their difficulties. Whatever effect these other suicides and the long use of morphine may have had on the mother and daughter, the occasion for the suicide is clearly that of threatened rupture of an intimate relationship upon which both depended.

CASE XXXII

Eleanor Parker, a girl of seventeen, came to Chicago from a nearby city with her uncle's chauffeur, a young man of twenty-five who was

[1] Coroner's inquest records, Cook County, 1923, and records of the United Charities of Chicago.

separated from his wife. Eleanor's mother knew of the attachment and had given the man money a short time before the elopement for him to return to his wife. When her daughter disappeared she suspected the elopement and traced the pair through a letter which the man sent to an aunt. She found the two living in a rented room as Mr. and Mrs. Brown. In reporting her meeting with the two, the mother said, "I asked him what he meant taking my daughter, the only thing I had in the world, and he said, 'I love Eleanor.' 'Well,' I said, 'it doesn't make any difference if you love her or not. You are going to pay for this.'" She then took her daughter with her in a cab to the station for the return home. On the way she said that she told Eleanor that she would have to go to school until she was twenty-one years of age, and that Eleanor said she did not want to go back. While the mother was out of the cab to make a telephone call, Eleanor took poison and died a few hours later.

The chauffeur in the meantime had returned to the nearby city and there on the following day learned from the newspapers that Eleanor was dead. He saw the coffin taken from the train and shortly afterward was found dead back of the girl's home. He left several notes, in one of which he told of taking poison from Eleanor several times. "I loved Eleanor and know she also loved me," one note read. "She told me she would give me her right hand and said that if her people forced her to leave me she would kill herself. . . . . When I asked her about the poison she would say that she always carried it, and if her mother came after her she would take some. I am going to take some as she did, as I have some which I took away from her." Another note states that once when he took poison from Eleanor he gave half back and kept half saying, "If you go, I'll follow."[1]

The process of development of the pact is clear. Eleanor's determination to kill herself if parted from her lover is identical with many cases already discussed. Her lover voluntarily adopted her interpretation of such a separation, and long before the separation came, a joint solution for it had been agreed upon.

[1] Coroner's inquest records, Cook County, 1922, and newspaper accounts.

There are other cases of pacts in which the participants are intimately associated but the crisis which precipitates the suicides is not a threat of separation.

CASE XXXIII

Five high school boys in a Michigan city agreed to kill themselves after they had been reprimanded by parents and teachers for skipping school. One boy died from his act, another made an unsuccessful attempt, and the remaining three did not keep their pledge.[1]

The situation here is that of friends accustomed to share their pleasure together who indulged in a forbidden day of joy. They apparently reacted in similar manner to the punishment, identified their difficulty as a common one, and planned a common solution.

In other cases the difficulty pertains to one member of the pact directly but is accepted by others in an intimate group as a common difficulty. Such was the case of the family in San Diego, California, all the members of which sat in a gas-filled room until death came, after two young daughters had been rescued from a hotel where they said they had been carried by several men after having been drugged. The father left a note to an official which reads:

CASE XXXIV

I am sorry, but myself and family are of the best southern blood. Death always preferred to dishonor to our women. We are wiping it out tonight. Rush this case, and if you can have the government avenge our wrongs, we will appreciate it where we go maybe. We thank you for your efforts.[2]

From these and other cases it seems apparent that the suicide pact develops when persons already in an intimate

[1] *New York Times,* May 30, 1924.

[2] The *Chicago Tribune.*

relation interpret some crisis in an identical manner. While the basis for this unity of attitude is in the relationship already existent, it is strengthened by the conscious expression and plans made between the two.

Suicides preceded by murder.—Suicides preceded by murder are much more numerous than suicide pacts. In 1923 among Chicago suicides were eighteen cases in which the person had killed or attempted to kill one or more persons before he killed himself. In addition there were cases of threats to murder without an actual attempt. From other years and other sources than the coroner's record, twenty-one unselected cases have been added to the list. When analyzed, these cases fall into several classes. In some the murder and suicide are part of the same act and apparently arise from the same motive. In others they are separated in time and a secondary motive intervenes between murder and suicide.

In the latter class are those cases in which a person commits murder, attempts to conceal the act, is later apprehended, and after arrest commits suicide.

CASE XXXV

Alfred Black was arrested after the body of his wife had been found in the forest preserves. He was questioned all night by the police and finally confessed to the crime, saying he had killed her because she would not get his breakfast for him and told him of other men who were "better" than he was. After the confession he appeared depressed, said he was sorry he had killed her, and was guarded because it was feared he might attempt suicide. When taken from his cell a few hours later, he evaded the guards and leaped from a window, killing himself by the fall. He had killed his wife two months before he was arrested.[1]

[1] The *Chicago Tribune.*

In this case and many similar ones the murder and suicide are not parts of one act. The motive for the murder does not enter into the suicide. Black, whose life as gambler, bootlegger, and roustabout had accustomed him to direct and crude action, apparently felt justified in killing his wife, who "was going out with other men, anyway," and who would not perform what he considered her duty of preparing his breakfast. The murder was the fulfilment of a threat, her punishment for lack of devotion to him and his needs, his riddance of someone who had become a nuisance and who had slighted him for other men. His feeling of sorrow and remorse was not apparent until after his arrest, after his resistance had been broken down by persistent questioning, and he had confessed to a crime which he must have known would in all probability result in his execution. Such a suicide is no different from any suicide or attempted suicide by a criminal whose morale has been destroyed by long hours of official questioning and who knows he faces a court trial and perhaps a long punishment. The crime committed may have been murder; it may have been larceny. But the situation which caused the murder does not cause the suicide. Undetected, the murderer would have lived on. Fearful of an unknown but certain punishment, he escapes his fear, the uncertainty, and the public disgrace by suicide.

A pathetic type of murder-suicide case is that in which the person committing suicide visions someone as wholly dependent upon him and seeks to extend his protection by taking the dependent one with him in death.

CASE XXXVI

Jennie Walker, thirty-eight years old and the mother of two children, six and ten years old, was deserted by her husband, who wrote to her that he had "at last found the woman he liked." He wished his wife to earn her own expenses by working and to place the children with his sister. He also urged her to get a divorce, threatening to file a bill himself if she did not. Mrs. Walker told a neighbor that her husband "was not satisfied with her in the marriage relation," and also that he thought she "was not raising the children right." Finally he wrote her that he had no money to send her and she would have to take care of herself and the children. Mrs. Walker had begun to talk of "making an end of it all," and when this last letter came, said "There is not anything left on earth for me to do but end it." She would not leave the children and he would not "give in." Nevertheless she found work and planned to have someone care for the children, although she did not know whom to get, as the youngest child was timid. Before arrangements were made, however, she killed herself and the children by means of gas, leaving a note which read, "God says come ye unto me who are weary and heavy laden and I will give thee rest. Don't take the children from me."[1]

Another young mother, who killed herself while ill, also killed her two youngest children who were with her (an older child was in school), leaving a note that she was taking these children with her and was sorry for them. Another mother who gave her two youngest children poison and then took poison herself left a note which said: "It is better that the children go while little." In this case an older child had been sent to school before the suicide was undertaken.

These mothers apparently did not as yet regard their infant children as separate personalities with an independent right to life, but really as part of themselves, sharing their troubles and to be taken on with them into death. While these cases are usually ones in which a parent, often the mother, kills her children, they are not necessarily so. There is, in the 1923 series, a case of a man of eighty-one who killed himself after attempting to kill his wife. Both were in poor health and the man had said he would be better off if he

[1] Coroner's inquest records, Cook County.

were dead. The wife, who was only wounded, said her husband shot himself and her because he was tired of life and wanted to end it. Apparently he imposed in his own mind his attitude toward life on the wife with whom he had lived for many years. Had she accepted his attitude and consented to her death, the case would fall in the class of suicide pacts. These cases differ from the pacts in that while the person who does the killing identifies the interests of himself and his victim, the victim does not, or, in the case of children, cannot, accept the attitudes.

Except in the extreme ends to which it leads, this attitude of interpreting the interests and attitudes of another in terms of one's own interests is not abnormal nor even unusual. It is particularly common in intimate circles, between friends and in families. It occurs whenever a father wishes his son to train for the profession which he himself longed for when young, but was denied. Sometimes the son concurs in the wish and adopts the father's attitude that that profession is the desired one. More often he resists and rebels, and dissension results, unless the father can visualize his son as a distinct personality with independent interests, rather than merely as a reflection of himself.

In cases in which this attitude leads to murder before suicide the person committing the murder does not regard himself as doing anything criminal or even wrong. He is moved by love, pity, sympathy—he is removing someone from a wicked world before the wickedness has touched him. He is doing a kindness by removing the other from suffering which he has endured and which therefore the other also endures or will in time encounter.

Perhaps the most common type of murder-suicide case is that which involves an intimate relation of adults. In some of these cases one person has battered long and ardently at the affections of another but without arousing adequate and complete response.

CASE XXXVII

Ray, a young man of twenty-eight, who was night clerk in a hotel and lived alone, loved Laura, a woman several years his senior who lived with her sister and worked as a waitress. The sisters had known him for three years. After he had gone with Laura for a year and a half she discontinued the friendship because he wanted to marry her, as she thought him too young and without sufficient money. She told him to leave her alone and find some younger girl to marry. He became jealous, and finally after an evening with her during which they were heard to argue, he shot her and then himself. In his pocket was found a note. "I, Ray, will my saxophone to ——— [a friend]. I am going to kill myself and sweetheart, my sweetheart and true love, Laura. I will bid my friends goodbye, and may God bless them and keep them from the hell that I have gone through. For the sake of love and happiness, Ray."[1]

An attitude which is apparent in many of these cases is that held by the young man who declared as he shot a girl whose attention and affection he was unable to hold, "If I can't have her, nobody else can." Denial of a thing ardently desired may lead to suicide, but in most of the cases in which murder of the person desired precedes the suicide there has been more than mere denial. The person has been made to feel inferior, undesired, a failure. He has been spurned, told to leave, to find another girl. His conception of himself has been attacked, his pride and self-respect injured. If more than one person is involved, the affair may include the death of several people.

While many of these cases center around a love relation, others have to do with the standing of a person in some group whose respect he values.

[1] Coroner's inquest records, Cook County, 1923.

A very clear case of loss of status and attendant shame and anger is that of John Moore, who had worked for several years in a railroad roundhouse as assistant foreman. One day he refused to make out a report for the foreman under whom he worked and was summarily discharged. He did not tell his wife of his discharge, and the next day returned to the roundhouse and shot the man who had discharged him and then shot and killed himself.[1] Another case which brings out clearly the injured feelings and jealousy is that of a patient in a marine hospital who found his life bounded by contacts within the hospital. With the other patients he was dependent upon the nurses for friendship and praise and upon success in handwork for admiration. He was hurt because the nurse, after an absence from the hospital, shook hands with the other men in his ward but not with him. She stated later she had thought him asleep at the time. He became jealous of a fellow-patient who made more beaded bags than he had made. Puerile as these things may seem from the point of view of a well person in a normal environment, they were of great significance to a lonely patient in a hospital. The man attempted to kill his rival at beading bags and then left the hospital and killed himself.[2]

In the cases just given the people murdered have all clearly been connected in the suicide's mind with himself and his difficulty. From time to time a case occurs in which not one or two but a greater number of persons is killed. The person is said to "run amok," a term borrowed from a peculiar Malayian "custom" discussed elsewhere in this book, in which a man kills until he is himself killed. In the cases of interest here, the person, after his seemingly indis-

[1] Coroner's inquest records, Cook County, 1923.
[2] *Ibid.*

criminate killing, commits suicide. When these cases are examined in detail they cease to appear wholly irrational. Their beginnings are very similar to the cases just discussed.

CASE XXXVIII

A series of quarrels between Mr. and Mrs. Russell came to a climax regarding a farm which Mr. Russell wished to buy but which Mrs. Russell objected to because the house was not in good repair. The quarrel started at the farm and was interrupted when Mr. Russell forced his wife to get out of the automobile of the friend who had driven them out, and to walk back toward town. Finally he returned and picked her up, but the quarrel continued. Mrs. Russell begged her husband to return to his job in the city, and Mr. Russell told her she might return but he intended to stay and buy the farm. During the evening, at the friend's, Mrs. Russell became acquainted with a Mr. Garrett who had a soft drink parlor. Mr. Russell came in and gambled with Mr. Garrett and his wife, losing a considerable sum of money. Apparently Mr. Russell considered that there had not been fair play, for he jumped to his feet after losing, pounded the table, and shouted, "I'll get the two of you for this." He drove to town, bought a pistol, and returned. He kissed his two little daughters and said goodby to them, then he fired at Mr. Garrett, caught his wife as she tried to escape, and shot her. One baby girl reached for the gun, seemingly to play with it, and was in turn shot. The friend with whom they were staying started to take the other little girl away and was shot. Mr. Russell then placed the pistol to his own temple and killed himself.[1]

The immediate victims sought by the husband were his wife and Garrett, who, following the long domestic quarrel, had tricked and humiliated him. The others shot were those who impeded him at the moment of his emotional excitement. Other cases are similar. The emotion originally centered in one person leaps out to include anyone who interferes or seems an obstacle. Sometimes the person has previ-

[1] *New York Times,* 1925.

ously given evidence of instability of emotions; there is a suggestion here of a particular type of temperament which may under given circumstances lead to such acts.

Two other types of cases remain, in both of which the person is apparently not rationally responsible for the murder with which he prefaces the act of suicide. Neither type is frequent. In a few cases a man while drunk kills someone else and then himself. Usually the person killed is someone in the family, and there is here the suggestion of some previous difficulty and emotional tension which escapes inhibition when the person is under the influence of alcohol.

Finally, there are a few cases in which someone actually insane kills others and then himself. In Chicago in 1923, although there were fifty-eight persons with definite evidences of insanity who killed themselves, there is only one case of an insane person killing another first. A young man previously diagnosed by a physician as a paranoiac sufficiently dangerous to be confined shot his sister-in-law and then himself. He thought his sister-in-law wished to have him sent away[1]

It is probable that most insane people of dangerous tendencies, especially in urban places, have been discovered and confined in hospitals. For purposes of analysis the definitely insane should be distinguished from the people who under stress of circumstances may kill a number of people, some of whom have no connection with his particular difficulty. Such people are often thought of as insane. As suggested before, they may be emotionally unstable and easily lose control of themselves and be unable to inhibit their emotions. Insanity implies a more or less permanent disorganized state of emotions and usually of reasoning ability.

[1] Coroner's inquest records, Cook County, 1923.

In the other type the disorder is of the emotions alone and not of mental faculties. They belong to the "feebly inhibited" group of Davenport's studies.[1]

The question often arises whether murder and suicide are one act or whether, having committed the murder, the person realizes what he has done and then commits suicide in remorse or fear of punishment. The first case given under this section has been included for the explicit purpose of showing the distinction between the cases in which fear or remorse is the true motive for suicide. When such cases occur the suicide usually comes at a later period than the murder. In the other and majority of cases the murder and suicide seem part of one act. The person interprets his difficulty as sufficient to prohibit adjustment; he has, he believes, reached the end of the way, and suicide is a means of solution for him. But his happiness has been ruined or is prevented by some person. Before he kills himself he kills that person, in anger and revenge, or in jealousy and to prevent another from succeeding where he has failed. In several of the cases given previously the whole affair, murder and suicide, was premeditated and planned. In other cases it is more or less impulsive. But in general both murder and suicide seem to be the result of one emotional outburst, and there is no intervening of remorse or fear between the two acts.

The college "suicide wave" of 1927.—During the first two months of 1927, according to newspaper reports, twenty suicides occurred among college and secondary-school students. During the first part of March student suicides continued

[1] Charles B. Davenport, "The Feebly Inhibited, I, Violent Temper and Its Inheritance," *Journal of Nervous and Mental Diseases*, XLII (September, 1915), 593–628.

to receive notice in the newspapers. After the first six or ten college suicides had been given publicity, newspapers and periodicals dubbed the phenomenon a "suicide wave" or "epidemic." Cases were played up by the daily papers with spectacular headlines and full column accounts on the front page, often with a summary of all preceding cases. Periodicals carried articles by psychologists, physicians, educators, and others, each with its individual explanation of why college and high-school students should suddenly show a tendency to commit suicide.

The first question to be answered is the simple one of whether more students killed themselves than is customary. If students had continued throughout the year to kill themselves at the rate reported for January and February, 120 student suicides would have occurred. There are approximately 4,600,000 students in the United States.[1] The rate per 100,000 would be 2.5 suicides.

The rate for Chicago in 1924 for persons under twenty years of age was 1.7 suicides per 100,000.[2] The rate for the registration states of the United States in 1920 for the age group 10–19 years was 2.1 suicides per 100,000.[3] There is no reason to believe that these rates have changed materially in succeeding years.

[1] This figure is for 1923–24 and undoubtedly would be higher were more recent statistics available. It includes students in colleges, universities, professional, normal, vocational, preparatory and high schools. It does not include music and art schools. It may therefore be regarded as an understatement. This total was computed from statistics given in the *Chicago Daily News Almanac and Year Book* (1927), pp. 620–21.

[2] See Table XIII. So few children under ten years of age commit suicide that this rate may be considered as essentially the rate for the high-school and college age group.

[3] See Table XXIII.

It seems then that if student suicides were at all unusual in number in the early months of 1927 they were only slightly so, since the rate for student suicides is only slightly above the rate for people of approximately the same age group for the entire United States. It may be of course that in other years the rate for students has been less than the rate for other young people; but there are no data either to prove or disprove such an assumption. The conclusion seems valid from the figures given that there was in no sense a "wave" or "epidemic" of student suicides, except on the front pages of newspapers and in the imaginations of certain adult groups.

It should be noted also that the student suicides lack certain qualities usually regarded as typical of social epidemics. Epidemics of social phenomena involve an element of suggestion which causes the individual acts to resemble each other. The student suicides bear no particular resemblance to each other in the manner in which they were committed or in the situations causing suicide to occur. According to one newspaper summary of the suicides occurring up to March 9 (twenty-five in number), twelve students had shot themselves, four used poison, four gas, three threw themselves under trains, and two died by hanging themselves. The situations ending in suicide included worry over examinations, failure to obtain passing marks, love affairs which did not progress smoothly, physical illness, and general weariness with living and failure to adjust.

An examination of the newspaper accounts (the only records at present available) leads to the conclusion that the student suicides were not an epidemic in the sense of an unmotivated type of conduct sweeping people unwillingly into an act. Nevertheless, an element of suggestion may have entered into the situation. College suicides were "played up" in the leading daily papers in a manner equaled only by the Loeb-Leopold case, and with many of the same implications of the instability, the delving into mysterious philosophies, the unaccountability of that unworldly being, the college student. The college student is still a curiosity to the reading public, a being of another genus, and the newspapers throw around student life the glamor beloved of their readers. The following account of the treatment of student suicides for the daily of largest circulation in the United States may be regarded as typical of the way in which newspapers handled the accounts of student suicides.

The first two student suicides were reported on the same day. One was of a University of Illinois student, the other of a Sophomore from the University of Rochester, the son of a well-known psychiatrist. Both left notes indicating inability to find a guiding and unifying philosophy of life. The similarity of the two cases, the status of the families involved, and their almost simultaneous occurrence led to their receiving lengthy front-page notice. The third student was an obscure youth who killed himself because of a love affair; the fourth was a friend of the first student who committed suicide, and hence merited a front-page headline and full column. The fifth student was the son of a well-known poet and literary critic. The sixth student received a front-page headline and full column. Gradually treatment of the cases on the front page was dropped by this paper, but items on inside pages carried such headlines as "Co-ed Enters College List of Suicides," and "Honor Student Kills Himself," with frequent summaries of earlier cases. All types of students were included to swell the list: college, university, music school, high school, continuation school. Added to these reports of cases were reports of sermons denouncing modern methods of education, certain types of psychology, freedom of the sex mores, and many more factors alleged as causes of student suicides. Meanwhile, periodicals had begun to print articles with explanations of numerous types.

Suicide became—at least in the public eye, and, it may be, to some students—not only a spectacular method of ending difficulties, but an esoteric method, the prerogative of the collegian. Suicide became in some small degree a social pattern, the accepted way for a student to end his difficulties.

There is no indication that students in the early part of 1927 had more difficulties, were any more perplexed and confused intellectually, had any poorer health, any more love quarrels, any greater degree of failure in passing than in preceding years. A few who otherwise might have found other solutions for their problems perhaps seized on this new, conclusive, and heroic method of ending difficulties offered them by the newspapers. But for the most part the "epidemic" of student suicides in 1927 seems to have been a case of public hysteria illustrative, not of the dangers of modern education, but of the cleverness of newspaper reporters and the credulity of the reading public.

The "epidemic" ended when the newspapers dropped student suicides from the front pages and turned to other and newer "news."

CHAPTER XIII

THE EXTERNAL SETTING

Although the discussion thus far has been concerned with psychological processes, it is apparent that these processes do not take place in a vacuum. The value of an abstract statement lies in its greater universality. External and conditioning factors may vary, but the underlying process remains the same.

For the control of suicide the external setting in which the suicide process comes to its climax is important. These situations vary from time to time and place to place. The material given here is for Chicago, and while it is no doubt more or less typical of other urban centers and perhaps even of rural districts, it should always be held in mind that differences in social organization and traditions affect the external conditions of personal disorganization.

The external experiences or situations are related to suicide only indirectly. They indicate the experiences which, in a given society, lead to personal disorganization which may end in suicide.

It is difficult to give quantitative statements, to say which experiences are most likely to lead to personal disorganization. For such a statement it would be necessary to know, not only how many people had committed suicide due to such experience, but how many people had been exposed to the experience. It means nothing to say that a hundred people commit suicide following illness while only fifty commit suicide following a business failure, unless we also know how many people in the total population were ill and how many suffered business failures. These total numbers are not known. Hence it is difficult to estimate the potency of any particular type of experience for causing personal disorganization and suicide.

Nevertheless it is possible to indicate the relation of various types of social and psychological situations to the suicide process. The classification given here is based on the 391 cases which occurred in Chicago in 1923, with some supplementary material from other places and other years.

Does the suicide rate vary with economic changes?—The relations of economic conditions to suicide are varied. Mere poverty can scarcely be asserted to be conducive to suicide. The stress of living is most difficult in winter and the burden of poverty most heavy then. Yet the greatest number of suicides occurs consistently during the spring and early summer months. In New York City, in which conditions of poverty and relief are probably very similar to those in Chicago, a careful study of suicides for 1910–23 places the smoothed mean curve at less than fourteen suicides per 100,000 for July, August, and September, rising to slightly over fifteen suicides per 100,000 for November, December, January, and February, and then rising to more than sixteen suicides per 100,000 during May and June.[1] Earlier statistics for certain of the New England states indicate the same general monthly trend,[2] while an examination of the data for Chicago for eleven years, 1915–25 (Table XVIII) indicates that although the total for December exceeds that for any other month, the rate for the three spring months ex-

[1] Metropolitan Life Insurance Company, *Statistical Bulletin*, VI (August, 1925), pp. 1–3.

[2] Dewey, "Statistics of Suicide in New England," *Publications of the American Statistical Association*, N.S., III (1892–93), 171.

ceeds the rate for any other season.[1] So far as severity of the weather can be correlated with the pressure of poverty, there is little basis for a belief that poverty is conducive to suicide. Another type of indirect evidence comes from considering the groups among which suicide is most frequent and those among which it rarely occurs. As a group the

TABLE XVIII

SUICIDE BY MONTHS
CHICAGO, 1915–25*

Year	Jan.	Feb.	Mar.	Apr.	May	June	July	Aug.	Sept.	Oct.	Nov.	Dec.	Total
1915...	51	40	61	43	61	52	63	48	52	43	47	55	616
1916...	38	36	44	46	56	52	42	38	50	45	39	47	533
1917...	44	32	49	39	44	55	25	38	43	33	33	39	474
1918...	29	33	41	41	29	35	36	26	33	48	38	55	444
1919...	22	48	30	36	34	58	40	46	30	27	21	23	415
1920...	27	20	34	29	36	22	31	29	33	33	27	44	365
1921...	21	29	45	39	47	27	57	50	35	30	31	48	459
1922...	17	26	40	38	48	34	31	28	38	34	26	38	398
1923...	27	28	32	28	27	36	30	31	27	36	29	58	389
1924...	17	32	32	47	44	37	46	24	42	50	27	45	443
1925...	35	40	38	29	34	36	36	33	26	26	51	46	430
Total	328	364	446	415	460	444	437	391	409	405	369	498	4,966

*From the Chicago Department of Health.

Negroes are perhaps the least wealthy of any definite group in the United States. Yet their suicide rates in both North and South are consistently 30–90 per cent lower than the white rates in the same communities. In Chicago much of the charity work—an indication of poverty—is done with immigrant groups. Some of the immigrant groups with the lowest economic level, however, have the lowest suicide rates of any immigrants.

Poverty, ordinarily thought of in terms of capital and income, has a sociological connotation. People may become

[1] Chicago Department of Health.

inured to poverty; they may be born and bred to poverty. It is altogether possible for people to live in poverty, and so long as the actual starvation point is not reached, to feel no particular hardship. People become pauperized, they become accustomed to living on the ragged edge and perhaps depending upon charitable agencies for relief. To such people poverty presents no crisis. They expect little from life and hence are not disappointed when they receive little.

It is usually a change which causes an economic crisis, and this change may be of two kinds. Either the person may develop new interests which he is unable to satisfy on an income previously found satisfactory, or his income may be lessened or stop entirely, in which case he is unable to satisfy interests previously taken for granted.

In the case which follows, lack of finances places the young man in question in a position where he is unable to satisfy a new and ardent desire, and causes a definite wish for death.

CASE XXXIX

A young man of twenty-three years, a home missionary, writes as follows:

I think the idea of death has been in the background of my mind most of the time since I was about fourteen years old. At that time my father died; I was the oldest child, and had been very greatly influenced by my father. After his death the standards of the family were not quite so high. The death of my father led me to think more or less seriously, as a result of which death seemed to hold no terror for me. Death, I believed and still believe, would bring me into closer association with God. On the other hand, life itself seemed to have no purpose. . . . .

The burden of the family has fallen upon me in the last few years. Some of my most cherished plans have been defeated because of this responsibility. I had planned on being a foreign missionary; but the problem of supporting my family made that impossible. After teaching one year, I was able to have one year of theology looking to the ministry. But here again, the needs of the family were so great that I had to give it up. I had planned on being married, having set the approximate date, but I discovered debts that took my savings so that the marriage had to be postponed. This situation with the more or less hopeless outlook has led me to think of death from despair of the situation. I think that my sense of responsibility both to my family and to my fiancée has been the only thing that has prevented my attempting suicide. I have felt that if I could just quietly pass out without anyone ever missing me or realizing that I had gone, it would be such a relief. At one time, as a result of this situation, I had a very distinct fear of committing suicide on impulse, forgetting for a time my responsibilities, and I was glad that there were no means of committing suicide in my room.[1]

The sudden loss of money or of employment and income may have different connotations, and may be merely part of a more thoroughgoing situation of disorganization. In the first case which follows, grief and loneliness as well as poverty caused the wish for death, while in the second case money signifies care and consideration for a dependent family.

CASE XL

An Irish woman of thirty-seven, working for ten years in Chicago as a secretary, writes that at the age of eighteen she found herself a widow in a strange American city. Her husband had just died without leaving insurance, and she had no money. "His friends paid the funeral expenses," she writes," and I was in a strange city, lonely, friendless, and with a child coming." For several months she definitely wished she was dead. She managed to make a partial adjustment. "I managed to find a home and a position until money arrived from my mother. The baby was born on my way back to Ireland." Once among her own people, "I was taken care of and all desire for death left me."[2]

An iceman, who had wished not only himself, but his entire family, dead, writes, "four years ago I hurt my back carrying ice. My wife never worked except at home doing housework. My two children are crippled from infantile paralysis. If I were unable to work any more I would rather we would all be dead, than not know how my family was suffering when I would be gone or be helpless. I still

[1] Questionnaire No. 46.
[2] Questionnaire No. 186.

carry the worry and fear and sometimes pray that if anything should happen I would be the last to go."[1]

Sometimes merely the impersonal obligations contracted which cannot be met during a period of financial misfortune may cause depression and wishes for death.

CASE XLI

A young business woman of twenty-seven for several days wished for death after the following experience. During her roommate's illness she had paid the doctor's bills, the rent on their apartment, bought the food, and met the instalments on the furniture which they were buying. Her savings were almost gone when in a reckless moment she bought a much-desired fur coat. She came home one day to find her clothes and some of the furniture gone. She learned from the other tenants that her roommate had taken them and left without repaying the money spent during her illness. She writes, "I fainted, and on coming to certainly wished for death. No clothes, no money, and the rent due in a week. I was despondent for several days, and then, with help from the office, made the best of it."[2]

Financial difficulties have meaning chiefly with reference to the person's interests and wishes. A young European artist in this country found himself unable to support himself by his profession and was soon in debt. He took a job as a laborer, repaid the money he had borrowed, and then killed himself, leaving a note to the effect that life without his art meant nothing. He was able to support himself after a fashion by other work, but without sufficient money to satisfy his art interests he could not live.

The person's conception of himself at the time of the financial difficulty may be the crux of the situation. Failure in business or inability to find employment may mean not only inability to satisfy interests, but may lead to change

[1] Questionnaire No. 102.   [2] Questionnaire No. 207.

in the personality itself, for the man may come to regard himself as a failure. Such a conception of himself not only hinders adjustment, but may become so acute that adjustment seems impossible.

CASE XLII

A young man of twenty-six, of German parentage, found himself unable to obtain employment at his trade. He killed himself, leaving a note addressed to his wife: "You were the only girl I could love so I have lied to you for the last time, as you know I could not bear to see you suffer any longer. So this will be goodby, and hope the next man will be a real man, one that has a little money and has a good job as I have done my best to find work. So goodby and good luck." The lying he refers to apparently concerned his efforts to convince his wife that he would soon have work. His wife stated that she knew he was despondent because he could not find work.[1]

It seems then that while mere lack of money may not be said to be a fertile cause of personal disorganization, the loss of money and necessary change in mode of living, with perhaps a developing attitude of self-depreciation, is conducive to disorganization and hence to suicide.

Attempts have been made by statisticians to show the relation between suicides and economic conditions by means of correlations. A correlation between suicide in Massachusetts and a general index of business conditions in the United States indicates a rather close correlation between business conditions and male suicides, but none at all between business conditions and female suicides.[2] Apparently men feel the brunt of business failures; this suggests the personal definition which has already been mentioned. The wives of men who fail in business, as well as their husbands, are de-

[1] Coroner's inquest records, Cook County, 1921.

[2] Metropolitan Life Insurance Company, *Statistical Bulletin*, VI (May, 1925), 1 ff.

SUICIDES
and
BUSINESS CONDITIONS
in
MASSACHUSETTS
1910 *to* 1923

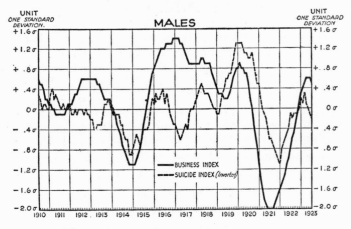

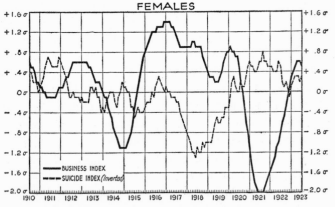

FIG. 4.—Statistical Bureau, Metropolitan Life Insurance Company, reprinted from the *Statistical Bulletin*, VI (May, 1925), 2, with the permission of the Metropolitan Life Insurance Company.

prived of their accustomed standard of living, but it is the men who have undergone the worry and who feel themselves to be failures. One factor in the Massachusetts statistics should be noted: the lowered male suicide rate during the war years, which corresponds to the bettered business condition of that period. It has been generally noted that during any war period the suicide rate tends to be low.[1] It is not possible to tell from this graph how much of the lowered rate is due to the good business conditions and how much to the attitude of participation in a social movement which seemingly accompanies a war period. The high rate in 1914–15 coincides with the marked business depression and unemployment situation of that period. It should be noted that there is a lag of about three months between the time of business depression and the corresponding variation in suicide. Apparently suicide does not follow immediately upon a business failure, but comes later, perhaps when attempted adjustments have failed and the accumulated failures have brought the full measure of discouragement and sense of defeat.

Arrests.—Probably there are more attempts than actual suicides among people who have been arrested and are in jail. Of both attempts and actual suicides there are quite a number. No one explanation suffices for all, for arrest has different meanings to different people. It may be that arrest so thoroughly disarranges accustomed habits and presents such an incomprehensible future that complete demoralization results.

---

[1] The decreased rate during war years was noticeable for certain of the United States during the Civil War and for England, France, and Germany, as well as other European countries, during the World War. See Table I, p. 8.

In some cases fear seems the dominant motive; in others, a feeling of disgrace. In the 1923 series of Chicago cases there are several instances of men of middle age, never before arrested, who found themselves arrested on some very trivial charge which at most would have entailed only a small fine. During the first few hours of jail, suicide occurred.

In other cases the factors are more complex.

CASE XLIII

Florence Green, arrested with her common-law husband for the murder of a night watchman of a building they had attempted to burglarize, attempted to commit suicide while in jail after her confession to the crime. When she found herself restored to life by the efforts of the police matron she burst forth into a tirade the theme of which was resentment over being separated from her husband and baby. She had previously been heard to debate with her husband the chances they had to escape legal execution for their crime and both had agreed that suicide would be preferable to execution.[1]

Arrest seems to lead to suicide through the thoroughly demoralizing effect of becoming entangled in a situation which becomes too complex for personal handling, through disgrace, through loss of personal relations, and through fear of an uncertain punishment. Remorse may enter in, but it is a strange remorse which waits until jail and punishment have come before it awakens.

Change of location.—Change of location differs somewhat from the preceding agents of disorganization in that it does not disrupt a social world in which the person is trying to live, but gives the person an entirely new and strange environment in which he must establish the relationships and contacts which constitute a life-organization. With his in-

[1] From the *Chicago Tribune*, 1923.

terests intact, but formed in another community, perhaps under different customs and moral codes, the person comes into a new community, there to adjust himself either by finding new satisfactions for the old interest or by modifying his interests to suit the new environment.

This change of location may be of almost any kind, but the tension is most acute when the change is from one type of environment and social custom to another type, particularly when the new type is different in a way which shocks and annoys. Every large city is full of people who have come from small towns and rural districts. Some of them make a normal adjustment, some of them achieve a makeshift adjustment, and some fail entirely. When the last happens, as with business failures, there is very apt to be a personal definition of failure.

CASE XLIV

Lois came to Chicago from a Wisconsin farm, where she had found herself at odds with her parents. She registered at a second-rate hotel in the "loop" and sought work. She could find none, her hotel bill was due, she was too proud to write to her parents. Poison was the solution. After swallowing the poison she regretted the act, called the hotel physician, and her life was saved. She said she could not face the hotel people and tell them she had no money. She also was "sick of the noise and dirt and the heat. God never intended us to live the way we live in a smoke-filled railroad yard." After the suicide attempt she decided to return home.[1]

It is quite generally conceded that immigrants coming to American cities from European villages find adjustment difficult. The suicide rate for foreign-born is much higher than the rate for native-born people in America, and is also higher than the rate in Europe.[2] Yet comparatively few of the foreign born commit suicide soon after their arrival (see

[1] *Chicago Tribune.*   [2] See pp. 33 ff.

Table XIX). Bolstered up by hope of the new country and incorporated usually into an immigrant community which is a small replica of their native land, disorganization of the suicide type does not usually come in the first years of American life. A parole officer with wide experience with

TABLE XIX

NUMBER OF YEARS SPENT IN THE UNITED STATES BY FOREIGN-BORN
PEOPLE COMMITTING SUICIDE IN CHICAGO (BASED ON SUICIDES
FOR THE YEARS 1919, 1920, AND 1921)

Country of Birth	Shortest Term of Residence at Time of Suicide (Years)	Median Term of Residence at Time of Suicide (Years)	Longest Term of Residence at Time of Suicide (Years)
Jugoslavia	1	10	39
Greece	8	10	17
Hungary	4	12	35
Poland	Less than 1	13	50
Russia and Lithuania	2	13	40
Italy	1	14	39
Austria	5	14.5	58
Ireland	9	25	50
Norway	3	26	53
Czechoslovakia	Less than 1	27	60
Sweden	8	27.5	57
Scotland	11	30	60
Denmark	12	30	65
Canada	9	31	60
Germany	3	33	67
England and Wales	11	37	60

delinquent boys in Chicago states as his conclusion that the period of greatest disorganization in immigrant families is not during the first period of adjustment to America, but ten, fifteen, or more years later, when the children grow up neither European nor American in their customs and morals, but queer hybrids who distress the parents and come into conflict with American institutions. The fact that new immigrants usually find here relatives, friends, people from their own village perhaps, at least people who speak their language and understand them, no doubt relieves the difficulty of early adjustment.

Illness and disease.—In a number of cases illness leads to suicide through inability longer to endure severe pain. Such a situation is especially apt to arise when the illness is incurable. It may become so acute that other interests for which the person would like to live longer are swept away.

CASE XLV

Jean Gray, after a somewhat unsatisfactory life with several successive husbands, found herself at the age of thirty-three deserted by her husband, estranged from her parents, and with an adolescent daughter. Cancer developed, and when Mrs. Gray could no longer work, her daughter found work which supported them, since relatives refused to assist. Mrs. Gray had tried to protect her daughter, planned on a business course for her, and refused to permit her to go to live with an aunt who would have allowed her to stay out late at night. When the cancer became serious, she committed suicide, leaving the following letters.

To MY DAUGHTER ALICE: Baby, please forgive me for not trying to struggle along any longer but I am at the end. It is of no use to try. Please try to live up to my teaching and be a pure sweet girl always and if you love Arthur and he is still willing to marry you, why you have my consent, although I realize that you are very young, but if you had someone to protect you and provide for you it would be a whole lot better for you, as, my dear, you will find this world a pretty hard place to live in, but be brave and make the best of things. I wish I could stay with you a while longer but it cannot be done. With love,

YOUR MOTHER.

To her doctors she wrote: "I know you have done all you could to try to save me but I realize it cannot be done. I thank you for all you have done and I know there is no use for me to try to struggle any longer."[1]

[1] Coroner's inquest records, Cook County, 1923, and records of the United Charities of Chicago.

The conflict of her love for her daughter and her weariness with the incurable pain is evident in these letters.

Even a severe pain of a temporary character may cause a definite wish for death or suicide. A young married woman of twenty-six writes of her experiences at the birth of her children, particularly the first time, when she had been frightened by the tales told her by other expectant mothers in the hospital where she had gone to await the birth.

CASE XLVI

I thought I would rather die than go on with the torturing pains I was enduring and cried aloud time and time again to let me die and not let me suffer so—love, marriage, etc., were not worth the agonizing time I was having. I really did want to die but did not think of a method—just wanted to be relieved—anything to be out of the peculiar pain. Forgot all about it after the birth of my baby. Had the same wish for death, only not so intensely, at the next birth. Rather vague, knew what was going to happen, but rather vaguely wished for death in that it would mean relief.[1]

This same woman writes further that during one of her hospital stays a young woman "suffered these pains for three days and with no relief in sight, since her doctor believed in natural birth; she became frantic in wishing for death and slipped into the operating room and committed suicide."

Compared with the total number of suicides in which illness of some sort seems to be a factor, the number of cases in which death is the direct result of unendurable pain is small. In the 391 cases for Chicago for 1923 Table XX shows the numbers and classes of cases related to illness.

The seeming difference in sexes is, except in (1) and (4) in accordance with the difference in suicide rates between

[1] Questionnaire No. 211.

the sexes for the total number for 1923. For each woman who committed suicide in Chicago in 1923, 2.5 men committed suicide. This relation of 2.5 to 1 is maintained in (2) and (3), foregoing. While the figures for suicide as the result of severe pain are too small to be conclusive, they suggest that men are less able to endure pain than women.

Into the second class of cases in which the illness is not incurable nor extremely painful at all times fall cases in

TABLE XX

RELATION OF SUICIDE TO ILLNESS

	Male	Female	Total
1. Suicide the result of pain.....................	10	1	11
2. Illness directly related to the suicide............	43	18	61
3. Illness asserted but relation to suicide not shown.	21	8	29
4. Menopause.....................................		8	8

which some definite illness interferes with a normal life. The person is not acutely ill; nor is he well. He can do some of the things he wishes, but not all.

CASE XLVII

Twenty-three years old, happily married, a young wife took poison and left the following note: "Dearest love: It is hard to part with you. But I am so ill. Always I am nervous, and it interferes with everything I want to do. Do not grieve, my love. How can I say what happiness it has been to have known and lived with you these precious years? B."[1]

The men's social worker in a clinic which handles cases of venereal disease states that many of the clients speak of suicide when their suspicions become a surety and they face a long series of treatments. The patients at this clinic are

[1] Coroner's inquest record, Cook County, 1923.

middle class and pay a moderate amount for the services they receive. Physically, they feel no worse after learning that they have the disease than they felt before. But the prospect of painful treatments extending over months, the desire to conceal the disease from family and friends, and the necessity for raising money for payments cause the disease to interfere seriously with their normal round of life. This tendency of a disease which might of itself be endured to interfere seriously with normal living is well illustrated in the case of a young college student who suffered from diabetes.

CASE XLVIII

A successful student, member of a well-to-do family, and a fraternity man, he found himself unable to adjust to the limitations which his illness set upon his activities, although it completely incapacitated him only occasionally. According to evidence at the inquest, he was often moody and depressed, and very sensitive about his illness, so that other members of the family dared not speak of it in his presence. He had concealed it successfully from his college friends and indulged in all the usual college pleasures of dances and parties, gradually, as he undermined his health, going to greater and greater lengths of drinking, wild parties, and orgies of food. He often took large doses of insulin, which gave him temporary relief but left him in worse condition, and at times caused him to lose control of his voice so that he talked too loudly or in a whisper, with resultant embarrassment and fear of ridicule. He left a letter to his parents and a diary, both of which were published in the daily papers and extracts from which are repeated here.

The letter which John Morton left to his parents when he committed suicide reads in part as follows:

I've tried everything and every plan. Each had its attraction simply because it was different from the rest; but after all, I can't live any of them.

I am only sorry that my condition did not put me in a position where I could show my appreciation of what you were doing for me; for I did appreciate it. I know you have done more for me than the average parents, and I would like to repay you, and feel that what I have done will repay you in a small way. I know how grandma fitted into life, a welcome member of the family—but a problem. . . . .

I've thought it all out; I'm not acting on the spur of the moment, or under stress of mind. It is the inevitable end, so why not now.

Please let the matter drop as soon as possible by knowing that I am at last happy and contented.

THE DIARY[1]

March 15. [About one year before he committed suicide.] Came home today from college. I hate like the dickens to drop out but I can't eat what I ought to and I'm just running myself to pieces. I'm flunking all my subjects so there's no use staying any more.

April 5. In bed. I'm so sick and tired of lying in bed and not being able to live on a diet of string beans, broth and bran cakes that I think I'll go nuts. Today I told dad I think I'll go to Rochester, whether he wants me to or not. He said he had been thinking about insulin too. But not as I've thought.

April 7. Went down to the . . . . hospital this morning. . . . . I don't know how I'll like it here but they have some good-looking nurses. Lights go out here at 9 P.M. My God, how will I ever get used to that? [The stay at the hospital is filled with comments on the small events of the day. He becomes friends with a girl patient, and after leaving the hospital calls on her. During the rest of the summer the entries in the diary are reports of successive "dates" with girls from a business school which he attended, girl ushers at theaters, girls met in parks, and the like. He reports his first drink and his first indiscriminate love-making. His illness receives no mention. In the fall he entered a college near his home.]

January 3. Got up at 7:30, went to campus and cashed check. On way home got a pint of port wine and drank one quarter of it. Home and took a shot. At college had waffles and candy. After supper got the girls and went to the theater. Took two shots before leaving home and they kind of got me in the show. Then went to café and had chop suey and danced. . . . . Smoked for the first time. Home at 3 A.M. and killed another quart of wine.

January 5. This morning I took my clothes and things back to my room. Returned home at 2 and had a lamb sandwich, an egg

[1] The diary has been checked by comparing the various newspaper versions of it.

sandwich, bread and jelly, and a glass of milk. The folks were out. Got a check from dad and left for campus again at 3. Stopped in town for three tubes of insulin and to see a show. Felt blue and thought it impossible to come to my room here and act happy when I felt so bad. I felt so blue I promised to stop eating and tell the boys, but I know I never will. I have to reduce, though, that is settled. In fact, I'm just tired of all things. I'd like to get away from it. One shot at three.

January 6. Resumed classes today. Had no breakfast or lunch and turned down L. and N. and B. in doing so. Had no supper last night either. This evening went to city with L. and had supper. Shrimp cocktail, bouillon and crackers, rolls, veal, potato, corn and ice cream. Then went to show. Took a shot before going and acted fine. . . . .

January 8. Was going to have a good day on eats but couldn't refuse L. supper at ———. Absolutely stuffed and have made a damn fool of myself. Laundry came today [from home] and in it six tubes. . . . . Every half-hour a shot. . . . .

January 9. ———, the swindler, died today of diabetes in the pen. The poor devil. He may have done wrong, but I pity him. A jail within a jail. It is better he has gone. Maybe some day I, too, will journey to that happy land where there is no sorrow, pain, joy or happiness. . . . . I only weigh 158 now, but am eating and going up again.

January 13. At five went to ——— banquet. . . . . H. looking awful. He says they tell him he has diabetes. O, God, the poor devil, if he has, I pity him from the bottom of my heart. To my room and took a shot and one-half. Almost caught by F. and had to jerk the needle out. Raining. Pretty bad, but will go to bed and hope for a good night.

January 17. In bed at 4:30 A.M. after day of cabareting and so forth.

Janury 23. Ate like hell today. Candy and all. Took two shots. had no supper and met M. at 7:30. He had dated two girls. Took them to the theater. Got back row seats and had one peachy mug. I guess it's the first time I've kissed in a show.

January 30. At 9 S. phoned and wants me to leave for ——— right after his German exam. I got my laundry and not enough insulin, but phoned dad and he was willing to bring laundry and three tubes tomorrow. I told him we were going on the train. I am up against it as to taking my medicine and will probably have to tell S. I have diabetes, I am sure. [This trip, taken between semesters, was a round of dances and drinking.]

February 8. I saw in the papers today where some big financier died from an operation for diabetes. God! I didn't know they could operate. As I think of my eating meals that a healthy person eats and also candy and drinks besides I don't see how I can last. It seems all right now, but I feel somehow that I am a goner—O, when, I can't say, but I believe within the next year. So, hell, I'm going to have a good time. No shots.

John Morton killed himself the first part of the April following this entry. While the published reports of his diary give no consecutive entries for dates later than February, scattered extracts indicate that he determined several weeks before the event to kill himself. John Morton's problem was not primarily to combat the disease. A good student, he wished also to be a debonair man of society, and with this latter ambition his disease interfered. His attitude toward the disease was that it was a personal weakness, something to be ashamed of and not acknowledged. In his effort to keep the pace set by his healthy friends, he violated all the rules for his physical care, and finally, shutting his eyes to the future, plunged deeply into sensual pleasures with the decision to take his own life when he could no longer stand the strain to which he subjected himself.

In twenty-nine cases in 1923, relatives or friends asserted at the inquest that the person had been ill. The evidence, however, showed no observable relation between the illness and the suicide, and it is not possible to state how much of a factor illness was, or whether it was a factor at all. There is a tendency for witnesses at an inquest to seek in their memories for something in the behavior or experiences of the deceased which might have caused him to commit suicide, and the occurrence of illness is accordingly recorded whether it had any relation to the suicide or not. Nevertheless, there are several ways in which illness may contribute indirectly to suicide. Illness is devitalizing, and in the following case led to definite wishes for death.

CASE XLIX

A young woman who thought seriously of suicide by gas for a period of three months thought that by her death she would obtain the rest and peace she desired. She says, "I had been ill and was not as strong as I had been. I tried to do as much as formerly and got very tired—so tired all the time that I wanted to be dead. Then, too, I was away from home at a girl's school and was lonesome."[1]

Illness may lead to a condition of hypochrondria, in which the person worries unduly about his health, foresees periods of ill health descending upon him, and at last, in a much perturbed and at times almost abnormal state of mind, commits suicide.

A number of cases also indicate that the illness, while apparently a factor in the situation, is only one of several factors. The last case quoted shows that not fatigue and illness alone caused the wish for death. This girl faced adjustment to a new environment and was lonely and homesick. Illness and unemployment often go hand in hand.

In four of the eight cases in 1923 in which suicide occurred at the time of the menopause no details are given; in one case a note stated that the woman was lonely; in two cases there was melancholia, and in another there had been definite signs of insanity and confinement in an institution. It is difficult to know to what degree the mental states at-

[1] Questionnaire No. 36.

tending the menopause contribute to suicide, for there is no
certainty that the eight cases are the only ones, of the total
of 391, in which the menopause was occurring. The relation
of melancholia to the menopause and the tendency to suicide
is discussed in chapter vii.

While pregnancy itself does not seem to be a factor in
causing suicide, it is probable that pregnancy outside of marriage is a factor. Among the 391 cases of suicide in Chicago
in 1923 there was only one in which pregnancy occurred, so
far as the coroner's records were concerned. It is always
possible that relatives and friends who might know of this
condition would suppress the facts. It is also possible that
in an urban environment pregnancy lacks the connotation
of disgrace which is usually thought to adhere to it. Not
only do people live more detached lives, so that there is less
community sentiment than in smaller places, but conceal-
ment of pregnancy and even of the birth of a child is possible; also, physicians and midwives who perform abortions
are easily found, and, as with most moral questions, the
urban attitude toward abortions is less severe than the rural
attitude. Only two cases have come to light during the
course of this study of girls who killed themselves because
they were pregnant and unmarried. One was a girl in a small
town, and the other a student in a girl's college. In both
cases the fact of the pregnancy was suppressed from the
newspapers and the general public. How many more cases
of this kind exist it is difficult to know.

Alcoholism.— Two types of cases occurred in the Chicago records in which alcohol was a factor. In one type, the
person, usually a man, who committed suicide was intoxicated at the time he killed himself. In many of the seventeen
male cases of this type the intoxicated man revived some

tension previously existing between himself and, usually, some member of the family. Intoxication has the effect of lifting inhibitions usually placed upon emotions and actions. Cases occur, therefore, in which a quarrel between husband and wife which has been smoldering quietly for some time is fanned into a flame during a period of intoxication on the part of the husband and may result in his attempt to kill his wife as well as himself. In a number of cases the point of contention was the husband's fondness for liquor.

In thirty-three other cases in 1923 the evidence showed that the man who committed suicide was accustomed to drink, but was not drunk when he killed himself. In such cases it is not possible to make out any connection between the drinking and the suicide; for although heavy drinking may be an indication of maladjustment,[1] it may be merely habit, or even, in the case of some immigrant groups, a social custom which has no relation to the state of mind of the individual. In many of these cases the drinking had led to quarrels or separation between husband and wife, which in turn provided the setting for the suicide.

The relation of alcoholism to suicide has been something of a controversial question among European writers on suicide. Morselli (1881) accepted the work of earlier investigators that the consumption of alcoholic beverages had a direct relation to suicide frequency. The basis of the proof lay in comparing statistics for alcoholic consumption and the rates of suicide for different European countries and for parts of one country for the same period of time, and also by comparing the trends of alcoholic consumption and suicide frequency over a period of years. The figures upon

[1] See p. 145.

which he based his conclusion that increased alcoholic consumption causes increased suicide are for the years 1849–70, and hence so far out of date that they are not quoted here.[1]

Durkheim (1897), using the same method of comparing statistics for two phenomena, came to the opposite conclusion from that reached by Morselli. The provinces of France which in 1875 had the highest consumption of alcoholic drinks are not those having the highest suicide rates, and the provinces with the most admissions to institutions for insanity due to excessive alcoholism do not coincide with the provinces of highest suicide rates. Moreover, by comparing alcoholic consumption with suicide rates for the countries of Europe for practically the same period of time as used by Morselli, he arrives at the opposite conclusion, that alcoholism is not a determinant of suicide.[2]

The lack of agreement between these two writers is not so much a matter of difference in statistics as difference in the particular statistics upon which emphasis is placed. Morselli emphasized the ones which supported his point; Durkheim, the ones which supported his. The value of the statistics in both cases is lessened by the fact that no direct relation can be shown between alcoholism and suicide. Only a study of actual cases can determine whether alcoholism and suicide are linked together.

In England, where it has been customary to place unsuccessful suicides in prison, a study of 142 such cases, representing most of the cases of attempted suicide in Liverpool in eighteen months, shows that of the 64 males in this group, 54, or 84.4 per cent, used alcohol, and that 56, or

[1] Morselli, *Suicide: An Essay on Comparative Moral Statistics*, pp. 288–91.

[2] Emile Durkheim, *Le suicide*, pp. 46–53.

71.8 per cent, of the females in the group used alcohol. It is not stated, however, that the people were intoxicated at the time of committing suicide, and it seems somewhat dubious to attribute to alcoholism all suicides occurring among people who may at some time drink in a country where drinking is so much a part of the everyday life as in England. This same investigator found that of 6,146 persons apprehended in 1896 in Liverpool for drunkenness, in 1.4 per cent of the cases the drunkenness was associated with suicidal tendencies.[1] It should be remembered that these figures are all based on *attempted* suicides and that it is altogether possible that the drunken man may be less sure of success in his attempts at self-destruction than the man in complete control of his mental faculties.

While wholesale statistics can be made to prove either that alcoholic consumption does or does not affect the suicide rate, the evidence from actual cases indicates that the number of suicides occurring during actual drunkenness is not large. Up to date no adequate studies have been made of the relation of the habit of drinking to suicidal tendencies.

The rupture of intimate relations.—Lovers quarrel; married people find themselves uncongenially mated and separate; husbands, wives, children, and parents die. In these ways some rift is occasioned in a relationship of intimacy, and suicide may result. Obviously, these occasions are not all of the same type.

One type of discord is that which results from the love which is not responded to. Of more common occurrence are cases in which there has been mutual affection either before or after marriage, with harmony of ideals and attitudes, and

[1] W. C. Sullivan, "Alcoholism and Suicidal Impulses," *Journal of Mental Science*, XLIV (1898), 259 ff.

for some reason this relationship is broken up, that is, new attitudes appear which conflict, or one of the pair does something which offends or conflicts with the ideals of the other. The dissension may be very open and crude, or it may involve different life-philosophies not fully realized or perhaps not developed when the friendship first formed.

CASE L

Mrs. M., aged twenty-one and married three years, killed herself after her husband who had been out all night, came in, and became drunk. He denied her accusations of having been out all night with another woman.[1]

CASE LI

A girl of eighteen, a model, was in love with a married man whose wife had filed suit for divorce. He was also in love with her and planned to marry her as soon as possible. The girl had a stepmother in Chicago but did not live at home. The girl had told her stepmother that if she "could not have" this man she would "just as soon be dead." One evening the girl and man had a quarrel, and according to the man's testimony at the inquest following the girl's death, she said he was not treating her right and cried. He described the quarrel as "just a few words." He was to call her at nine the following morning, but overslept, and when he called at eleven he found she had killed herself. She left the following letter addressed to him.

DEAR ALBERT: Surprised? I don't think so, because you might know I couldn't stand to let the mean things you do hurt and disappoint me any longer. I've always remembered the night that Helen came down to our house; how you told me you really loved me and asked me to give up the rest of my friends for you. I did gladly because I loved you. I thought you meant it when you spoke of making good, getting a divorce and marrying me; that has been all I have hoped and lived for since then—to make things pleasant and comfortable for you would have given me all I'd want of life, but I know from the indifferent way you've acted and talked, nothing is further from your thoughts than that, and I'm sorry.

Now you'll probably feel free to go back to Helen and not have to worry about me, and that hurts, to think you wouldn't tell me ages ago how

[1] Coroner's inquest records, Cook County, 1923.

you felt toward her. I could have forgotten then, but now I care too much—more than you can ever know. . . . .

I've made an awful mess of my life, Albert, and if I'd never met you how different things would have been.

I still love you, Albert, but please don't ever do to another girl what you've done to me.

The letter is signed with her name and the statement, "The one girl who would have given you fair deals and made you the best pal you ever had, if you'd only given her half a chance."[1]

CASE LII

Anna Gabriele was an Italian woman who had come to this country when a young woman as the wife of a man to whom she was not married but with whom she lived for years in common-law marriage. They had three children. Finally the man left her, and in a short time she married Joe Gabriele, a laborer for the city. Four children were born in the next few years, one of whom died. From time to time conflict became apparent, the symptoms being drunkenness on the part of the husband, beatings from the husband, threats of the husband, to leave, refusal of the husband to work. Underlying this was sexual incompatibility and jealousy. Mr. Gabriele was jealous of his wife because she was attractive to other men, and because she had had three children with a man to whom she was not legally married. At one time he left home because of the presence of a man boarder in the house. The husband believed that his wife had men visitors when he was away, although he was never able to prove anything. His attitude was one of continued jealousy and suspicion. The wife on her part stated that the quarrels occurred when her husband wished her to have intimate relations with him and she refused because she did not want the children to observe. The suicide attempts were on the part of Mrs. Gabriele, and occurred twice, once because of cruelty, the second time when her husband deserted her and she was without funds.[2]

[1] Coroner's inquest records, Cook County, 1923.

[2] Records of the United Charities of Chicago.

In this case the conflict centered about inability to adjust sexual relations. The more obvious signs of discord were secondary and symptomatic of the true conflict of attitudes.

In a number of cases drunkenness or cruelty on the part of the husband led to the wife's refusal to live with him, and his suicide followed when she remained obdurate.

An Italian woman refused to have her husband return home because of periodical drunkenness which he seemed unable to avoid. He told the social agency which was advising his wife that he loved his wife dearly and would kill himself if he could not return home. An adjustment was found before he made an attempt at suicide.[1]

A young husband whose wife left him because he struck her while drunk told his mother he would take his wife's life and his own if she did not return to him, as he could not live without her. He committed suicide, but did not carry out his threat on his wife's life.[2]

Cases could be repeated almost indefinitely in which quarrels and dissensions growing out of conflicting opinions regarding family conduct led to separation and finally to suicide, usually on the part of the less aggressive one, whether husband or wife. While one can scarcely generalize on the data at hand, it is significant that it is not always the mistreated wife who kills herself because her husband is cruel to her, but rather the drinking husband who has been discarded by his wife.

Somewhat more subtle are the cases in which the difficulty is of long-continued incompatibility due to widely different interests.

[1] Records of the United Charities of Chicago.
[2] Coroner's inquest records, Cook County, 1923.

CASE LIII

A young business man killed himself on his wedding anniversary after one serious business failure involving poor management which verged on dishonesty and several less serious failures which occurred in his efforts to re-establish himself. Back of these failures and back of his efforts to make money lay the conflicting interests and ambitions of himself and his wife. He was apparently a man who loved a quiet home and whose ideal recreation was in camping, hunting, and fishing. His wife, on the other hand, liked a social life and gayness of dance halls and cabarets. Extracts from the letter he wrote to his wife just before killing himself follow:

I suppose you thought I would forget the day, but I cannot forget. I have tried to live away from you, but it is no use. I never can forget that you are mine now as ever will be from the day we met until eternity, and although we cannot get along, I do not know why, I still love you and you are the only woman I have ever really loved. . . . . I cannot stand it any longer. . . . .

Do you remember when we moved to Broadway in our little flat? O, honey, I was so happy then, and when I had such a bum toothache you were so tender and kind to me. And how proud I was of you then. [He describes their various moves upward in the social scale and their vacation trips.] Then our trip to Florida. I thought you would be happy down there, but it only turned out to be a bad dream. Every time you corresponded with G. and H. and they told you about Chicago and the M. cabaret, when I wanted to forget them, it just made me sick, but you have them now, your dear friends, and you can go out with them, because you are free again.

He then denied in the letter the charge that he was a "lazy bum," and asked to have his body, dressed in his hunting clothes, cremated, and to have a simple funeral, without flowers. He wished his ashes to be scattered in the woods "where I will always be happy in the great outdoors where I have spent the happiest hours of my life. Then take my gun and fishing tackle and sink it all in Ghost lake where it cannot be recovered."[1]

In the cases which have just been quoted the feeling is either resentment, when the person feels aggrieved at the quarrels and desertion which he feels are unjustified by his behavior, or shame, chagrin, and grief, if the person feels

[1] From newspaper accounts.

that he has failed to reach the ideal of his mate or if he finds himself unable to live alone. In all cases there remains an emotional relation. If there were indifference, an adjustment could probably be made to a separation. But so long as the other person is loved and his respect a thing of value, it is difficult and in many cases impossible to find life endurable without harmonious relations.

In another class of cases the husband or wife has died and the one remaining feels that life cannot be lived without the other.

CASE LIV

A man of fifty-five who was taken from the river into which he had jumped and who lived for some time told the officer who rescued him that he wanted to die, his wife was dead, his daughter had returned to Europe, and he had no home and nothing to live for.[1]

CASE LV

Five months after his wife died the father of two children, thirty-three years old, killed himself, leaving a note which asked his children and relatives to forgive him. "I am sick of living without my wife so take care of the kids."[2]

In such cases the suicide has apparently organized his whole life in the other person, whose death means the loss not only of a beloved companion but of means of satisfaction for many interests. Stated concretely, the husband whose wife dies loses not only his mate but his housekeeper and homemaker, his companion in recreation, the one who encourages him when he fears failure, who praises him when he succeeds, who cares for his children. The more narrowly the life is organized about one person and a few interests, the more complete is the personal disorganization which follows the collapse of this one element in the life-organization.

[1] Coroner's inquest record, Cook County, 1923. [2] *Ibid.*

It sometimes happens that the emotional break is not between husband and wife, or dependent child and parent. In a few cases a mature and married son or daughter found the death of a parent so distracting that despondency and suicide followed. These are apparently cases in which the emotional dependency which is natural and normal in childhood has never been broken; the child has never really achieved independence, but still leans on the parent.

As with other cases, death may come simultaneously with other difficulties and the suicide result from the cumulative effect of several disturbing experiences happening at the same time.

The inarticulate suicides.—The discussion thus far has covered the main external situations in an urban center which lead to personal disorganization and suicide. In addition, a number of scattered and miscellaneous situations were found: unfounded accusations of theft or misconduct, loneliness and friendlessness, separations due to the insanity of husband or wife, and the like. In other social groups other concrete situations might be found to dominate in causing personal disorganization.

In addition to the cases in which some definite factor or factors could be isolated, there was in 1923 in Chicago a group, comprising somewhat more than one-fourth of the cases for the year, in which the inquest did not disclose the circumstances leading to the suicide (see Table XXI). The assumption here is not that there were no contributing and exciting causes of suicide, but merely that they were not brought out at the inquest or were unknown to anyone except the suicide himself.

In an effort to discover whether any peculiarities adhered to this group it was compared to the entire group for the year with reference to such things as sex, age, nativity, and marital condition.

The relation of males to females for the entire year was 2.5 male suicides to every one female suicide. For this special group the relation is 2.9 male to one female suicide; that is, there is a slight predominance of males in this group over the number to be expected.

In age grouping there are more of the very young ages and of the ages between fifty and seventy in the special

TABLE XXI

AGE GROUPINGS OF INARTICULATE SUICIDES

Age	PERCENTAGE OF TOTAL NUMBER OF SUICIDES	
	Total for 1923	Inarticulate Suicides
Under 20.............	2.6	4.6
20–29................	13.8	11.0
30–39................	23.4	19.2
40–49................	19.1	19.2
50–59................	16.6	19.2
60–69................	14.8	17.4
70–79................	3.1	2.7
80–89................	2.3	.9
Age unknown........	4.3	5.6

group than is to be expected. There are fewer of the young mature group (20–40) and of the old (70 and over).

When compared with all cases for 1923, the inarticulate group is found to have more than its share of people born in the United States and too few of the foreign born (see Table XXII).

It is somewhat surprising that more can be discovered about the suicides of immigrants than of native-born people, but so the percentages indicate. It is almost obvious that those whose birthplace is unknown would be apt to fall into the group about whom little or nothing is known.

With reference to marital condition, the inarticulate group has more than its share of the single and widowed, almost exactly its proportion of divorced, and fewer mar-

TABLE XXII

FOREIGN BORN AMONG INARTICULATE SUICIDES

	PERCENTAGE OF TOTAL NUMBER OF SUICIDES	
	Total for 1923	Inarticulate Suicides
Born in United States..	37.3	39.4
Foreign-born..........	57.1	49.5
Birthplace unknown....	5.5	11.1

ried than would be expected from the percentages for the year (see Table XXIII).

While it is perhaps to be expected that in cases of married persons who commit suicide more would be known of the details, since persons may be summoned to the inquest

TABLE XXIII

MARITAL CONDITION OF INARTICULATE SUICIDES

	PERCENTAGE OF TOTAL NUMBER OF SUICIDES	
	Total for 1923	Inarticulate Suicides
Single................	19.4	24.7
Married..............	54.1	39.4
Widowed.............	13.8	14.7
Divorced.............	3.3	2.7
Unknown.............	9.3	18.3

who have lived in daily contact with the suicide, the number of single and widowed in the inarticulate group suggests that the cause of suicide may have been connected with their manner of living. Married persons are incorporated into a family group; they have contacts and opportunity for responses of various sorts. Unmarried and widowed persons may easily become isolated and find in their loneliness cause for dissatisfaction and eventually suicide.

In so far as the inarticulate group varies from the total group of cases it may be said they include a slightly larger proportion of men, somewhat more of the very youthful and of the ages between fifty and seventy, a larger proportion of the native born and of the single and widowed than one would expect. In all cases, however, the variations are relatively small. It seems safe to assume then that these cases probably would fall into the same general classes as have already been discussed, except that they may contain more cases in which an isolated life has contributed to the suicide by its lack of intimate contacts and responses.

Attempted suicides in England.—The external situations ending in attempted suicide have been listed by one English investigator who made a study of one thoussand consecutive cases of people awaiting trial in prison because of attempted suicide. These cases came from the county and city of London, the counties of Middlesex and Surrey, and the small adjacent areas of Hertford, Kent, and Essex, mixed urban and rural communities, and occurred between April 1, 1907 and the latter part of December 1910.[1] The classification shows well the plurality of factors contributing to disorganization in any one case. In the majority of cases physical conditions were ruled out, even as contributing factors, since 709 of the 1,000 cases were found upon examination to be in

[1] W. Norwood East, "On Attempted Suicide, with an Analysis of 1,000 Consecutive Cases," *Journal of Mental Science*, LIX (July, 1913), 428 ff. For analysis of suicides in Massachusetts, see A. W. Stearns, "Suicide in Massachusetts," *Mental Hygiene*, V (1921), 752.

good or fair physical condition. The "causes" or external situations are listed as follows.

1. Alcoholic impulse with amnesia:

Number of Cases

This cause alone...................... 85

With other causes:

Out of work.................. 18

Quarrels and temper........... 11

On arrest.................... 10

Debt........................ 5

Losing work.................. 2

Losing money................. 1

Wife unfaithful............... 1

Business worries.............. 2

Bereavement.................. 1

Love trouble................. 1

Deserted by wife............. 1

Destitute.................... 1

Children ill.................. 1

Depression from syphilis........ 1

—

56

2. Alcoholic impulse, memory retained:

Number of Cases

This cause alone...................... 35

With other causes:

Out of work.................. 42

Quarrels and temper........... 52

Debts........................ 13

Wife left.................... 5

Destitute.................... 2

Bereavement.................. 2

Loss employment.............. 9

Loss money................... 2

On or to avoid arrest........... 6

Love troubles................ 2

Despondent from phthisis...... 1

—

136

3. Post-alcoholic depression:

Number of Cases

This cause alone...................... 5
With other causes:
On arrest..................... 1
Out of work.................. 5
Debts........................ 7
Quarrels, temper.............. 5
Loss or fear of loss of employment 5
Love troubles................ 1
Shame 1
Post-influenza depression....... 1
———
26

4. Out of work:

Number of Cases

This cause alone...................... 77
With other causes:
Exhaustion................... 19
Quarrels and temper........... 9
Drunken wife................. 1
Influenza.................... 1
Bereavement.................. 2
Phthisis..................... 1
Pneumonia.................... 1
Fear of going mad after dog bite 1
———
35

5. Destitution:

Number of Cases

This cause alone..................... 30
With other causes:
Exhaustion................... 30
Influenza.................... 1
Pneumonia.................... 1
Phthisis..................... 1
Pain from ulcer.............. 1
———
34

6. Domestic trouble:

Number of Cases

In temper or during quarrel..... 39
To gain sympathy or frighten
  relatives.................... 51
Love troubles................. 30

———

120

7. Ulterior purpose:

Number of Cases

To obtain work or relief....... 47
To get shelter of prison........ 13
To get out of army............ 1

———

61

8. Fear of imprisonment or on arrest:

Number of Cases

Offenders against person........ 22
Offenders against property...... 13
Various summonses............ 6

———

41

9. Business worries:

Number of Cases

This cause alone.................... 18
With other causes:
  Influenza.................... 3
  Quarrels..................... 5
  Bereavement................. 1

———

9

10. Depression from various causes:

Number of Cases

Feared loss of employment....... 2
Bereavement................... 1
Phthisis...................... 5
Influenza..................... 6
Pain......................... 2
Cancer....................... 1
Inability to work (illness)........ 2
Illness of wife................. 1

———

20

11. Other causes:

Number of Cases

Shame	5
By mistake when confused by alco-hol	1
Not known	1
	7

12. Weak-mindedness:

Number of Cases

This cause alone	o

With other causes:

Alcohol impulse:

Amnesia	8
Memory retained	4
General	1
Out of work	2
Post-alcoholic depression	1
Out of work	7
Out of work and quarrel	1
Destitute	5
Temper	3
To obtain charitable relief	3
Fear of arrest	1
Debt, etc.	3
To get into prison	2
Bereavement	1
Fear of losing employment	1
Being teased	1
To gain notoriety	1
Sudden responsibility	1
	46

13. Neurasthenia	8
14. Epilepsy (with other causes)	10
15. Borderline cases	18

16. Insanity:

Alcoholic:

Delirium tremens	9
Probable delirium tremens	4
Delusional	20

Depression:

   Without delusions............. 44
   With delusions............... 39
   Stupor........................ 3
   Delusional.................... 4
                             ―――

                                123

                              1,000

The meaning of the external circumstances.—The external situations outlined for Chicago and for England have no value for suicide except in so far as they cause personal disorganization. In other words, these situations apparently are, at a given time and place, the ones to which it is difficult for people to adjust, and the maladjustment of which leads to discouragement and the feeling that life is intolerable. If the various aspects of the suicide problem thus far discussed were to be put into schematic form they would be arranged in this fashion:

A pre-existing favorable attitude toward suicide plus the encountering of a critical situation for the solution of which accustomed habits are inadequate leads to emotions aroused by the disturbance of accustomed routine and to the dominance of attention by the disturbed phase of life; this condition creates the feeling that the situation is both intolerable and irremediable, which results in the arousal of the pre-existing attitude that death is a favorable solution to problems, and finally suicide is committed.

The question at once arises whether all types and classes of people are equally subject to an attitude favorable to suicide and to personal disorganization.

The question of an attitude tolerant of suicide is in part a question of the customs, traditions, and ideals of the society where the person is reared. Whether or not certain types of temperament more readily adopt a "give-up" attitude than other types there are no objective data to show. In their acquired attitude on life people certainly differ; some are aggressive and optimistic, and look forward to new plans when old ones fail; others are easily discouraged and give up without much effort. How much of this difference in attitude toward life is due to innate temperament and how much is due to social experience it is impossible to judge.

With regard to proneness to disorganization, people differ greatly, both in their ability to adjust to difficult situations and in their exposure to experiences which tend to be disorganizing. The latter difference especially is reflected in the varying rates for classes of people, such as the groups by sex, age, different marital standing, and occupation.

CHAPTER XIV

CLASSES OF PEOPLE WHERE DISORGANIZATION
PREVAILS

Men more suicidal than women.—The almost unvarying
relation of sex to suicide frequency has long been noted.
Esquirol is credited by Morselli with being the first to point
out the fact that for every woman who commits suicide in
European countries three or four men commit suicide.
Morselli's own tables, covering all of the principal European
countries separately for periods varying from 1831–1871,
demonstrate conclusively the constancy of this relation of
the sexes to suicide in Europe.[1] Table XXIV gives the figures
for a more recent period than Morselli's book covers and
also shows both the slight variations from year to year and
the variations between countries in Europe. These rates assume an equal number of men and women in each country;
while this assumption is of course not entirely accurate,
tables corrected for the exact number of men and women
show essentially the same relation, namely, one female suicide to every two to four male suicides. That the relationship does not remain exactly constant is shown by the
statistics for Sweden (Table XXV), in which figures corrected for the number of men and women in the population
show that while in 1781–90 one woman killed herself to every
three men, in 1901–10 the ratio had, by a gradual shifting,
become one female suicide to every five male suicides.

For the United States essentially the same relationship

[1] Morselli, *Suicide: An Essay on Comparative Moral Statistics*, pp.
89–204.

holds as for Europe. In the registration area in 1910 there were 29.5 female suicides to every 100 male suicides, and in 1920 there were in the registration area of that year 38.1 female suicides to every 100 male suicides.[1] Whether these

TABLE XXIV

FEMALE SUICIDES PER 100 MALE SUICIDES*

	1881–85	1886–90	1891–95	1896–1900	1901–5
German Empire.........	24.5	26.0	25.1	26.9	27.3
Austria.................	26.1	27.3	29.2	27.9	29.1
France.................	26.1	27.4	27.0	30.0	30.2
Italy..................	23.6	23.6	23.5	26.2	26.5
England and Wales.......	33.4	33.6	34.2	33.7	33.0
Norway................	27.5	27.0	29.3	23.8	22.2
Sweden................	28.9	28.6	26.1	22.3	21.8

*G. von Mayr, "Selbstmordstatistik," in his *Statistik und Gesellschaftslehre*, III, 298, quoted by Miner, "Suicide and Its Relation to Climatic and Other Factors," *American Journal of Hygiene, Monographic Series, No. 2*, p. 30.

TABLE XXV

SUICIDES PER 100,000 OF EACH SEX IN SWEDEN*

	Male	Female	Female Male
1781–90............	3.42	1.12	.33
1791–1800..........	3.85	1.23	.32
1801–10............	5.02	1.65	.33
1811–20............	6.86	1.82	.27
1821–30............	9.83	2.36	.24
1831–40............	10.37	2.45	.24
1841–50............	10.94	2.66	.24
1851–60............	10.28	2.69	.26
1861–70............	13.04	3.30	.25
1871–80............	13.94	3.72	.27
1881–90............	17.21	3.88	.23
1891–1900..........	21.24	4.84	.23
1901–10............	25.36	5.38	.21

* Miner, *ibid.*, p. 31.

[1] *Mortality Rates* (1910–20), p. 625.

figures show an actual increase of female suicides or are due to chance variation or to differences in sexual distribution it is not possible to state.[1] Figures for separate states and for individual cities at a much earlier period (about 1890) show a lower proportion of female to male suicides, namely, approximately 20 female to 100 male suicides; however, figures for certain of the same states (Massachusetts, Rhode Island, Vermont, Connecticut, Michigan) for a still earlier period (1851–70 for Massachusetts, 1866–80 for Rhode Island, and 1876–80 for the other states) show a much higher proportion of women to men, varying from 23 to 39.6 female to 100 male suicides.[2]

The variations already noted for both Europe and the United States indicate that the propensity of men to commit suicide is probably not inherent in their sex, a conclusion further supported by figures for the Orient. For instance, in Japan the proportion of women who commit suicide is much higher than for Europe or America. The situation in India is yet more at variance with the relations noted for the Occident.

The Chicago cases for 1923 were examined in an attempt to determine whether men are subject to critical and trying situations from which women are protected. Men and women were found to have almost equal percentages of each type of disorganization as outlined in chapter ix. With regard to the external situations the same statement holds true with only a few exceptions. Cases of suicide while the person was thoroughly intoxicated were confined to men. Women had

---

[1] The registration area varies from year to year as more states are added to it.

[2] Frederick L. Hoffman, "The Sex Relation in Suicide," *Publications of the American Statistical Association,* IV (1894–95), 21.

slightly more than their due proportion of suicides following change of location and following quarrels. Suicide accompanying the menopause is confined to women. The number of women who committed suicide in each of the situations

TABLE XXVI

FEMALE SUICIDES PER 100 MALE SUICIDES IN JAPAN*

1884–85	1886–87 1889–90	1891–95	1896–1900	1901–5
55.0	59.0	62.1	64.2	63.1

* G. von Mayr, "Selbstmordstatistik," in his *Statistik und Gesellschaftslehre*, III, 298, quoted by Miner, "Suicide and Its Relation to Climatic and Other Factors," *American Journal of Hygiene, Monographic Series, No. 2*, p. 30.

TABLE XXVII

FEMALE SUICIDES PER 100 MALE SUICIDES IN INDIA, 1907*

Madras	134.4
Bombay	108.5
Agra and Oudh	193.3
Punjab	127.1
Bengal	177.1
Central Province	99.9
Burma	85.7
East Bengal and Assam	149.0
N.W. Border Provinces	183.0
Whole empire	171.4

* G. von Mayr, *ibid.*, III, 300, quoted by Miner *op. cit.*, p.31.

named in chapter xiii was of course not the same as the number of men. But in each type of situation the same relation of the sexes was maintained as was found for the entire number of suicides: that is, for every woman who killed herself because she failed to attain the lover she wanted, or found herself an economic failure, or was ill, two or three men in the same situation committed suicide. It must be assumed either that more men are subjected to these critical situations or that men are less able to adjust to them. There is no way of knowing the relative number of men and women who are disappointed in love each year, or who suffer physical pain, or become economic failures. And without some such knowledge any explanation of the variation in rates between men and women is a matter of conjecture.

The suicide rate increases with age.—That specific types of conduct correlate with age is commonly known. Thus delinquency is an attribute of later adolescence, and ganging, of the entire adolescent period. Even certain psychoses typically appear at certain ages: dementia praecox usually appears between the twelfth and thirtieth years, and melancholia in middle age. The clustering of definite types of conduct about certain age groups is no doubt in part due to physiological changes (as adolescence or the menopause); but it is also due to social strains which adhere to certain periods of life in any given society. For instance, in America adolescence is not only a period of rapid physiological development and adjustment to new impulses, but is also a period when children achieve a certain independence in their conduct and often experience conflict with their parents who desire to supervise them too closely. So, too, the period of the menopause is not only a time of physiological change and adjustment, but has a psychological concomitant: youth has gone; the opportunity or the burden of child-bearing has gone; old age approaches.

As with other types of conduct, so with suicide: it bears a definite relation to age. The tables and charts which follow are illustrative.

Statistics for European countries, both for the middle of

the nineteenth century[1] and for the early years of the twentieth century[2] show the same general tendency that appears in the statistics and charts for Americans, namely, no suicides during the early years of childhood, a rapid increase in the rate during the years of adolescence, a more gradual increase until middle age, a more or less stationary rate until old age, when a tendency appears for the rate to drop. The chief variation seems to be in extreme old age, for which the rate occasionally continues to increase. The variation here may be, however, partly chance, since both the number of suicides and the number of people upon which the rate is figured are small, and a chance variation of two or three cases from year to year may change the rate from high to low or vice versa. By combining the figures for a number of European countries and several places outside of Europe Miner[3] has constructed a graph which shows for both males and females a rapid increase from the tenth to the twentieth year, an almost stationary rate to the thirty-ninth year, and from that year on a slight but steady increase.

A tentative classification by age groups of the external situations leading to suicide in Chicago in 1923 indicates that illness is a more dominant situation in the older age groups, and that the two emotional situations, love affairs and domestic difficulties, are more common in early maturity. Exact percentages are not given because the nature of the data (inquest records) calls for a considerable amount of

[1] Morselli, *Suicide: An Essay on Comparative Moral Statistics*, pp. 204-26.

[2] Miner, "Suicide and Its Relation to Climatic and Other Factors," *American Journal of Hygiene, Monographic Series, No.* 2, pp. 33-39.

[3] *Ibid.*, p. 33.

personal interpretation, and in addition the number of cases for one year is too small for a sound classification. More detailed and extensive data would make it possible to deter-

TABLE XXVIII

SUICIDES PER 100,000 BY AGE GROUPS FOR THE REGISTRATION STATES OF THE UNITED STATES FOR 1920*

Age	Total Population (by Hundred-thousands)	Number of Suicides	Rate per 100,000
Under 9.........	180.0	1	....
10–19............	156.8	335	2.1
20–29............	148.4	1,415	9.5
30–39............	130.8	1,789	13.7
40–49............	100.7	1,860	18.5
50–59............	70.0	1,582	22.6
60–69............	42.5	1,104	26.0
70–79............	19.1	515	27.0
80–89............	4.8	162	34.0
90–99...........	.4	11	27.5
100 over........	.03	0	....
Age unknown.....	1.2	16	....

* Computed from data given in *Mortality Statistics* (1920), pp. 310 ff., and in *Mortality Rates* (1910–20), pp. 638 ff.

TABLE XXIX

SUICIDES PER 100,000 BY AGE GROUPS, MASSACHUSETTS, 1881–85*

Age	Males	Females
10–20............	.8	1.2
20–30............	12.5	4.0
30–40............	17.4	5.5
40–50............	24.4	6.1
50–60............	35.5	7.7
60–70............	42.4	12.6
70–80............	60.0	7.6
Over 80.........	21.9	2.3

* From Dewey, "Statistics of Suicide in New England," *Publications of the American Statistical Association*, III (1892–93), 158–75.

mine the critical situations in each age group which are associated with suicide.

Children are non-suicidal.—From time to time startling statements appear in newspapers and magazines regarding

TABLE XXX

Age	Male	Female
10–14............	.27	....
15–19............	4.12	7.24
20–24............	11.23	11.36
25–29............	15.38	8.11
30–34............	27.25	10.79
35–39............	29.92	13.52
40–44............	35.73	15.00
45–49............	42.89	14.93
50–54............	40.60	18.22
55–59............	53.83	16.98
60–64............	58.00	16.56
65–74............	71.00	21.21
75–84............	150.00	14.55
85 over..........	30.00	30.00

* Based on coroner's records, Cook County, and United States census.

TABLE XXXI

SUICIDES PER 100,000 BY AGE GROUPS,
ADMINISTRATIVE COUNTY OF
LONDON, 1922*

Age	No. of Suicides	Rate
5–15............	1	....
15–25............	29	4.00
25–45............	159	12.00
45–65............	229	26.00
Over 65..........	87	34.00
Total........	505	11.00

*From *London Statistics* (1921–23), XXVIII, 46.

the suicide of children both in this country and in Europe. Such statements frequently give the absolute numbers of child suicides, rather than the rates. In the United States,

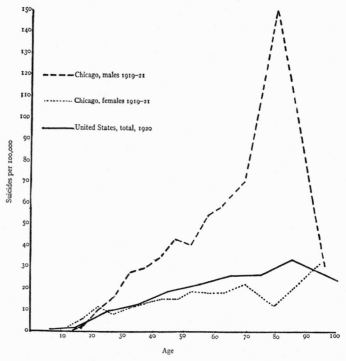

FIG. 5.—Suicides per 100,000 in the United States and Chicago, by age periods (Based on Tables XXIII and XXV).

as judged from the registration area, children under ten years of age do not commit suicide; only occasionally is there a suicide between the ages of ten and fifteen; and the rate for adolescents under twenty is exceedingly low as compared with the rates for other ages (see Table XXVIII).

In Europe for the first decade of the twentieth century the situation parallels that in the United States, with the exception of Denmark, France, and Germany, all of which had a rate of from 2 to 5 suicides per 100,000 boys between the ages of ten and fourteen, and .6–2.6 suicides per 100,000

TABLE XXXII

SUICIDES PER 100,000 BY AGE GROUPS,
AUSTRIA, 1910*

Age	Total	Males	Females
Under 15.......	.5	.9	.2
15–19..........	18.3	24.1	12.7
20–29..........	27.8	39.6	16.5
30–39..........	23.3	35.8	11.4
40–49..........	30.4	50.7	10.7
50–59..........	39.0	65.9	13.8
60–69..........	38.4	66.7	13.2
70——..........	46.2	79.4	18.6
Unknown......	.1	.2	.2
Total......	19.2	29.8	9.0

*From *Österreichisches Statistisches Handbuch* (1916–17), p. 35.

girls.[1] But it must be remembered that these countries had at that period the highest suicide rates for Europe,[2] and the somewhat more frequent suicides of children in these countries is apparently but a part of the general conditions that caused many suicides. Italy and Sweden, both with low suicide rates, have few suicides of children.[3]

There is, however, a suicidal tendency among children. In the first place there are the attempted but unsuccessful

[1] Miner, "Suicide and Its Relation to Climatic and Other Factors," *American Journal of Hygiene, Monographic Series, No. 2*, pp. 34–35.

[2] See Table I.

[3] Miner, *op. cit.*, pp. 34–35.

suicides of children. How many of these occur each year there is at present no way of ascertaining. More important, it is in childhood that in many cases the favorable attitude toward suicide as a means of solving problems is established. Of 147 instances of wishes for death in some form or other, as recorded by teachers and college students, in which age was specified, 45 occurred prior to the age of thirteen, 49 between the ages of thirteen and eighteen, and 53 after eighteen years of age. The persons answering these questionnaires were for the most part in the twenties and early thirties.

The occasions upon which children under thirteen wished to be dead include a long list of punishments actually undergone, or feared, especially when felt to be unjust; in a number of cases a parent had died, leaving the child facing tremendous readjustments; in several cases the death of a beloved brother or sister aroused the wish for death; in other cases a feeling of inferiority, or of jealousy, or of injured feelings was excited, making the child feel insignificant; illness caused the wish for death in a few children; in other cases the child had "set his heart" on having some specific gift, or indulging in some definite activity, and was forced to relinquish the desire.

In the next age group, from thirteen to eighteen years, there were a few cases of punishment and also cases of deaths in the family, cases of illness, and of some event which gave a feeling of inferiority, as well as thwarted temporary wishes. In addition, we find confusion when ideals are found not to correspond with the world; irritating conflicts with older members of the family and thwarting by the family of plans and wishes which involved the future work of the boy or girl. Denial by parents of such wishes as to attend college, to study dancing, or to go on the stage caused the wish for death.

If the situations calling forth the wish for death in both groups are combined, it is seen that they include cases in which the entire routine and habits of living have been destroyed, as in the case of illness or the death of parents; cases in which some cherished plan, involving ideals and ambitions either of an immediate or far-reaching sort, was thwarted; and cases of various types in which the child's conception of himself was affected, as when older brothers and sisters ran away from a younger child, or when punishment, felt by the child to be unjust, was inflicted.

These disturbances in the child's life are very similar to the crises which cause suicide in adults. Their main difference is that for the most part they are more temporary—a matter of an hour or a day, rather than of weeks—and that most of them affect only a small segment of the child's life or round of interests. Nevertheless, the thought of death accompanying these little crises establishes a habit of thought, an attitude of mind, favorable to suicide later in life when serious crises occur.

The widowed and divorced have high rates.—The relation of suicide to the various relations of the sexes has been so thoroughly worked out that it can be stated in almost categorical manner. Morselli, using data for the 1860's and 1870's from such European countries as had available statistics, found that for Italy, France, Saxony, Württemberg, Switzerland, Piedmont, Lombardy, Venetia, and Emilia, the suicide rate for married men stood lowest; that for the unmarried, second; for the widowed, much higher; and for the divorced, in countries where divorces were found, highest of all. For the women of Italy, France, and Switzerland the rate for the unmarried was slightly lower than that for the married.[1] Morselli also investigated the effect of children on suicides in France for the years 1867–76, and in Prussia for 1869–75. He came to the conclusion that children restrained married and widowed people, especially mothers, from committing suicide, but that their presence tended to increase suicides among divorced women. This was due, Morselli concluded, to the fact that children of divorced parents were usually given to the father to rear, and the mother was thus deprived of them.[2]

Quoting more recent material for European countries, Miner makes the general statement that "in both sexes and all ages the rates for the married are lower than those for single or widowed."[3]

Morselli's conclusions regarding the effect of children are also confirmed by more recent data (also drawn from France).[4] It can only be presumed that data for other countries would confirm the French findings that children act as a deterrent to suicide among married and widowed people.

For America only general statements can be made regarding the effect of marriage and family life on suicide.[5] For Chicago, so far as marital condition holds, the relationship found by Morselli fifty years ago for European countries is duplicated (Table XXXIII).

[1] Morselli, *Suicide: An Essay on Comparative Moral Statistics*, pp. 231 ff.

[2] *Ibid.*, pp. 237 ff.

[3] Miner, "Suicide and Its Relation to Climatic and Other Factors," *American Journal of Hygiene, Monographic Series, No. 2*, pp. 40–41.

[4] *Ibid.*, p. 46.

[5] The United States mortality statistics do not give such data. They must be gathered directly from the various coroners' offices—an arduous task.

It is evident that while marital condition has an effect, it is not the only factor involved, for the rate for women in each class is lower than the corresponding rate for men. While data are not available to explain the differences in rates between single, married, widowed, and divorced, the logical explanation from the point of view of this study would be that the low rate of the married is due to the relatively

TABLE XXXIII

SUICIDES IN CHICAGO BY SEX AND MARITAL CONDITION, 1919–21

	Single	Married	Widowed	Divorced	Unknown
Males:					
Population in Chicago 15 yrs. of age and over*..	362,178	578,949	40,023	6,609	....
Average annual number suicides†............	77.6	158.6	31.0	9.6	15.3
Rate per 100,000.......	21.5	27.4	77.5	146.5	....
Females:					
Population in Chicago 15 yrs. of age and over*..	274,924	560,645	110,299	8,938	....
Average annual number suicides†............	26.0	70.3	17.0	4.6	.6
Rate per 100,000......	9.5	12.5	15.5	53.6	....

*Fourteenth Census of the United States, II (1920), p. 473.
†Computed from coroner's records, Cook County.

greater degree of incorporation into an intimate group which they experience. Membership in a family group not only provides opportunities for expression of wishes otherwise difficult to obtain, but also acts as a means of control over the member. The widowed and divorced are in a particularly trying condition because their habitual life-organization has been destroyed and they often suffer in addition from grief, and, in the latter case, perhaps social disgrace.

Occupational and educational groups.—It is impossible to separate occupation and education as factors in their rela-

tion to suicide. The professional groups, certain official and
executive positions, and a few other occupations include
practically all of the highly educated persons, particularly

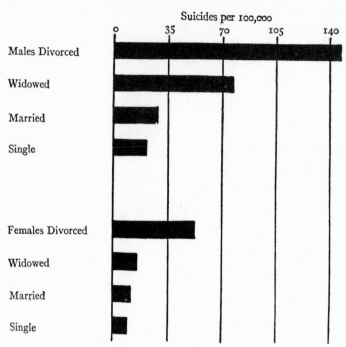

Fig. 6.—Suicides in Chicago by sex and marital condition, 1919–21

among men. In some communities there is a further correspondence of religion with education and occupation. For
instance, in many American cities the newer recruits of immigrants fall into one group, the older immigrants and native
born into another. It so happens that poor education, un-
skilled occupations, and the Catholic religion mark one
group, while good education, skilled and professional occupa-

tions, and the Protestant religion characterize the other. In such a situation it is extremely difficult, if not absolutely impossible, especially with the scanty data available, to determine the relative importance of these factors, although logically all three may be important.

The mortality statistics for the United States do not give suicides by occupations, education, or religion. Such material is available for other countries and some of it is quoted here (see Tables XXXIV and XXXV). In considering this material another caution should be heeded in addition to the one already given. There is no magic in any profession which causes or prohibits suicide, and professions or occupations classed under the same title in different countries may be very different in the demands they make upon the people in them, in their standing in the community, in the amount of money they pay, and in other respects, all of which are factors having their due effect upon the people in them.

The low rates for agricultural people suggest that another factor enters into the situation: the social organization, to which the occupation is incidental. Rural rates of suicide are everywhere lower than urban rates, and it is probable that it is not because men till the soil that they do not commit suicide, but rather because of the integrity of the social organization in rural communities which provides for the individual in such a way that disorganization is less apt to occur than in the confusion of social groups in cities.

The key to varying rates.—Such concepts as age, sex, marital condition, and occupation, when used to denote classes of people with varying suicidal tendencies, seem to relate closely to the social conditions into which the groups are thrown. While there are no objective data on the matter, general knowledge indicates that there is no reason to believe that men find adjustment to difficulties more trying than women; in fact, men, by reason of their broader experience,

TABLE XXXIV

SUICIDES PER 100,000 OF EACH OCCUPATION IN ITALY, 1897–1911*

Priests and monks	6	Printers and binders	34
Farmers, foresters, and shepherds	9	Soldiers and sailors	37
		Physicians	41
Fishers and mariners	11	Police and inspectors	43
Spinners and weavers	20	Capitalists	48
Professors and teachers	24	Hotel and café personnel	48
Servants	30		
Barbers	34		

*Miner, "Suicide and Its Relation to Climatic and Other Factors," *American Journal of Hygiene, Monographic Series, No. 2,* p. 47.

TABLE XXXV

SUICIDES PER 100,000 OF EACH OCCUPATION IN BAVARIA, 1902–6*

Agriculture and forestry	13.7
Mining and manufacturing	34.8
Commerce	48.0
Personal service	19.0
Care of the sick	18.9
Military and police	31.3
Education	23.0
Officials	45.4
Church officials	13.2
Art, literature, journalism	56.7

*Miner, "Suicide and Its Relation to Climatic and Other Factors," *American Journal of Hygiene, Monographic Series, No. 2,* p. 49, quoting G. von Mayr, "Selbstmordstatistik," in his *Statistik und Gesellschaftslehre,* III, 331.

are often thought of as more capable of handling difficult problems than women. There is, however, reason to believe that men face more crises than do women, or perhaps that more men than women face crises. Illness, for instance, to the man means not only physical discomfort and the thwarting of personal plans, but often means also the loss of employment and consequently a sense of failure and distress over inability to provide for family needs. One masculine habit leading indirectly to suicide is intoxication. Many of the domestic quarrels ending in suicide in Chicago in 1923 originated in the husband's habit of drinking to excess and the wife's refusal to live with a regularly intoxicated husband. While the wife was involved in these difficulties she held the offensive position, and the husband, on the defensive, found his position belittled and the respect of his wife gone.

With reference to age, suicide really begins at about the age when young people leave the protection and guidance of their parents and start out on independent life. The variance of motives with reference to age which has been mentioned is probably due to the fact that love affairs and domestic adjustments are more common to the years of early than of late maturity, and that illness is more general among the old than among the young. With respect to the increase of suicide with advancing age, an unsolved problem arises as to whether this increase is due to an increased number of problems which come with advancing years, or whether the hope and courage of youth gradually die down, leaving a hopeless outlook as men and women realize that the height of their vigor has left them.

Divorce and widowhood of themselves constitute problems; old habits of living must be abandoned and new ones established; usually, too, the adjustment is full of emotion, of tearing sentiments from old objects and finding new objects to which to attach them. Moreover, the divorced and widowed often live alone. The well-adjusted family has long been recognized as one of the most satisfactory groups for comfortable and happy living. Not only may the family provide the intimacy which most people crave, but in addition companionship, praise, and security, and it may become the means of gaining wider recognition in the community. It is these latter attributes of family life which probably prevent restlessness and disorganization.

Occupation is in many instances an indication of the type of social organization within which the person lives, of his social and economic class. Hence, in addition to any strains inherent in the occupation, occupation also indicates strains inherent in other social relations of the person and may even hint at a point of view toward life held by a social class. The high suicide rate of professional people coincides with the high suicide rate of the more highly educated classes, and can be thought of as due only in part to strains in the professions themselves. Personal disorganization is in part due to the number and kind of interests which the person has; and the person with wide social experience and education tends to have more interests than the uneducated man or one who lives a narrowly circumscribed life; hence he has more opportunities for unsatisfied interests and for finding life incomplete. Moreover, members of a cultural stratum or an occupational group may develop common attitudes and a common philosophy of life. It is possible that the attitude to regard suicide as commendable human conduct may vary in educational and occupational groups. In so far as this may be true, education and occupation become criteria of true social groups with traditions and customs which tend to control the members.

CHAPTER XV
THE CONTROL OF SUICIDE
(Summary Chapter)

With apparently few exceptions, suicide in contemporary America has one connotation. It is a symptom of complete loss of morale, a result of personal disorganization.

The process by which the wish to die becomes dominant in the experience of a person involves some major disturbance in that constantly shifting adjustment between the interests and ambitions of the person and the external social environment in which these interests normally should be realized. These breaks in a carefully balanced relationship in which the person seeks fulfilment for his interests in an environment which constantly modifies old interests and stimulates to new ones may take several forms. The most amorphous is an indefinite restlessness, a vague craving without a definite object. Occasionally this dissatisfaction becomes so acute, so irritating, yet so unnamable, that life ceases to have value, and relief is sought through suicide.

Somewhat more definite in character is the wish for a specific object or type of experience which can be named and is sought but not found. The boy has an ambition to become a writer, the lonely woman longs for a home, the girl sees all life in terms of a projected stage career. Yet for some reason, seemingly beyond the control of the person, the ambition cannot be realized. Again suicide may result.

It seems to be a psychologically sound principle that the more specific and well defined a wish or interest becomes, the more tense is the desire for its satisfaction, the more distressing its lack of fulfilment. Certainly in suicide cases some of the most poignant ones are those in which the person has found the object or means which he thinks would satisfy his most intense desires and cannot effect a response. The desire of a man for someone to care for him is slight compared to the desire of a man for a particular woman whom he can see, hear, talk with, caress. When such specific wishes cannot be satisfied, the emotional reaction is apt to be violent, and intense despair, and in some cases suicide, is the result.

Before an interest can come to fruition in an overt act, it is necessary that a certain adjustment take place between it and other interests already held by the person. If the whole scheme of a person's interests cannot be made harmonious in some way, discord results, and the conflicting interests block each other and prevent action. There are various ways of adjusting conflicting interests. One may be resigned in favor of the other; or one may be fulfilled in one circle of relationships, as in business; another, in a different set of relationships, as at home; or one may be modified—the person may alter some ideal or attitude—to accommodate the other. But if both remain in full force and are incompatible, mental conflict results. Extreme distress and suicide may result from long-continued conflict of dominant but incompatible interests.

Perhaps the most frequent type of crisis culminating in suicide is that in which a previously satisfactory life-organization has been broken through forces outside the control of the person: through the death of someone important to him, through illness, through economic failure, through quarrels, and the like. Such disturbances seem more liable to affect a whole system of interests and relationships, rather than merely one interest, and adjustment is correspondingly difficult.

This linking of suicide with personal crises is confirmed not only by analysis of cases of suicide, but by study of situations in which the person wishes for death but does not carry the wish to the overt act of suicide. Even the wishes and day dreams of death experienced by children are connected with crises.

Suicide has relation to two types of social factors which influence its occurrence. One is an attitude favorable to death, and particularly to suicide, as a commendable means of ending crises. The testimonies of university students show that the wish for death is relatively common at times of crisis. Recurrent wishes for death may lead to a habitual way of reacting so that at every crisis the wish for death may arise. The case of Marion Blake shows clearly the recurrence of what began as an ephemeral wish for death until it became a permanent attitude, leading at last to suicide. Whether or not a wish to die in times of difficulty is spontaneous or not cannot be said. But beyond doubt it could in America be acquired from the social environment, and certainly the attitude toward suicide as desirable or repulsive is built up out of personal and social experiences.

The second type of factor contributing to suicide is the experiences the person has had with reference to their disorganizing effects. The experiences found to lead to disorganization and suicide in Chicago in 1923 include: unemployment and economic failure, arrests, change of location, illness and disease, alcoholism, insanity, the rupture of intimate relations through quarrels, death, or separation.

The statistics of suicide show that not all classes and types of peoples commit suicide with the same frequency. The

question at once arises whether the social attitudes toward
suicide as a means of adjustment and the subjection to sufficiently severe crises can account for the variations in rates.
A survey of the literature on insanity and suicide suggests
another factor, the person's temperamental and personality
type. For some people adjustment is especially difficult.
While the process of disorganization resulting in suicide does
not differ materially from other cases, certain people become
disorganized over relatively trivial difficulties and hence are
more liable to become disorganized than those with more
flexible personalities. It is of course impossible to know how
much of the difficulty is due to innate characteristics and
how much to previous social influence which may have
effected a rigid and custom-bound character which finds
changes difficult to meet.

There are only speculative and common sense interpretations of the prevalence of male suicides over female and of
the increase of rate with age. The higher rate of widowed
and divorced persons over married suggests that the dis-
ruption of married life is at the root of the trouble in these
cases.

Attitudes toward suicide and personal disorganization
are not matters of the individual person. They are social
in origin. The effect, on the occurrence of suicide, of group
attitudes toward suicide seems evident from historical and
ethnological material, although it is often difficult to dis-
entangle this factor from that which relates to the prevalence
of disorganization. The Orient prior to Western contacts
and Europe in the Middle Ages offer an interesting contrast.
Both were rigidly organized with stable customs and attitudes and a high premium was placed on conformity to conventional modes of thought and action. The customs of the

Orient decreed that suicide should occur on certain specific occasions, often with a maximum of pain, yet people regarded it as a mark of honor to conform and to kill themselves in the ways prescribed. In Europe the church condemned suicide and he who committed suicide was regarded as a worse sinner than a murderer. Suicide became almost non-existent. If, then, a community is homogeneous and the members are completely incorporated into a consistent set of mores, the people will conform and either commit suicide or abhor it, as the customs decree.

Even in static Europe, however, suicide tended to appear at times of social crises, such as epidemics of disease, and among classes subjected to severe personal crises, as among the witches. It was found more particularly at periods of great social change, such as at the time of the decline of power in Greece, at the fall of the Roman Republic, and at the time of the Renaissance.[1] Periods of social change free the people from traditional attitudes and from group allegiance. They give people an opportunity to adopt personal codes at variance with the prevailing social code, and to place individual interests above group interests. At the same time they break up stable customs and institutions, and make it difficult for people to obtain satisfactory contacts and relationships.

In Europe and America the traditional attitude has been to hold suicide in disfavor. This attitude is still held in groups which have remained relatively isolated and hence conservative. At the same time such groups have routinized life in such a way that personal disorganization is of infre-

[1] War is not wholly a time of social change, although it is often thought of as a disorderly period. War is conflict between groups, and tends to unify each group. Social disorganization results from changes within the group.

quent occurrence. Thus, in communities organized on a religious basis and in small towns and rural sections the suicide rate is low, apparently both because the old traditional attitudes against suicide are still held there, and because there is little occasion for confusion of interests and purposes.

Cities, on the other hand, tend to be in a perpetual state of disorganization, and the multiplicity of contacts and diverse codes of conduct permit liberation of the individual from traditional ways of thinking and at the same time often make it almost impossible for him to achieve satisfactory relationships for fulfilment of his interests.

The relationship of suicide to social disorganization is further evident in the contrast between preliterate and civilized groups. The preliterate village, as the rural, is well organized and all the major interests of life are provided for in the customs of the group. A similar contrast is seen in the conditions of European peoples and of European immigrants in American cities, whose rates of suicide are two or three times as high as in their parent-countries.

Perhaps in the study of suicide in Chicago the relation between personal and social disorganization is best illustrated. The two terms are not synonymous but they denote related phenomena. Social disorganization is the loss of control of the mores over the members of the group. A certain amount of social disorganization does not disrupt the group, and is in fact common to all but the most static groups. Persons who are uncontrolled by the mores may be personally disorganized, or they may have elaborated a more or less individual scheme of behavior which permits satisfaction of interests, and an efficient life, even while it is not entirely conventional. It is true, however, that when social disorganization exists there is liable to be a greater amount of personal disorganization than in a static community. People's lives are ordinarily organized on the basis of definitely taught rules of right and wrong. When the social organization which taught them these rules disintegrates and the rules no longer apply, people are often unable to formulate for themselves substitute attitudes and habits. In Chicago the communities with high suicide rates are those communities in which there are other indications of both personal and social disorganization.

While this study has been concerned mainly with the psychological and sociological processes leading to suicide, rather than with methods of preventing suicide, several facts pertinent for its control stand out. Suicide may be controlled and all but eliminated when the social organization is maintained in fairly small, isolated, undisturbed units. Rural and primitive villages, in their typical undisturbed state, have few suicides because there are few occasions when individuals are faced with insurmountable problems and left by society to solve them alone. But the tendency of present-day society is away from small, isolated groups. People from widely divergent races and cultural groups are mingling as never before. Customs and ideals of opposing character are being brought together and become part of the personalities of the same people.

While this intermingling of people has its disastrous effect on certain members of society, it is, on the whole, considered beneficial. One of the ideals of men is to progress, to obtain more, to learn more. The centers of invention, of stimulation to investigation, of the production of industry and art, have been the places where men of different customs and traditions have met. The Mediterranean no doubt owed its early culture to the ease with which contacts could be had between countries. Modern cities are the centers of art and industry for the same reasons.

Small, isolated group life as a means of controlling suicide is not compatible either with the present trend of social life or with present ideals of progress.

From the point of view of attitudes which constitute personality, suicide might be eliminated to a large degree, even among disorganized persons, by cultivating attitudes unfavorable to suicide. If suicides could be made repulsive enough they would not occur so frequently. In former times religious scruples and the legalized mutilation of bodies tended to make suicide repulsive to people. But individualism has swept away the strict adherence to religious dictates, and the temper of Europeans and Americans has changed so that mutilation of dead bodies as a deterrent to would-be suicides is no longer thinkable. There are other possible attitudes toward life and death which, if inculcated, might act as a deterrent, such as the attitude that the lives of individuals belong to society and that it is a sacrilege to waste them. This attitude is in reality a modern version of the old religious attitude which regarded individual life as belonging to God. The religious attitude was bolstered up by fear of hell. The social attitude has no such supporting buttress. Such a prohibitive attitude regarding suicide would not, however, prevent disorganization of some type from occurring, however much it might prevent the disorganization from ending in suicide.

Of more practical and far-reaching value would be methods of education and training which would develop in the first instance resourceful, reflective characters—characters not dependent solely on rule-of-thumb methods of regulating life. Modern civilized life is too changeable for any one rigid set of rules to apply for long. The need is for certain social ideals or aims, with wide capacity for obtaining them. But even with the most Utopian education and training of character there would no doubt be persons who would become disorganized. For such persons there is need for agencies and trained psychologists and sociologists to study, analyze, and diagnose the trouble before the person has become so despondent that adjustment seems impossible and suicide the only relief. There is a growing recognition of the need for this type of service, but up to date provision for this service is so limited that only the more advanced stages of disorganization are handled. As the work develops it will no doubt cover milder phases of disorganization and check the process before the person has become demoralized and unable to redeem himself.

APPENDIX A

QUESTIONNAIRE BLANK

In the interest of a study in social psychology your co-operation is requested in filling out the following questionnaire, the purpose of which is to obtain data on possible methods of adjustment to individual crises.

One possible reaction in times of stress is the contemplation of death. In some cases this leads to an actual attempt at suicide. In others, a satisfactory adjustment is made aside from self-destruction.

The scientific value of this questionnaire depends upon the absolute frankness and honesty with which you answer the questions. The information given will be treated as strictly confidential.

Nationality   Age   Sex   Married

Education   Profession

Has your life been spent in country   Town   City   Chicago

Have you father   Mother   Children   No. of brothers   Of sisters

Do you live at home   Away from home   Where   How long

Religious affiliation or belief: Catholic Protestant Jewish Other None

Have you ever, even vaguely, wished that you were dead?

Or not been born?

Had a sudden impulse to commit suicide, as to jump off when on a high building?   Threatened to commit suicide?

At what age did this first occur? (Specify which of the above)

On this occasion:

What did you think would happen if you were dead?

Was the desire for death vague or definite?

What method did you plan to use?

How long did the desire last?

What was the situation or cause of this wish?

At the time the wish was dominant, what was your emotion? (Despair, grief, hopelessness, loneliness, friendlessness, wish to cause sorrow, revenge, or what?)

What influence caused you to abandon the idea? (Fear of death, removal of initial cause, religious teachings, prayer or confessional, advice of some friend, dread of disgrace to family, interest in some new activity, unwillingness to be a quitter, day dreaming, going to a new locality, or what?)

IMPORTANT.—If the contemplation of death or suicide has recurred at other ages, describe each occasion on the attached sheet, according to the above questions. Write freely.

Are you willing to have a conference on this subject, if desired?

If so, sign your name.

APPENDIX B

RESIDUAL PROBLEMS

A survey such as this study of suicide, which attempts to test theories advanced by earlier investigators and to isolate certain general factors which influence the suicide rate, cannot but uncover problems of a specific character worthy of detailed and intensive study. Certain such problems follow:

1. Statistical study of suicide in the United States. Such a study would consist in the main of the correlation of suicide rates with other phenomena, such as indexes of economic conditions, mobility, religious adherence, community unity, family life, vice, and many more social phenomena. The significance of the study would rest in large part on the ingenuity used in obtaining indexes for types of social organization and disorganization usually thought of as without a numerical equivalent.

2. Studies of suicide in a number of cities, similar to the one presented here for Chicago, would throw light on the high urban rate of suicide.

3. Suicide in small towns and rural districts has been neglected, probably because the rates are low. A study of suicides in these places would, by contrast with urban studies, add to knowledge of the factors contributing to personal disorganization and to suicide.

4. Suicides of insane people in the United States have not been studied. German psychiatrists have given this problem extended attention, but few of their studies have been translated. On the basis of their studies the situation in the United States could be investigated and their conclusions checked. Such a study would require a trained psychiatrist.

5. Suicides of children have been given attention in Germany and France. In the United States there are few child suicides; yet those which do exist and the attempts which prove unsuccessful merit attention, for the maladjustments of childhood often lead to permanent maladjustments.

6. Perhaps the most important study would be of attempted but

unsuccessful suicides. A preliminary reading of case records at the Cook County Hospital indicates that a study of such records would throw added light on conditions culminating in suicide, and would also make possible an investigation of readjustment to the difficulties which the person meant to escape through death.

In general the need is that future studies should utilize case histories of actual suicides and should center around specific social environments. Only with such a basis of numerous detailed cases can the errors of loose generalizations be avoided.

BIBLIOGRAPHY[1]

I. BIBLIOGRAPHIES OF SUICIDE

Index-Catalogue of the Library of the Surgeon General's Office, U.S. Army. Vol. XVII. Washington, D.C., 1912.

Index Medicus, a monthly classified record of the current medical literature of the world. Washington, D.C., 1913.

Psychological Index, an annual bibliography of the literature of psychology and cognate subjects. Princeton, New Jersey.

Rost, Hans. *Bibliographie des Selbstmords.* Literar. Institut Haas & Grabherr, Augsburg, Bayern.

II. SOCIOLOGICAL, PSYCHOLOGICAL, PSYCHIATRIC, AND STATISTICAL STUDIES AND INFORMATION

Abstract of the Fourteenth Census of the United States, 1920. Washington, D.C., 1923.

Abstract of the Thirteenth Census of the United States, 1910. Washington, D.C., 1914.

Adler, Alfred, *et al.* "Über den Selbstmord, in besondere den Schüler-Selbstmord," *Diskussionen Wiener psychoanalytischen Vereins.* Wiesbaden, 1910.

Annuaire Statistique, Quarantième Vol., 1924. Paris, 1925.

Annuaire Statistique de Finlande, 1925. Helsingfors, 1925.

Annuaire Statistique de la Belgique et du Congo Belge, XLVII, 1920–21. Brussels, 1923.

Annuaire Statistique de la Norvége, 1922. Christiania, 1923.

Annuaire Statistique de la Suède, 1921. Stockholm, 1921.

Annuaire Statistique de la Ville de Paris, 1920. Paris, 1924.

Annuario Statistico Italiano, 1917–18. Rome, 1919.

Asnaourow, F. "Der Selbstmord auf Sexualler Basis," *Sex-Problème,* VIII (1912), 621.

Backus, Ogden. "A Case of Suicidal and Homicidal Melancholia," *American Journal of Insanity,* XLI (1885), 309.

[1] This bibliography is selective rather than inclusive. For additional references see the indexes listed under I, Bibliographies of Suicide. The bibliography compiled by Rost contains 3,622 titles on suicide.

Bailey, William B. *Modern Social Conditions*. New York, 1906.

Behla. "Report on Suicide among School Pupils in Prussia," *Medizinische Reform*, 1909. Abstract in *Journal of American Medical Association*, LIV (1910), 479.

Brachelli, H. F. *Die Staaten Europas. Statistische Darstellung*. Leipzig, 1907.

Census, Fourteenth, of the United States. Vol. III (1920). Washington, D.C., 1922.

Census, Thirteenth, of the United States. Vol. I (1910). Washington, D.C., 1913.

Davenport, C. B. *The Feebly Inhibited. Inheritance of Temperament, with Special Reference to Twins and Suicides*. Washington, D.C., 1915.

DeGreef, G. "Introduction to Sociology," *American Journal of Sociology*, IX (1903-4), 69.

Dewey, D. R. "Statistics of Suicide in New England," *Publications of the American Statistical Association*, n.s., III (1892-93), 158.

Dexter, E. G. "Suicide and the Weather," *Popular Science Monthly*, LVIII (1900-1901), 604.

Durkheim, Émile. *Le Suicide*. Paris, 1897.

Diefendorf, A. R. *Clinical Psychiatry*. New York, 1915.

East, W. Norwood. "On Attempted Suicide, with an Analysis of 1,000 Consecutive Cases," *Journal of Mental Science*, LIX, (1913), 428.

Eulenburg, A. "Schülerselbstmord," *Ztschr. f. pädagog. Psych.*, etc., IX (1907), 1.

Fishberg, Maurice. *The Jews: A Study of Race and Environment*. New York, 1911.

Frenay, Adolph Dominic. *The Suicide Problem in the United States*. Boston, 1927.

From the Jaws of Death (fifth-year report of the operation of the Anti-suicide Bureau of the Salvation Army). London, 1912.

Gamble, S. A., and Burgess, J. S. *Peking: A Social Survey*. New York, 1921.

Gaupp, R. *Über den Selbstmord*. Munich, 1905.

Harper, A. "The White Australia Policy," in *Australia, Economic and Political Studies*, by various writers. Ed. by Meredith Atkinson. Melbourne, 1920.

Healy, William. *The Individual Delinquent*. Boston, 1915.

Hoffman, Frederick L. "The Sex Relation in Suicide," *Publications of the American Statistical Association*, IV (1894–95), 20.

——. "Suicides and Modern Civilization." *Arena*, VII (1893), 680.

——. "Suicide as a Factor in Life Insurance," *Spectator* (August 6, 1896), p. 61. See also *Spectator* for July 1, 1897, September 5, 1907, October 1, 1908, July 6, 1911, November 30, 1916, November 1, 1917, December 2, 1920, March 9, 1922, December 21, 1922, July 17, 1924, and July 30, 1925.

Jewish Encyclopedia (New York, 1905), XI, 581.

Kellner, A. "Über Selbstmord von ärztlichen und anthropologischen Standpunkt," *Ztschr. f. d. ges. Neur. u. Psychiat.*, XXIX (1915), 288.

Kempf, Edward J. *Psychopathology*. St. Louis, 1920.

Knibbs, G. H. "Suicide in Australia: A Statistical Analysis of the Facts," *Journal of the Royal Society*, XLV (1912), 225.

Kollarits, J. "Ein Erklärungsversuch für die Selbstmordhäufigkeit der Protestanten," *Ztschr, f. d. ges. Neurol. und Psychiat.*, XLIX (1919), 357.

Kraepelin, Emil. *Lectures on Clinical Psychiatry*. Revised and edited by Thomas Johnstone. 2d. English ed. London, 1906.

Krafft-Ebing, R. V. *Lehrbuch der Psychiatrie*. Stuttgart, 1893.

Leffingwell, Albert. *Illegitimacy and the Influence of Seasons upon Conduct*. London, 1892.

London Statistics, 1921–23. Vol. XXVIII. London, 1922.

MacDonald, Arthur. "Statistics of Child Suicide," *Publications of the American Statistical Association*, X (1906–7), 260.

——. *Statistics of Crime, Suicide, Insanity, and Other Forms of Abnormality*. . . . . Document No. 12, 58th Congress, Senate, Special Session. Washington, D.C., 1903.

Miner, J. R. "Suicide and Its Relation to Climatic and Other Factors," *American Journal of Hygiene, Monographic Series, No. 2*, 1922.

Morselli, Henry. *Suicide: An Essay on Comparative Moral Statistics*. New York, 1897.

Mortality, 1900–1904. Washington, D.C., Government Printing Office, 1909.

Mortality Rates, 1910–20. Washington, D.C., Government Printing Office, 1923.

Mortality Statistics, 1909, 1910, 1918, 1919, 1920, 1921, 1922, 1924. Washington, D.C., Government Printing Office.

Nagle, J. T. *Suicides in New York City during the Eleven Years Ending December 31, 1880.* . . . . Cambridge, 1882.

New Zealand Official Yearbooks for 1913–1923. Wellington.

Noble, John. "A Glance at Suicide as Dealt with in the Colony and in the Province of the Massachusetts Bay," *Massachusetts Historical Society, Proceedings,* Set 2, XVI, (1903), 521.

Nordisk Familjebok. Konversations Lexicon och Realencyklopedi. Vol. XXV. Stockholm, 1917.

Österreichisches Statistisches Handbuch, 1916–17. Wien, 1918.

Pfeiffer, H. *Über den Selbstmord.* Jena, 1912.

Population and Vital Statistics. Commonwealth Demography, 1924 and previous years. Bulletin 42. Melbourne.

Proal, L. *Le Crime et le Suicide Passionnels.* Paris, 1900.

Proal, L. *L'éducation et le suicide des enfants.* Paris, 1907. Reviewed under heading "Child Suicide" in *Nation,* LXXXV (1907), 28.

Redlich, E., and Lazar, E. *Über kindliche Selbstmörder.* Berlin, 1914.

Religious Bodies, 1916. Part I. Washington, D.C., Government Printing Office, 1919.

Résumé Statistique de l'Empire du Japon. Tokio, 1925.

Ring, A. H. "Factors in Suicide," *Boston Medical and Surgical Journal,* CXXXV (1921), 650.

Ross, E. A. *Principles of Sociology.* New York, 1920.

Rost, H. *Der Selbstmord in den Städten,* review of. *American Journal of Sociology,* X (1905), 562.

Sichel, Max. "Zur Psychopathologie des Selbstmordes," *Deutsch. med. woch.,* XXXVII (1911), 445.

Statistical Bulletin, Metropolitan Life Insurance Company, I (June, 1920), No. 6; II (February, 1921), No. 2; II (August, 1921), No. 8; IV (April, 1923), No. 4, and (December, 1923), No. 12; V (March, 1924), No. 3; VI (May, 1925), No. 5, and (August, 1925) No. 8; VIII (April, 1927), No. 4.

Statistique des causes de Décès de l'Empire du Japon, 1917, 1918. Tokio, 1920 and 1921.

Statistique du Danemark. Annuaire Statistique, 1924. Copenhagen, 1924.

Statistisches Jahrbuch der Schweiz, 1922. Bern, 1923.

Statistisches Jahrbuch für das Deutsche Reich, 1924–25, 1923, 1917.
Berlin.

Stearns, A. W. "Suicide in Massachusetts," *Mental Hygiene*, V (1921),
752.

Stelzner, H. *Analyse von 200 Selbstmordfällen.* Berlin, 1906.

Styles, G. "Suicide and Its Increase," *American Journal of Insanity*,
LVII (1900), 97.

Sullivan, W. C. "Alcoholism and Suicidal Impulses." *Journal of Mental Science*, XLIV (1898), 259.

———. "Relation of Alcoholism to Suicide in England," *ibid.*, XLVI
(1900), 260.

Sumner, W. G. *Folkways.* Boston, 1906.

———. "Suicidal Fanaticism in Russia," *Popular Science Monthly*,
LX (1902), 442.

Terman, L. M. "Recent Literature on Juvenile Suicide," *Journal of
Abnormal Psychology*, IX (1914), 61.

Tosti, G. "Suicide in the Light of Recent Studies," *American Journal
of Sociology*, III (1898), 464.

Viallon. "Suicide et folie," *Annales Medico-Psychologiques*, Vols.
XIV–XVIII (1901–3), series of twelve articles.

Wassermeyer. "Über Selbstmord," *Arch. f. Psychiat. u. Nervenkr.* L
(1912), 255.

Weichbrodt, R. "Der Selbstmord," *Abhandlungen aus der Neurologie,
Psychiatrie, Psychologie, und Ihren Grenzgebieten*, Heft 22 (1923).

Westcott, W. *Suicide.* London, 1885.

Williams, T. A. "The Prevention of Suicide," *American Journal of
Insanity*, LXXI (1915), 559.

III. AUTOBIOGRAPHIES GIVING PERSONAL ACCOUNTS OF WISHES FOR
DEATH AND ATTEMPTED SUICIDE

Barbellion, W. N. P. *The Journal of a Disappointed Man.* London,
1916.

Botchkareva, Maria. *Yashka, My Life as Peasant, Officer, and Exile.*
New York, 1919.

Hasanovitz, Elizabeth. *One of Them.* New York, 1918.

Riis, Jacob A. *The Making of an American.* New York, 1902.

Tolstoi, Count Lyof N. *My Confession and the Spirit of Christ's Teaching.* New York, 1887.

IV. HISTORICAL AND ETHNOLOGICAL SOURCES

Adams, James Truslow. *The Founding of New England*. Boston, 1921.

Alabaster, Ernest. *Notes and Commentaries on Chinese Criminal Law.* . . . . London, 1899.

Backhouse, E., and Bland, J. O. P. *Annals and Memoirs of the Court of Peking*. New York, 1914.

Ball, J. D. *Things Chinese, or Notes Connected with China*. London, 1904.

Bancroft, H. H. *The Native Races, I*. San Francisco, 1882.

Barrett, W. E. H. "Notes on the Customs and Beliefs of the Va-Giriama . . . . British East Africa," *Journal of the Royal Anthropological Institute*, XL, 20.

Beech, M. W. H. "Suicide amongst the A-Kikuyu of East Africa," *Man*, XIII (1915), 56.

Boas, Franz. "Ethnology of the Kwakiutl," *35th Annual Report, Bureau of American Ethnology*, Washington, D.C., 1921.

———. Tsimshian Mythology," *31st Annual Report, ibid*. Washington, D.C., 1916.

———. "The Central Eskimo," *7th Annual Report, ibid*. Washington, D.C., 1891.

Bogoras, W. "Chuckchi of Northeastern Asia," *American Anthropologist*, III (1901), 80.

Brinkley, F. *A History of the Japanese People*. London, 1915.

———. *China: Its History, Arts, and Literature*. Boston and Tokyo, 1902.

Budge, E. A. W. *Egyptian Sudan: Its History and Monuments*. London, 1907.

Byington, Cyrus. "A Dictionary of the Choctaw Language," *Bureau of American Ethnology, Bulletin 46*. Washington, D.C., 1915.

Cameron, V. L. *Across Africa*. New York, 1877.

Codrington, R. H. *The Melanesians*. Oxford, 1891.

Commission of Indian Affairs, *Annual Reports of the Department of the Interior*, from 1898 through 1906. Washington, D.C.

Coomaraswamy, A. *The Dance of Siva: Fourteen Indian Essays*. New York, 1918.

Cooper, J. M. "Analytical and Critical Bibliography of the Tribes of Tierra del Fuego and Adjacent Territory," *Bureau of American Ethnology, Bulletin 63*. Washington, D.C., 1917.

Crantz, David. *History of Greenland*. London, 1767.

Cyclopedia of India and of Eastern and Southern Asia. Vol. II. London, 1885.

Dalton, E. T. *Descriptive Ethnology of Bengal*. Calcutta, 1872.

Dorsey, G. A. *Traditions of the Skidi Pawnee*. New York, 1904.

Dorsey, J. O., and Swanton, J. R. "A Dictionary of the Biloxi and Ofo Languages," *Bureau of American Ethnology, Bulletin 47*. Washington, D.C., 1912.

Dubois, J. A. *Hindu Manners, Customs, and Ceremonies*. Oxford, 1906.

Duruy, V. *History of Rome*. Vols. IV and VI. Boston, 1883.

Dutt, R. C. *A History of Civilization in Ancient India*. London, 1890.

Eastman, Mary. *Dahcotah, or Legends of the Sioux*. New York, 1849.

Ellis, A. B. *Ewe-Speaking Peoples of the Slave Coast of West Africa*. London, 1890.

———. *The Tshi-Speaking Peoples of the Gold Coast of West Africa*. London, 1887.

Ellis, Gilmore. "The Amok of the Malay," *Journal of Mental Science*, XXXIX, 331.

Fletcher, A. C., and LaFlesche, F. "The Omaha Tribe," *27th Annual Report, Bureau of American Ethnology*. Washington, D.C., 1911.

Frazer, J. G. "The Dying God," *The Golden Bough, Part III*. London, 1911.

———. "Sati," *Encyclopedia of Religion and Ethics*. New York, (1922), XI, 207.

Gann, Thomas W. F. "The Maya Indians of Southern Yucatan and Northern British Honduras," *Bureau of American Ethnology, Bulletin 64*. Washington, D.C., 1918.

Gowland, William. "The Burial Mounds and Dolmens of the Early Emperors of Japan," *Journal of the Anthropological Institute*, XXXVII, 10.

Gray, J. H. *China*. London, 1878.

Green, Laura C., and Beckwith, Martha W. "Hawaiian Customs and Beliefs Relating to Sickness and Death," *American Anthropologist*, XXVIII (1926), 176.

Griffis, W. E. *The Mikado's Empire*. New York, 1895.

Grimshaw, B. *Fiji and Its Possibilities*. New York, 1907.

Hara, Katsuro. *An Introduction to the History of Japan*. New York, 1920.

Harada, Tasuku. "Suicide," *Encyclopedia of Religion and Ethics*. New York (1922), XII, 35–37.

Hecker, J. F. C. *Epidemics of the Middle Ages*. London, 1859.

Heeren, A. Vander. "Suicide," *Catholic Encyclopedia*. (New York, 1912), XIV, 326.

Hewitt, J. N. B. "Iroquoian Concept of the Soul," *Journal of American Folklore*, VIII (1895), 109.

Hobley, C. W. *Bantu Beliefs and Magic*. London, 1922.

Hocart, A. M. "The Cult of the Dead in Eddystone of the Solomons," Part I. *Journal of the Royal Anthropological Institute*, LII, 71; Part II, *ibid.*, LII, 259.

D'Holbach, B. *System of Nature*. Vol. II. Boston, 1889.

Hopkins, E. W. *Religions of India*. Boston, 1895.

Hose, Charles. "A Journey up the Baram River to Mount Dulit and the Highlands of Borneo," *Geographic Journal*, I (1893), 193.

Hrdlicka, A. "Physiological and Medical Observations among the Indians of Southwestern United States and Northern Mexico," *Bureau of American Ethnology, Bulletin 34*. Washington, D.C., 1908.

Hume, David. *Philosophical Works*. Vol. IV. London, 1826.

Hutton, J. H. *The Angami Nagas*. London, 1921.

——. *The Sema Nagas*. London, 1921.

Janssen, J. *History of the German People at the Close of the Middle Ages*. Vols. VI, XVI. London, 1903.

Jenks, A. E. *The Bontoc Igorot*. Manila, 1905.

Jones, Peter. *History of the Ojebway Indians*. London, 1861.

Johnson, Samuel. *The History of the Yorubas*. London, 1921.

Johnston, Sir Harry. *The Uganda Protectorate*. New York, 1902.

Joyce, T. A. *Central American and West Indian Archeology*. London, 1916.

——. *Mexican Archeology*. New York, 1914.

Junker, W. *Travels in Africa during the Years 1875–78*. London, 1890.

Lasch, R. "Die Behandlung der Leiche des Selbstmörders," *Globus*, LXXVI (1899), 63.

——. "Rache als Selbstmordmotiv," *ibid.*, LXXIV (1898), 37.

Lecky, W. E. H. *History of European Morals from Augustus to Charlemagne*. 2 vols. New York, 1880.

Leonard, A. G. *The Lower Niger and Its Tribes*. London, 1906.

Lowie, R. H. *Primitive Religion*. New York, 1924.

Lumholtz, Carl. *Through Central Borneo*. 2 vols. New York, 1920.

McClintock, W. *Old Indian Trails*. Boston, 1923.

MacDonell, A. A. "Vedic Religion," *Encyclopedia of Religion and Ethics* (New York, 1922), XII, 601-18.

MacLeod, W. C. "Certain Mortuary Aspects of Northwest Coast Culture," *American Anthropologist*, XXVII (1925), 122.

Mair, A. W. "Suicide (Greek and Roman)," *Encyclopedia of Religion and Ethics* (New York, 1922), XII, 26-33.

Malcolm, L. W. G. "Notes on Birth, Marriage, and Death Ceremonies of the Etāp Tribe, Central Cameroon," *Journal of the Royal Anthropological Institute*, LIII, 388.

Mallery, G. "Pictographs of the North American Indian," *4th Annual Report, Bureau of American Ethnology*, Washington, D.C., 1886.

Malo, Davida. *Hawaiian Antiquities*. Honolulu, 1903.

Man, E. H. "On the Aboriginal Inhabitants of the Andaman Islands," *Journal of the Anthropological Institute*, XII, 111.

Marshall, H. I. "The Karen People of Burma: A Study in Anthropology and Ethnology," *Contributions in History and Political Science, Ohio State University Bulletin*, XXVI, No. 13 (1922).

Martin, J. *An Account of the Natives of the Tonga Islands in the South Pacific Ocean, Compiled and Arranged from the Extensive Communications of Mr. William Mariner*. Boston, 1820.

Matthews, Washington. "Ethnography and Philology of the Hidatsa Indians," *U.S. Geological and Geographical Survey*. Washington, D.C., 1877.

Matignon, J. J. *Superstition, Crime et Misère en Chine*. Paris, 1902.

Mooney, James. "Calendar History of the Kiowa Indians," *17th Annual Report, Bureau of American Ethnology*. Washington, D.C., 1898.

Murdoch, James. *A History of Japan, from the Origins to the Arrival of the Portuguese in 1542 A.D.* Vol. I. Asiatic Society of Japan, 1910.

Murdoch, James, and Yamagata, Isoh. *A History of Japan during the Century of Early Foreign Intercourse (1542-1651)*. Kobe, Japan, 1903.

Murdoch, John. "Ethnological Results of the Point Barrow Expedition." *9th Annual Report, Bureau of American Ethnology*. Washington, D.C., 1892.

Nansen, F. *Eskimo Life.* London, 1893.

Niblack, A. P. "The Coast Indians of Southern Alaska and Northern British Columbia," *Report of the U.S. National Museum, 1888.* Washington, D.C., 1890.

Nitobe, I. O. *Bushidi, the Soul of Japan.* New York, 1905.

Pasha, R. G. *Seven Years in the Soudan.* London, 1892.

"Personal Narrative of Captain Thomas G. Anderson," *Report and Collections of the State Historical Society of Wisconsin,* IX (1882), 137.

Prescott, W. H. *History of the Conquest of Peru.* 2 vols. New York, 1850.

Ratzel, F. *History of Mankind* (trans. by A. J. Butler). London and New York, 1898.

Rivers, W. H. R. *The History of Melanesian Society.* Cambridge, 1914.

———. *The Todas.* London, 1906.

Rogers, Charles. *Social Life in Scotland.* Edinburgh, 1884.

Roscoe, J. "Further Notes on the Manners and Customs of the Baganda," *Journal of the Anthropological Institute,* XXXII, 25.

———. "Notes on the Manners and Customs of the Baganda," *ibid.,* XXXI, 117.

———. *The Baganda: Their Customs and Beliefs,* London, 1911.

———. *The Soul of Central Africa.* London, 1922.

Rose, H. J. "Euthanasia," *Encyclopedia of Religion and Ethics* (New York, 1922), V, 598–601.

———. "Suicide," *Encyclopedia of Religion and Ethics* (New York, 1922), XII, 21–24.

Ross. E. A. *The Changing Chinese.* New York, 1911.

Roth, H. L. *Natives of Sarawak and British North Borneo.* 2 vols. London, 1896.

Roth, W. E. "An Inquiry into the Animism and Folklore of the Guiana Indians," *30th Annual Report, Bureau of American Ethnology,* Washington, D.C., 1915.

———. "An Introductory Study of the Arts, Crafts, and Customs of the Guiana Indians," *38th Annual Report, Bureau of American Ethnology,* Washington, D.C., 1924.

Russell, R. V. *The Tribes and Castes of the Central Provinces of India.* Vol. II. London, 1916.

Sahagun, Bernardino de. *Historia General de los cosas de Nueva*

España. Vol. I. Ed. by Carlos Maria de Bustamante. Mexico, 1829.

Saito, Hisho. *A History of Japan.* London, 1912.

Schetelig, H. "Traces of the Custom of 'Suttee' in Norway during the Viking Age," *Saga-Book of the Viking Club,* 1910. Reviewed in *L'Anthropologie,* XXI (1910), 559.

Schopenhauer, A. *Selected Essays.* London, 1891.

Schrader, Otto. *Prehistoric Antiquities of the Aryan Peoples.* London, 1890.

Seligmann, Charles Gabriel. *The Melanesians of British New Guinea.* Cambridge, 1910.

Sheane, J. H. W. "Some Aspects of the Awemba Religion and Superstitious Observances," *Journal of the Anthropological Institute,* XXXVI, 150.

Smith, A. H. *Village Life in China.* New York, 1899.

Smith, E. W., and Dale, A. M. *The Ila-Speaking People of Northern Rhodesia.* London, 1920.

Stannus, M. B. "Notes on Some Tribes of British Central Africa," *Journal of the Royal Anthropological Institute,* XL, 285.

Steinmetz, S. R. "Suicide among Primitive Peoples," *American Anthropologist,* VII (1894), 53.

Stevenson, R. L. *The South Seas.* New York, 1913.

Sumner, William. *Folkways.* New York, 1906.

———. "The Yakuts, Abridged from the Russian of Sieroshevski, 'Yakuty,'" *Journal of the Anthropological Institute,* XXXI, 65.

Swanton, John R. "Early History of the Creek Indians and Their Neighbors," *Bureau of American Ethnology, Bulletin 73.* Washington, D.C., 1922.

———. "Indian Tribes of the Lower Mississippi Valley and Adjacent Coast of the Gulf of Mexico," *Bureau of American Ethnology, Bulletin 43.* Washington, D.C., 1911.

Theal, G. M. *History and Ethnography of Africa, South of the Zambesi.* London, 1907.

Thomas, N. W. *Anthropological Report on the Edo-Speaking Peoples of Nigeria.* Part I, "Law and Custom." London, 1910.

———. *Anthropological Report on the Ibo-Speaking Peoples of Nigeria.* Part IV, "Law and Custom," London, 1914.

———. "Some Ibo Burial Customs," *Journal of the Royal Anthropological Institute,* XLVII, 161.

Thwaites, R. G. (editor). *Early Western Travels, 1748–1854.* Vol. XXII, Part I of *Maximilian, Prince of Wied's Travels in the Interior of North America, 1832–34.* Vol. XV. *S. H. Long's Expedition, 1819–20.* Vol. XXIV. *De Smet's Oregon Mission and Travels over the Rocky Mountains, 1845–46.* Cleveland, 1906.

Torday, E., and Joyce, T. A. "Notes on the Ethnology of the Ba-Huana," *Journal of the Anthropological Institute,* XXXVI, 272.

Tregear, Edward. *The Maori Race.* Wanganui, New Zealand, 1904.

Tremearne, A. J. N. "Notes on the Kagora and Other Nigerian Head-hunters." *Journal of the Royal Anthropological Institute,* XLII, 136.

Turner, George. *Samoa a Hundred Years Ago.* London, 1884.

Turner, Lucien M. "Ethnology of the Ungava District, Hudson Bay Territory," *11th Annual Report, Bureau of American Ethnology,* Washington, D.C., 1894.

Tylor, Edward B. *Primitive Culture,* Vol. I. New York, 1877.

Wake, Staniland. *The Evolution of Morality.* 2 vols. London, 1878.

Weeks, J. H. *Among Congo Cannibals.* London, 1913.

———. *Among the Primitive Bakongo.* London, 1914.

———. "Anthropological Notes on the Bangala of the Upper Congo River," *Journal of the Royal Anthropological Institute,* XXXIX, 97.

Westermarck, Edward. *The Origin and Development of the Moral Ideas.* 2 vols. New York, 1906.

Wheeler, J. T. *The History of India.* 2 vols. London, 1867.

Williams, Thomas. *Fiji and the Fijians.* Vol. I. London, 1858.

Yarrow, H. C. "Study of the Mortuary Customs of the North American Indians," *1st Annual Report, Bureau of American Ethnology,* Washington, D.C., 1881.

V. THEORY AND GENERAL INFORMATION

Anderson, Nels. *The Hobo.* Chicago, 1923.

Brill, A. A. *Fundamental Conceptions of Psychoanalysis.* New York, 1921.

Chicago Daily News Almanac and Yearbook for 1927. Chicago Daily News Company.

Cline, Leonard. "Dope Peddlers Rarely give Addicts Chance," *Chicago Daily News,* March 6, 1926.

Davenport, Charles B. "The Feebly Inhibited. I. Violent Temper and Its Inheritance," *Journal of Nervous and Mental Diseases*, XLII (1915), 593.

Dewey, John. *Human Nature and Conduct*. New York, 1922.

Faris, Ellsworth. "Social Psychology" (MS).

Hapgood, Hutchins. *Spirit of the Ghetto*. New York, 1909.

Hart, Bernard. *The Psychology of Insanity*. Cambridge, 1922.

Healy, William. *Mental Conflicts and Misconduct*. Boston, 1917.

Johnson, Humphrey J. "Race, Language, and Nationality in Europe, in Kroeber, A. L., and Waterman, T. T. *Source Book in Anthropology*. Berkeley, 1920.

Kroeber, A. L. *Three Essays on the Antiquity and Races of Man*, Univ. of Calif. Syllabus Series, No. 119, 1920.

Mercier, C. A. *Conduct and Its Disorders, Biologically Considered*. London, 1911.

Mowrer, E. R. *Family Disorganization*. Chicago, 1927.

Myerson, Abraham. *The Foundations of Personality*. Boston, 1921.

Oakesmith, John. *Race and Nationality: An Inquiry into the Origin and Growth of Patriotism*. New York, 1919.

Park, R. E., and Miller, H. A. *Old-World Traits Transplanted*. New York, 1921.

Queen, S. A., and Mann, D. M. *Social Pathology*, New York, 1925.

Shonle, Ruth. "Social Psychologists and the Method of the Instinctivists," *Social Forces*, V (June, 1927), 597.

Thomas, W. I., and Znaniecki, Florian. *The Polish Peasant in Europe and America*. 5 vols. Chicago, 1918.

Thurstone, L. L. *Nature of Intelligence*. London, 1924.

White, W. A. *Outlines of Psychiatry*. Washington, D. C., 1918.

Znaniecki, Florian. *The Laws of Social Psychology*. Chicago, 1925.

Zorbaugh, H. W. "The Dweller in Furnished Rooms: An Urban Type," *American Journal of Sociology, Papers and Proceedings of the 20th Annual Meeting*, XXXII, No. 1, Part II (1926), 83.

INDEX

351

F